D1785316

# Social Control and Political Order

# Social Control and Political Order

## European Perspectives at the End of the Century

edited by

Roberto Bergalli and Colin Sumner

SAGE Publications
London • Thousand Oaks • New Delhi

© Roberto Bergalli 1997
Henner Hess 1997
Dario Melossi 1997
Massimo Pavarini 1997
Sebastian Scheerer 1997
Colin Sumner 1997

First published 1997

All rights reserved. No part of this publication may be
reproduced, stored in a retrieval system, transmitted or utilized
in any form or by any means, electronic, mechanical,
photocopying, recording or otherwise, without permission in
writing from the Publishers.

 SAGE Publications Ltd
6 Bonhill Street
London EC2A 4PU

SAGE Publications Inc
2455 Teller Road
Thousand Oaks, California 91320

SAGE Publications India Pvt Ltd
32, M-Block Market
Greater Kailash – I
New Delhi 110 048

**British Library Cataloguing in Publication data**

A catalogue record for this book is
available from the British Library

ISBN 0 8039 7558 9
ISBN 0 8039 7559 7 (pbk)

**Library of Congress catalog card number   96–068422**

Typeset by M Rules
Printed in Great Britain by Biddles Ltd,
Guildford, Surrey

# Contents

# Preface

This book began as a lively panel debate over two days between the six contributors to this volume, mostly in English although a little in Spanish, in front of about a hundred people as a conference convened at the University of Barcelona by Roberto Bergalli. As friends as well as colleagues, we were able to move forward with a little more constructive frankness than is usual at an academic conference and Roberto's excellent choice of restaurants in the evening accentuated this advantage. Hopefully, the spirit of this debate, and its spin-offs, has been captured within these pages. In editing the book, we have also deliberately tried to maintain the European, trans-linguistic and interdisciplinary flavour of our exchanges. The chapters within are, of course, a development of the papers and exchanges at the conference and, therefore, differences may have been reduced and positions converged a little because we have taken notice of each other's observations in Barcelona. Overall, we may not have solved any of the world's pressing problems and we are all conscious of the real difficulty in thinking through the cobwebs and blockages of the past, but, as a result of the conference, we are now at least clearer on what the questions actually are. Hopefully, the essays help to clarify the issues around the concept of social control for a much wider group than met in Barcelona, and also to indicate the significance of this quite American concept for the new political orders developing in contemporary Europe. The title of the book tries to anchor this and to indicate the fact that we see the concept of social control as being deeply connected with the construction of new political orders.

The editors began work on the book during a week together in Oñati, a small town in the Basque country where community, solidarity and respect are very important, but where so too are independence, self-determination and group culture. This is a country with a small 'c': where society begins at home, where not even the language spoken in some households is comprehensible to those from other households, where the common language is Euskera and Spain sometimes seems a long way away in Madrid. Nationalism is strong here, the revolutionary movement active, even 'terroristic', and the

Basque government not entirely as stable as it would like to be. At a more particular level, this book began life in the Oñati International Institute for the Sociology of Law, on one of its many high-tech computers. The editors of this book also communicate with each other regularly by fax and e-mail, perhaps being in touch more often than with several of their respective academic colleagues in Barcelona and Cambridge. One of our colleagues from Barcelona was here in Oñati on the day of writing this to discuss policing arrangements in Spain with representatives of the Basque government, and no doubt consistency of approach to social control between Madrid and Donostia is on the agenda. An American professor from California was also visiting the Institute that week, joining the Venezuelan scholar on sabbatical and the Master's students from Argentina, Spain, Italy, Finland, Mexico, Costa Rica, Ecuador and Brazil. All in all, here in the small town of Oñati, life is peaceful, orderly and lively, despite all the complexity in the situation; clearly, the topic of social control is not a simple issue. Clearly also, people from all over the world do care about bonding, community, participation and self-regulation. Social control, in this Parkian sense (Park, 1921), does matter but does calling what we experience social control make sense to us any more? Or is Park's view of social control just one possible view of a more general phenomenon which includes much more coercive regulatory systems?

The book opens with two essays, by Colin Sumner and Roberto Bergalli respectively, which were written specially for this volume by way of an introduction. Sumner's opening chapter attempts a broad outline of the history of the concept of social control and its related politics, with a view to setting the scene and defining some of the key issues. In Chapter 2, Bergalli comments upon the reception and usage of the concept of social control in Latin America before moving into an exploration of the significance of the concept for Spain, a country in full flow of developing a new political order. Chapter 3 sees Dario Melossi arguing a strong case for the value of the concept of social control in understanding democratization and for the importance of the concept in relation to the decline of the value of the idea of the state, especially in the formation of the new political arena in contemporary Europe. In Chapter 4, Massimo Pavarini, writing from within a kind of left-realist position, considers the importance of rethinking concepts of crime prevention in terms of a developed notion of social control, with a view to outlining the kind of social control which will both serve democratic ends and the necessity of crime prevention in contemporary Italy. Sebastian Scheerer and Henner Hess, in Chapter 5, present a thoroughgoing analysis of the value of the concept of social control as a general concept in social science. Their account amounts to a defence and reformulation of the concept in the light of the emergence of postmodernity. On the contrary, in Chapter 6, Colin Sumner suggests that the concept is not capable of a strong defence, arguing that any reworking of the idea of social control must be reconnected anew to political projects aimed at restricting élite power and reconstituting the discipline of resistance in an increasingly polarized and globalized social order. Finally, in Chapter 7, Roberto Bergalli sums up his conclusions from our debate and, as a good chairman does in certain cultures, tries to show that we were all right, to a point, and that we agreed on many things, before going on to outline some of the difficulties facing social control at the end of the century.

# Acknowledgements

We would like to acknowledge the financial support of the Goethe Institute in Barcelona and its director, Dr Karl Niggestich, in bringing our German colleagues to the conference; and also of the Departament de Dret Pénal I Ciències Pénals and the Instituto de Criminología, both of the Universitat de Barcelona, in enabling this conference to take place. In particular, our colleagues, Prof. Dr Iñaki Rivera Beiras (Universitat de Barcelona), Profra. Encarna Bodelón González (Universitat Autónoma de Barcelona) and José Luis Domínguez Figueirido made a big contribution to the organization of the seminar. Prior to the conference, a long period of collaboration between the editors had been funded by the Spanish Ministry of Education: our thanks to them for their generosity and to the University of Barcelona for making that collaboration such a productive one. Finally, the last stages of the publication process were made much easier by the skilled assistance of Ben Sumner, Mark Fenwick and Richard Jones in compiling the reference database; they have our gratitude in coping with such a complex list of references. Keith Hayward did the index – our thanks to him. Of course, as usual, our publishers deserve many thanks for their support, especially Gillian Stern, who has been a model of patience.

*Robert Bergalli and Colin Sumner*
Oñati, 1996

# 1

# Social Control: the History and Politics of a Central Concept in Anglo-American Sociology

*Colin Sumner*

Social control is the central fact and the central problem of society.
(Robert Park, 1921: 20)

Social control is an important concept within sociology, arguably one of the most important. However, it has become one of those that sociologists have recourse to when all else fails; just about everything and anything has been seen in recent years as an instance of social control. The concept has, at least in part because of this, lost most of its vitality. Sociologists have lost conviction in using it and it has come under substantial criticism.

But how did this come to pass? How did a concept which once stood for the very process of making a society out of a war of all against all, or at least out of a fierce class struggle, come to lose its potency? What does this tell us about the sociological project today? Indeed, do we still hold to a concept of society? If societies can be said to exist, what now binds them together? Does binding things together matter any more and does anyone care about it anyway? A look at the history and politics of the concept of social control should at least suggest the right questions to ask. This introductory chapter attempts that task and will discuss key moments, features and issues within that history. It is inevitably selective, aiming at an elucidation of the general picture rather than attempting a comprehensive, detailed, analysis. Focusing on Anglo-American sociology, the chapter describes several materials and issues which the rest of this book will keep returning to. It is written in conjunction with Roberto Bergalli's Chapter 2, in a conscious attempt to highlight the historical, cultural and political specificity of the original meanings of the concept of social control.

Sociologists writing about social control in the first quarter of this century in the USA were concerned about the dizzying effects of rapid change, increased mobility and transport, the new technologies of mass communications, the residential divisions of the city, the growing gap between urban and rural values, the violence of contemporary culture, the increasing distance of children from their parents, the effects of vast labour migrations within countries and internationally, and the apparent lack of an overweening moral force to guide people towards co-operative, peaceful and harmonious adaptations to this maelstrom of modernity. They were also fundamentally concerned about the evils of unrestrained capitalism and the freedom of the market. All these processes and patterns are still with us. Indeed, their speed has accelerated and their impact is more defined. Looking back at the early writings on social control, even Park, that great modernist, assumed a certain fixity of place and time – a location – as the foundation of social control. Today, the word fixity seems inappropriate and the word flexibility often jumps more readily to mind. Fixity may not even be a precondition of community any more; but flexibility might be. The time–space continua have shifted. They are maybe no longer best understood as continua.

Today, we often exist briefly in temporary points on an international grid before moving quickly to another; on a star trek going where no one has gone before. We communicate through means which connect us to others anywhere at any time, more or less. These means can be technological but they must also include the internationally known symbols which convey the intended message. We are connected as much by spectacle as by interaction. Indeed, we would no longer assume that interactivity required personal presence in a conversation between two or more human beings. Symbolic interaction in 1995 is very different from that of Mead's day, the first quarter of the twentieth century. But it is not just the links between people that are being transformed, it is also the spaces, times and identities they occupy. Boundaries are disappearing in some places, while in others the residents fight each other to the death in order to preside over a territory whose boundaries will dissolve soon after the fighting stops. Times come in zones and phases, and the seasoned traveller can experience most of the temporal variations since late feudalism within one lifetime. Moreover, even in stable territorial organizations, national identity seems constantly insecure, or at least socially divisive, constantly subverted by cross-national, inter-cultural, market-linked allegiances and the enduring recalcitrance of class, gender and ethnicity.

Individuals, individuated from others and divided within, are increasingly only briefly connected by money, cyberspace and friendship – cash, cables and consciousness. They recognize few boundaries, times and obstacles. So who or what regulates these treks into the deep, vast, space of hypermodernity? Is social control dead or is it simply a virtual reality? Has the time for the Parkian sociological project passed? Has the fundamental character of social interaction changed so much that all previous theories of regulation are redundant? Are they too just part of a new virtual reality? Or are we about to discover some timeless truths about the human condition? What about the eternity of real emotions, the recalcitrance of certain old values, the maturity of cultural knowledges and the mysterious unity of the universe? Were they ever reducible to being merely discursive themes of certain grand ideologies and are they any more compactible to convenient file protocols on an electronic network? No doubt, our book will only be able to make a start at suggesting answers to such deep questions, but even such a modest objective is necessary at a time when the very possibility of the classical sociological project is challenged and when the reality of our existential condition seems more virtual than virtuous. This necessity is compounded by the resurgence of political and cultural movements all over the world which not only emphasize the importance of a new democratization but also have great difficulty in appealing to our old values of community, family and co-operation through the prisms of a culture dismembered by the international media of spectacle.

## What was the sociological concept of social control about?

Strangely, given its centrality to the sociological project, the concept of social control has not been subject to a great deal of attention. In our view, it is due for a reassessment – if only because the concept has been tied to the concept of social deviance for the last 50 years and that latter concept is now, arguably, theoretically bankrupt (see Sumner, 1994). But there are deeper reasons (see also Scheerer and Hess, and Melossi, *infra*). The political problematic of the social control movement may no longer exist as a global foundation for sociology. The space and time which that politics occupied need scrutiny: possibly, they have gone forever, leaving no simple conceptual replacement as appropriate. We may have to develop general concepts which are more appropriate to our time and place. We may have to go further and approach issues of social regulation from a completely different standpoint or theoretical framework. Indeed, maybe there are no 'issues' but merely a set of disparate agendas linked to different standpoints and theories. But it may also be the case, as Scheerer and Hess suggest, that social control was a valid attempt at a general concept within sociology and is simply in need of reformulation. In this case, therefore, it may be that the concepts are already available, born in the womb of the parent and living a rebellious adolescence, which will ultimately rework our thinking about the character of the social and about the constitution of order in societies.

Janowitz once described the concept of social control as 'central' within sociology for 'analyzing social organization and the development of industrial society' (1975: 82). As such, he argued, social control performed several functions within pre-1930s sociology:

- it linked empirical sociological analysis to values and philosophies of progress;
- it signalled a desire to reduce scientifically the amount of 'irrational' behaviour in society;
- it was a way of talking about a society's ability to regulate itself.

Since 1930, Janowitz quite rightly maintained, its meaning has narrowed to refer to the processes of producing conformity through socialization or repression. Always, however, in my view, the concept has been a tool for analysing, or sensitizing sociologists and lawyers towards:

1   the combination of social forces aimed at giving 'society at least a trend toward an ideal' (Vincent, 1896: 490);
2   the study of societies as discrete wholes in movement;
3   the normative integrity of the nation-state; and
4   the need for understanding, identity, empathy and co-operation between citizens in multicultural democracies.

As such, in our view, it has always tended to focus on the integration of social systems, to neglect the negative forces or contradictions which push towards conflict, and to remain in the parochial rather than the global sphere of reference. Homely talk about societal disintegration involves a very different picture to that conjured up by internationalist declarations about class exploitation, super-profits and ethnic suppression. Social control discourse also sounds to me like talk from the top. In social control-speak, workers' resistance to harsh exploitation became system disequilibrium requiring rational management rather than self-protection requiring a lot of courage. Right from the beginning, I have to wonder whether such a general concept could ever be successfully reformulated to avoid the deeply problematic implications of its social and political origins and functions.

In its earliest forms in American sociology, however, the concept of social control was definitely not an expression of a conservative political standpoint. Its adherents were sometimes socialists, sometimes progressives or liberals. Typically, they were unimpressed with the inability of free-market economics to deliver a self-regulating society. They were unlikely to be of the view that 'the individualistic pursuit of economic self-interest' could explain or produce 'collective social behavior', 'social order' or 'the achievement of ethical goals' (Janowitz's phraseology). On the other hand, the concept of social control was certainly not part of a radical critique of capitalism.

Again, Janowitz's words convey the flavour of the concept. The early use of the concept, he said, paralleled sociologists' interest in 'value maximization', their commitment to the values of reducing the use of coercion by authorities and of eliminating human misery, and their wish to rationalize societal goals. In this early use of the concept, social control represented partly a critique of coercion and partly a critique of the free market. Janowitz goes so far as to say that its opposite concept was coercive control. If he is right, and I think he is, then the 'social' in the early uses of social control really meant consensual and collaborative. Thus there are unacknowledged parallels with the concept of hegemony as developed by the Marxist thinker Gramsci. Clearly, any exhaustive history of the concept of social control would need to attend to the very different social-isms that emerged in the USA, Germany and the USSR in the 1930s as solutions to the massive and complex crises of that time. What is clear to us now in the 1990s, with the benefit of hindsight, is that the concept of social control has two big problems: one concerning the nature of control and the other, much less discussed one, concerning the character of the social. Right up to the late 1980s, sociologists remained focused upon the problems of control, law and regulation; yet the challenge for us now, since the fall of the Berlin Wall, is to recognize that the concept of social control cannot easily move on or be reformulated, or even replaced, without an extensive discussion of the values and possibilities of the competing social-ist philosophies. Social control is partly about establishing control but, it seems to me, it is just as importantly about establishing an order which is in some way truly social.

In these early days before the Second World War, American sociology was concerned to do empirical research into various forms of social control to determine which were the most effective in enabling social groups to regulate themselves 'in terms of legitimate moral principles' with the result of reducing 'coercive control' (Janowitz, 1975: 85). This provides us with another way of grasping what the concept was always about. It can be seen, in Foucauldian terms, to be internal to the disciplinary project whose central mechanism was always 'mildness-production-profit' (Foucault, 1975: 219) and whose central object was/is self-discipline. Social control research can be understood as pseudo-scientific investigation into the mechanics of disciplinary power; 'pseudo' because the studies always worked within an acceptance of the parameters of capitalism, imperialism, patriarchy and state power. Self-discipline was rarely, if ever, defined in terms of what might be healthy for the individual (like not being alienated, oppressed or forced to conform, or, more positively, like being stimulated to growth and fulfilment).

Social control is not particularly concerned with the enormous self-discipline involved in the conducting of an insurgent military struggle against imperial capitalism. It is indefinitely more interested in the forms of self-discipline which imperial capital can instil into a population to pre-empt the emergence of such revolutionary action. This may seem obvious but no one has commented upon it. In brief, the ultimate values behind the purpose of the exercise of social control were rarely analysed rigorously and were usually taken for granted. After the 1939–45 War, such values were probably not even seen as having a foundational role as the concept became subsumed within the anodyne language and bureaucratic pyrotechnics of societal and international management strategies – such as welfare statism and the politics of the Cold War – and thus its original biases were doubly hidden from view.

From the outset, social control was about social discipline; from the outset its originating values were taken for granted; and so, not surprisingly, the norms which should tell us what social control is for have never ever been discussed. For the whole of the twentieth century, the foundational values of social control have remained sacred, beyond debate, and outside of scrutiny. But, what is societal order for? The preservation of capitalism? The maintenance of gender domination? The reproduction of the species? Psychological security? Since, at the end of the century, few of us now want to regulate anyone else in the name of these values, we have to ask what are the functions of order, stability, peace and harmony and whether conflict, subversion and ecstasy are not more productive of societal equilibrium.

As Janowitz baldly and revealingly put it, 'social control is not the achievement of collective stability' (1975: 85). In other words, the concept of social control was never a revolutionary conception, it was always a reformist one linked to practical social policy debates. It was part of the intellectual work directed towards mitigating the worst excesses of industrial capitalism. It belongs utlimately, in my view, to the hundred years in Europe and the USA between 1880 and 1980. It is not surprising, therefore, to find that its strongest, most attractive and clearest expressions are to be found in the middle of this period (see the discussions of Park and the Roosevelt era in Melossi, 1990; and Sumner, 1994). Janowitz's revealing comment shows that this is a concept linked to the politics of welfarism, the welfare state, and social democracy. It is not about long-term solutions to problems of alienation and oppression, marginalization and exploitation, conflict and violence. It is a concept which was at its most meaningful within a particular historical/political conjuncture. It is a metaphor for pragmatic thinking about morality and social solidarity in times of acute societal tension. It is a metaphor which has lasted for most of this century and which could be held partly responsible for the fact that we enter the next century like the last, with one writer after another calling for either a new ethics, or a reconstruction of social morality, or a politically informed social justice, or a new moral vision. However, as others more cynical may observe, it may also be partly responsible for the fact that we enter the next century at all.

Let us listen again to Janowitz:

> The vital residue of the classical standpoint is that social control organizes the cleavages, strains and tensions of any society – peasant, industrial or advanced industrial. The problem is whether the processes of social control are able to maintain the social order while transformation and social change take place. (1975: 85)

Social control is then a holding operation, not a solution. As Janowitz also observed, it is 'parallel' to repression: the difference from repression is that effective social control motivates whereas, he implies, quite rightly, repression politically demotivates populations (see also Thomas, 1984: 95). Social control, in its fundamentals within American sociology, is, therefore, part of the process of domination – but a part which is about the construction of hegemony; a part which deals in the discursive currency of regulation, conformity, assent, participation and balance rather than the register of repression, pacification, conquest, censure and censorship. While the earlier formulations were much further away from this latter register than those following 1940, the vision of social control throughout this century, one could say in summary, accepted that domination was not going to disappear overnight but hoped to minimize its coercive features in favour of a more 'civilized', more peaceful, more democratic, more reasonable and more effective approach.

Given the horrific violence of the twentieth century, the inconceivably savage scenes constructed by the 'civilized' world in the battles of the Great War of 1914–18, the Holocaust, the genocide in Indonesia, the gulags of the Soviet Union, the dictatorships of Latin America and the apartheid of Southern Africa, we might reflect that the social control project was a relatively enlightened influence, if a somewhat ineffective one. If the major problem with the intellectual conception and the political project of social control lay within the economic, political and normative parameters it accepted as axiomatic for its operationalization, one can imagine that there could – in principle, if we change the parameters – be a renewed and, in my view, transformed concept of social control in the next century which would focus upon both the values necessary for human health *and* the systematic daily contravention of those values and ethics by people in powerful but anti-social institutions and systems. Could there be a social control in the next century concerned with the reconstruction of societies around fundamental moral values at the expense of more economic, rational or political criteria?

## The limits to violence

Ross's book, *Social Control* (1969), was enormously influential in American sociology and politics. It has been frequently acclaimed as the stimulus for the growth of a whole sub-field of sociology around the concept of social control. Indeed, Ross is often seen as one of the founding fathers of American sociology. Some attention to his classical but rarely closely analysed text is therefore in order and, as we shall find, reveals many essential aspects of the American sociological conception of social control. But, before we do that and before we slip into the parameters of his discourse, we would do well to remember that in so far as societies exist at all prior to the emergence of the discussion about the need for social control, they exist as conquered territories ruled through the state machine. Violence, in the form of military conquest and repression, is a precondition for the subsequent emergence of a move to 'civilize' domination. The social character of 'control' was put on the political agenda by people in territories where the means of production, the means of 'legitimate' violence, and the means of mass communication were in the hands of élites and specialists (to use Elias's term: Elias, 1987) whose power derived in one way or another from the violent suppression of alternative claims on those resources.

As Melossi has acidly commented, the democracy of the 'natural community' in the United States of America meant that 'Americans' could progress as a community of people with equality and rights 'reserving violence for those who were excluded from it by (lack of) birthright or by "choice", such as the original inhabitants of the place, the slaves, and the criminally or socially "deviant"' (1990: 101). Popular sovereignty was the homely inheritance of true Americans; the rest of the population were the targets of regular violence aimed at sustaining the nation-state which had been established by an earlier violence of a distinctly international character. The democracy based on freedom observed by Tocqueville, wherein compliance is voluntary and stimulated by a free press, was 'one in which violence and coercion had been withdrawn from the center of the polity, and sent to preside over the internal and external borders of the white men's convenant' (Melossi, 1990: 102).

Ross openly feared that traditional ideals would be swept asunder by the processes and consequences of industrialization if there were not liberal changes in institutions and sanctions inspired by the progressivist masthead of science, reform and progress. This approach echoed Durkheim's work and was developed further in the well-known work of Roscoe Pound (see especially Pound, 1930). It later became axiomatic within liberal American legal philosophy, and was echoed by many a sociologist (for example, Tannenbaum, 1938). Like Durkheim, Ross wanted to see restrictions on economic individualism and the promotion of social welfare through the state. Like Maine, Tönnies and Durkheim, he saw community being transformed into society. The binding of living tissue' was being replaced by 'rivets and screws' (Ross's words, 1969), and there was a growing need for conscious planning and social control to sustain social order. The massive poverty sitting right alongside the huge accumulated capitals of the conquerors of aboriginal America signalled the weaknesses of raw capitalism. Ross clearly saw the problem of order as part of the white man's burden, since he appeared to see only Western Europeans as the bearers of civilization. The earlier civilizations, and the native American aboriginals, did not have an order problem, in his view, because their interrelations were 'natural' – that is, automatic, spontaneous and instinctive. In this tortuous logic, the civilization of the white man was unproblematic even though it required 'societal domination' – that is, the domination of society over its own acquisitive ruling marauders, through specifically created institutions of social control, to prevent social deviation and the domination of private interests – whereas uncivilized societies were seen as problematic even though they could evolve peacefully without recourse to specific institutions of social control. Of course, it was not untypical of the white middle-class male to see the world in this upside-down way at that time (see also Durkheim's observations on women's lack of inclination to suicide, and the general commentary in Sumner, 1994: Chapters 1–3, on the equally ethnocentric, imperialist and ideological concept of social deviation).

It is worth noting, however, that Ross actually saw colonizing ventures as not only destructive of the traditions of the colonized or 'the traits that make order a matter of course' (1969: 16) but also, interestingly, of those of the first colonists. The savage violence of the colonizers, for Ross, amounted to the loss of an innocence which was never recovered. He looked longingly at aboriginal culture thus:

> The most astonishing fact brought to light by the ethnologist, is that frequently the savage is not, save in his mode of warfare, 'savage' at all, but is, on the contrary, amiable and peaceful . . . We find them living in joint families or house communities with an intimacy and peaceableness we cannot attain to . . . The children of the Siberian savages 'never fight' . . . 'Scorning, scolding and rough words are absolutely unknown in Aleut life'. (Ross, 1969: 15)

The concept of social control, then, can be seen to be an intellectual or ideological outcome of the second imperialism, in particular the conquest of the American and Canadian aboriginals. How deeply ironic that Ross should bemoan the need for that social harmony which had just been destroyed in such a racist and irresponsible fashion.

Like G.H. Mead, Ross emphasized the importance of being able to sympathize with others as a condition of social order. The breakdown of traditional family values and the family itself tended, in his view, to destroy this ability to sympathize and the willingness to sociability, leading to 'misbehaviour and injustice', resentment and a sense of inequality. This was a classic modernization thesis, and was later to be repeated *ad nauseam* in the literature on underdeveloped countries (see Sumner, 1982). 'The breakdown of social control leads to crime' became a familiar refrain within American criminology. It proclaimed that moral relations were no longer interpersonal. In the 'natural order' with its 'natural control', 'nonconformity' had been 'directly censured' and neither 'police nor crime existed' (Weinberg et al., 1969: xxiii–iv). Again, we hear 'a loss of innocence' thesis rather than a more scientific and less idealistic analysis of the structural characteristics of the *longue durée* of capitalism and the civilizing process. Mr Hyde had simply turned into Dr Jekyll.

The new 'social' order of industrialism, in Ross's neo-Darwinist thesis, was seen as a product of centuries of 'selection'; as based on 'violence and aggression, the propensities of predatory man' (Ross, 1969: 16). These 'vast societies' shelter 'the bad man', he insightfully observed.

> With conquest and state-building begins a protracted régime of force, status, and exploitation, which strengthens self-seeking and clannishness, undermines the primitive instinct of friendly association, and leaves an emulative, individualistic stamp upon nearly all the institutions of the Teuton. (ibid.)

The American, and the Western man in general (and Ross did mean men specifically), had individualism in his 'blood and bone' (ibid.: 17). He produced a highly differentiated society where instinct had been replaced by reason, the ethical by the economic, feeling by intellect, simple mass by division of labour, and amiability by ferocity. Clearly, a close reading of Ross betrays crude portrayals of him as a conservative defender of order! No doubt there is a racism in his writing, sometimes a reverse one, but his character as a critic of the new social world, as well as a boy from an Idaho farm displaced to the city, is obvious:

> Or take that wonder of our age, the growth of cities. The modern commercial or industrial city, with its lack of neighborliness, its mutual

indifference, its mingling without fellowship and its contact without inter-
course, its absence of communal opinion, its machinal charities, its
vicarious philanthropy, its dismal contrasts of wealth and poverty, its
wolfish struggle for personal success, its crimes, frauds, exploitations, and
parasitism – surely this strange agglomeration is the work of the economic
man, not the social man! (ibid.: 19)

The instinct to sociability had become 'jaded' in this anonymous,
mass, divided and fast world. It was a world, for Ross, that produced
an 'hereditarily criminal class'; a world that needed a new 'social control' to mitigate the destruction of the 'natural control' of
undifferentiated, simple societies.

Men of violence, Ross argued, cannot be reconciled by 'the affec-
tionateness of Tahitans or Lepchas', but only by the 'voluntary
limitation of one's claims that flows from a sense of fairness' (ibid.:
29). Nature has given us reflexivity and self-control, and we have to
develop them as restraints on violence, to become 'the conscientious
individualist' (ibid.: 30). We must recover our better nature, urged
Ross (the contrasts here with Nietzsche are stark at times and, sometimes, interesting). The virtues of the civilizing warrior-races, like
honesty and directness, can produce a healthy sense of justice and
fair play, but they are forever in danger of being reduced by 'pro-
longed domination' to the 'vices of the master' such as brutality,
bullying, fraud and treachery. Like Durkheim, Ross felt that the principles of equity and justice had to limit the predatory violence of
economic man, and that unchallenged rule was a recipe for corruption
and abuse of power. Similarly, the will to justice and the compunction
to self-protection is deadened in those accustomed to sustained
unfreedom: 'the poor so far as they feel themselves unfairly beaten in
the battle of life; the subjects of arbitrary will, such as women, ser-
vants, and slaves; the classes, castes, and peoples that lie under the
harrow.' (ibid.: 31). Instead, 'they stoop to guile and cunning'" echoes
of Nietzsche's *ressentiment*.

At times, Ross sounded a little like an exponent of the colonial
ideology, but he was more like Arnold and Ruskin than Lord Lugard.
His insistence on fair play, democracy and rights was a strong one and
made it clear that social control for him was as much, if not more, an
ethical limitation on the power of the predators as on their resentful
victims. This is a sense of social control which somehow got lost after
1945, and has never been recovered. Maybe, now is the time. For the
end of this century reminds us of the last: the corruption of regimes
and governments too long in insufficiently limited power, the lack of
effective rights and consequent apathy of disenfranchised publics, the
lack of fairness and the absence of sympathy in national cultures, the
absorption and resistance of national cultures within supranational

economic blocks, the spectacle of horrific and often arbitrary violence, and the reluctance to provide welfare for the poor. The 'conscientious individualist' has had his day and has failed to defeat or control the conscientiously anti-intellectual, anti-social, predators of the city.

At a minimum, it is a time for moral and ethical renewal, as it was a hundred years ago. For Ross, part of the rot was the fact that the just had come to be identified with the praiseworthy and the unjust with the blameworthy (ibid.: 32). Conscience had been manufactured to order, as society domesticated justice by eliminating it from politics. The modern state, he said, had thus been inimical to the growth of an international morality. We have made righteousness the standard, instead of humanity; rules rather than equity; rights rather than common sense. The Teutonic sense of fair play, said Ross, enabled us to rule 'dependent peoples' with some justice and to obey general rules, but it does not originate 'mutual restraints' or recognize group interests. The 'arbitration of a gun' and 'shoot-at-sight' cause little deep anxiety, Ross claimed. The generation of 'social order' requires much more than a respect for rules and regulations. It requires positive, social, moral sentiments from within, plus a sympathy for the injustice and suffering of others.

For Ross, to produce society as an all-inclusive group, inspired by the sentiments of sympathy and justice, it is necessary to find methods of assimilating and reconciling different people and groups, and these methods had to inspire consciously created, specialized and authoritative systems of social control which had the support of the bulk of society. Societies had to develop these institutions of social control, and unless they were supported popularly they were not social. And develop them they did: in the form, said Ross in his famous but curious list, of public opinion, law, belief systems, education, custom, 'social suggestion', religion, ideals, ceremony, art, unique and dominant personalities, élites, illusions and values. Some of these social controls were internal, some external; and when operating in conjunction, they founded a system of social control.

The objectives of this social control for Ross were both individual self-control and the restraint of others; the latter being the greater 'service' to society (ibid.: 63). It was a form whose content, weight and tone varied with exact societal conditions. Its necessity, for example, is increased when social power is concentrated in the hands of a few and, under those conditions, it is more likely to affect sharply the direction of society. Similarly, the character or 'tinge' of this social control will depend on which group actively monopolizes power (for example, whether it be clerics or generals; a point also strongly emphasized by Elias, 1987), and the relative unity of the ruling minority will determine the degree of unequivocal 'class selfishness' displayed within the social control. In his own United States of America, what was needed of social control was 'the formation of an official body . . . to become a seat of social power'; ' . . . to protect ourselves against the lawlessness, the insolence, and the rapacity of overgrown private interests, we shall have to develop the state, especially on its administrative side' (Ross 1969: 88).

Ross's book on social control was influential in national political circles as well as in sociology. It could count President Theodore Roosevelt and Oliver Wendell Holmes as two of its admirers. Its optimism, particularly regarding the nationalization of social control institutions, was attractive. The editors of its modern reprint observe that Ross, as 'a Populist turning Progressive', was 'frightened and repelled by class conflict' (Weinberg et al., 1969: xxxvii). As a spokesman for the 'secure middle class', they say, his work owed far more to Durkheim than it specifically acknowledged, and Ross had clearly read Durkheim's *Division of Labour* (1893). They continued: 'Class control, in contrast to democratic social control, he considered to be destructive of individual freedom, immoral, and, in the long run, ineffective' (Weinberg et al., 1969: xxxvii). Class control, for Ross, threatened egalitarian competition; social control would maintain a balance between individual desires and social needs. Social control was to offer 'the most welfare for the least abridgment of liberty' (Ross, 1969: 427).

The book had outlined a theory of social control in direct, open and vibrant terms, but it had a glaring absence, as his modern editors observe. Ross had offered some general principles but had said very little about the nature of the norms which were to be the criteria and foundations of social control (Weinberg et al., 1969: xlii). It was an absence of some considerable significance: social control was being founded more on pragmatism, common sense, goodwill and negotiation than on decree, prohibition, coercion, moralizing and rectitude.

## Park, normative incorporation and the city

Assimilation might have been the watchword for Robert Park's social control project. Like Ross, he distinguished between a spontaneous, informal, 'natural' control and a more contrived, public and formal social control – and both were seen as formative of assimilated communities. Indeed, Park defined sociology itself as merely a 'method for investigating the processes by which individuals are inducted into and induced to co-operate in some sort of corporate existence which we call society' (1921: 20). Social control was absolutely central to his sociological work, and his writings on the subject developed the concept further along the lines initiated by Ross. But, like Durkheim, Park was dizzied by the extent and speed of social change:

> We are living in such a period of individualization and social disorganization. Everything is in a state of agitation – everything seems to be undergoing a change. Society is, apparently, not much more than a congeries and constellation of social atoms. (Park et al., 1967: 107)

Park's own sociology drew much attention to the role of mass communications as means of social control in the new urban societies of the twentieth century. Always concerned with the assimilation of the races and the formation of multicultural communities, and always emphasizing the value of strong informal bonds based on democratic communication and participation, Park defended the pluralism of the American press of his time and urged against isolationism and xenophobia (see Smith, 1988: 116; Park, 1950). Social control in this new world depended, for Park, upon agencies which would bring diverse cultures together and not divide them against each other. Without it, there would be a local 'civil' war (an idea reflecting closely the social reality of Chicago in the 1920s), and even a world conflagration (see Sumner, 1994: 45). Modern social control in this way reflected, and had to continue to reflect, the existence of a politically organized public with a shared universe of discourse, language, statements of fact and news (Park, in Turner, 1967: 216). Newspapers and news were, therefore, particularly important means of social control because news enabled the large populations of modern cities to 'readjust' quickly to constantly changing circumstances and to a procession of social crises (in Park et al., 1967: 19, written in 1925). In general, unless control institutions were underpinned by 'the mores' and public opinion, their chances of success were not great – and Park saw the failures of colonialism as testimony to that (Park, in Turner, 1967: 222).

Without this integration of custom, institutional morality and public opinion, there was much less chance of the development of a clear superego within the individual or a strong sense of what Mead conceptualized as 'the generalized other'. This social psychological dimension of social control theory is very important. The Chicagoan sociological utopia of a harmonious multi-ethnic community hinged always upon co-operation, consensus, participation and individual commitment. This, in turn, depended on the formation of moral conscience as a reasonably comfortable compromise between the experience of the individual and the feelings of the community. As Coser summarized Mead's account of the 'generalized other':

> a person's self-image, the 'me', becomes aware of and susceptible to the expectations and appraisals of others in his or her significant environment. The attitude of 'significant others' becomes internalized and broadens out to constitute the 'generalized other' . . . in this reflexive

manner, the expectations of others in society form the character of the individual. (Coser, 1982: 15)

What is less often noticed is that for this process to work well there had to be a substantial amount of tolerance of others' difference in a multicultural situation and, in the USA of the 1930s, such a degree of tolerance was a hope not a fact. Wirth's preface to Mannheim's *Ideology and Utopia* of 1936 is damning testimony to the absence of a shared universe of discourse and meaning, and, by 1940, he had concluded that there was very little consensus and such as there was had been constituted through propaganda (see Wirth, 1936 and 1940). The Chicagoan vision was, we should never forget, utopian, and it was nowhere near realization even by the time of Pearl Harbor in 1941 (see Sumner, 1994: 90–100). The social control project of liberal progressivism was at best only half complete, as millions remained unemployed. It took the full militarization of American society and the growth of a permanent arms economy, plus a massive dose of post-Holocaust amnesia (see ibid.: 146–50), before social control stopped being a negotiative project and was declared a social-systemic reality. The citizenry had to internalize the political significance of Superman, Donald Duck and *Fantasia* before Disneyland could be opened; and Walt Disney had to collaborate covertly with the FBI, J. Edgar Hoover, Senator McCarthy, and the House Committee on UnAmerican Activities. . . .

For Park, in the 1920s, the modern city was accompanied by the increasing importance of 'secondary', or indirect, relations over 'primary', or face-to-face, relations. Social control was, 'for the most part', a spontaneous, direct, personal 'accomodation' to 'personal influences and public sentiment' (Park et al., 1967: 24; see also Park, in Turner, 1967: 212–15). These 'immediate and unreflecting' interactions between members of a community were its foundations. However, in Park's modern city, the family is less important than the school, the church less influential than the 'printed page', and stability less powerful than changing labour-market patterns, with their accompanying changes of residence and heightened interpersonal distanciation. Intimate relations are weakened and 'the moral order which rested upon them is gradually dissolved' (Park et al., 1967: 24). City life is 'distintegrative' and leads to 'the increase of vice and crime'. Moreover, it is full of 'little colonies' of immigrants. Under these conditions, social control 'based on home mores' breaks down 'in the second generation' (ibid.: 27): 'the old forms of social control represented by the family, the neighborhood, and the local community have been undermined and their influence greatly diminished' (ibid.: 107).

Park was clear that the rapid increase in crime in the cities was not due to a lack of assimilation of American values by immigrants because second-generation crime was typically of an American type rather than of a type familiar to the immigrant's original culture. The social control applied to these crimes was also of an American type: 'positive law' was becoming more important than 'home mores'. Here was Park's decisive contribution to the theory of social control: formal criminal law was not the type of social control which would bind citizens together into a corporate community, because 'corporate action' required communication between group members whereas criminal courts were increasingly taking on an administrative, functional character.

Tannenbaum later made the same point even more directly and forcefully (in 1938; see Sumner, 1994: 124–8). The 'dramatization of evil' involved in the increasingly punitive world of the 1930s would, for him, merely heighten the sense of injustice felt by the target groups and increase the likelihood of their distanciation from the community. Park, too, seemed to fear the increase in 'positive restrictions on the individual' apparent in Germany of that time and the possibility of their bringing about 'a condition approaching socialism' (Park et al., 1967: 31). The growth of centralized power and the 'political machine' alarmed him as a means of controlling primary groups. While he felt that 'civilization', 'in the interests of common welfare', demanded the suppression sometimes, and the control always, of 'wild' 'passions, instincts, and appetites', he was concerned that the imposition of 'discipline' suppressed emotions of great social value. Such emotions needed to be 'purged' from the individual through the cathartic activities of sport, play, and art, or even through strikes, wars, elections and religious revivals, or else their suppression could be dangerous (ibid.: 44). Roosevelt's federal art programmes, not to mention the popular adulation of Babe Ruth, during the America of the 1930s were deafening echoes of the Parkian theme (see Sumner, 1994: 58–66).

Nevertheless, Park witnessed what he saw as 'segregation of the poor, the vicious, the criminal, and exceptional persons generally' within the city (Park et al., 1967: 45), and he perceived this as leading to a 'social contagion' which bred 'in soul and body' and anti-social moral traits which explained the 'persistent and distressing uniformity of vice, crime, and poverty'. Combining Le Bon's contagion theory of collective behaviour (1960, 1892) with the distinctively Chicagoan analysis of crime in the city, Park demonstrated that his social control project was still, sadly, locked within a very old class problematic. The city was still the breeding ground for some of the 'vicious' habits of the dangerous classes and a key reason for the development of a system of social control:

> Our great cities . . . are full of junk, much of it human, i.e. men and women who, for some reason or other, have fallen out of line in the march of

industrial progress and have been scrapped by the industrial organization
of which they were once part. (Park et al., 1967: 109)

To deal with this new urban crime, societies, said Park, were developing new social agencies and he gives the examples of the juvenile
courts, the Boy Scouts, and playground associations. These new organizations of social control were based on reason rather than sentiment
and tradition, and thus replaced primary forms of social regulation.
As he noted, they were experimental and, as many commentators have
reported since, they rarely succeeded in the tough working-class areas
they were most aimed at (see Sumner, 1994: 49).

These reflections on Robert Park's writings on social control, and
the studies of the Chicago School of sociology which those writings
inspired, draw to our attention the often neglected fact that the concept of social control is very closely linked to the Rooseveltian,
social-democratic, political project (see Pfohl, 1985; Melossi, 1990;
and Sumner, 1994). This New Deal was an attempt to repair the central damage of the *laissez-faire*, free-market economics of the 1920s. It
supported the development of social work, community development
schemes, art projects, and more liberal attitudes to working-class, especially juvenile, crime. The concept of social control worked during
this period of American history as a metaphor for the social-democratic politics of multicultural assimilation. Page after page of the
classical texts reminds us constantly of the backdrop of (a) immigration to America and (b) the migration of black people from the deep
South to the cities and car factories of the North. In Ross's discourse,
there was a clear smell of the gunsmoke and violence of colonial conquest; in Park's, there was a feel for its consequences during the
ensuing phase of sustained proletarianization. Ross spoke for a social
control by public reason; Park for a social control by sympathetic
negotiation. Neither wanted an authoritarian élitism, and neither
wanted to subvert the authority of the élites.

## Colonialism

The problems with the concept of social control become starkly and
painfully obvious when we consider the process of colonization which
so affected Ross's thinking. Colonialism is founded upon military
pacification, and it amounts to the capture and exercise of the administrative power of a territory. Its early forms of policing are
militaristic. Its separation of powers is minimal. The penality of ter-
ror, not disciplinary regulation, is its modality of power. Only when
resistance has been pacified does policing become part of a hegemonic project (see Ahire, 1991). The shift from militaristic to civil
policing is gradual and depends on the overall military control of the

territory. The rule of law exists in both modes but it is the rule of raw power and owes little to Enlightenment jurisprudence. Policemen act as magistrates, magistrates are plantation managers, tax collectors are judges; sentences are brutal and physical; courts are regulation of the last not the first resort; legislative councils are unrepresentative of the majority of the population or those whose land they stand on; judges impose the culture of a foreign society; and the police are hired hands from antagonistic groups. The only assimilation that is practised is that belonging to the strategy of indirect rule. Power is exercised through local chiefs and enemy tribes, as custom is warped to justify the needs of foreign power and capital.

There is very little sense in which this system of foreign domination could be described as social control even though it is an organized attempt at producing peace if not conformity. Even in the later stages of colonialism, when there were black faces to be seen occasionally on legislative councils, this domination is only social in the sense that the colonialists have imposed a society on the groups and territories they have conquered. By redrawing the map, they created a new administrative unit – a society in this sense only. Passage of time does little to dull the sharp impression gained, for example, from observing the Masai in Tanzania, that societies cannot be created by just drawing on maps. Nor does visiting Dar es Salaam quell the feeling that foreign domination is a mere rental; it confers little real control. Of course, as Fanon, Memmi and others have argued (Fanon, 1967; Memmi, 1965), the biggest damage done by colonialism lay in the minds of the colonized. Nevertheless, the psychological mutilation involved was not the same as control; incorporation was structural at best and the indigenous soul escaped hegemonization into the culture of Babylon. Even those who subsequently volunteered for Babylon's way had not been truly captured or assimilated; a tortured mimicry never lost its sense of opposition.

Social control, in its origins in Ross and Park, is then a very particular idea. It supposes a voluntaristic integration of citizens into a compact of co-operation, compromise, communication and self-policing. In that sense, it is predicated upon a will to peace and an equality of position which has never yet obtained on a mass scale in human society. Like colonialism, this notion of social control was never going to survive the ethnic mixing and cleansing which the Second World War brought about.

The transformation of the various European imperialisms into the new international economic order after 1945 wrought a globalization of economics, politics and culture – notably the economics, politics and culture of the USA. That new order of things was frequently represented as the basis of freedom, the stimulant of a development take-off, and the unity of civilized cultures. International regulation had been born. But still it could not easily be understood as social control. Korea, Vietnam and the Cold War merely left the feeling that social control was the military strategist's metaphor for the construction and mutilation of enemies. Again, Spencer's sense of the importance of military action in understanding social control comes to the fore: social control developed a softer, more 'cultural', sense after 1945 but the history which was its subtext had always been bloody and coercive. Cultural assimilation and construction only seem to arise in human history after conquest, annihilation and humiliation. If these are all aspects of social control, then it is a very generic category indeed.

## Social control and social systems after the Holocaust

Both the Parkian social control project and the earlier ideas of social control were left behind by post-1945 social systems theory. As Lewis Coser commented:

> The liberal era of the nineteenth century could indulge in a Panglossian vision of the present, and even more of the future, in which force and coercion were successfully minimized, and benign social guidance on utilitarian principles came to prevail over the barbarous coercive regimes of the past. But this rosy version found it hard to survive the impact on laymen and scholars alike of two world wars, the Holocaust, Gulag, and Nazi concentration camps. (1982: 19)

By 1990, the 'classical' idea of social control could be (mis)represented to refer to state-centred regulation as the main instrument for producing social order (see Horwitz, 1990: 1). Horwitz even argues that Marx, Weber, Durkheim and Parsons were all alike in seeing the state as 'the key development in the evolution of social control' (ibid.: 2). What a shift this was from the distrust of the state in the work of Ross and Park!

State law in this caricature of classical social control theory became the means whereby societies lifted themselves above the limits of private justice, small communities and status relationships. Legal order was to overcome the problem of diverse moralities in modern, highly differentiated, societies by constituting a neutral public forum applying general rules equally to all. Its autonomy, professionalization and centralization were to function to provide a legal culture with its own logic 'distinct from economic, political, religious or scientific norms and interests' (ibid.: 3). The world of the small, rural, community was not to be left behind entirely however, as we can see when Horwitz observed that, even when it takes legal forms, 'the logic of social control is based on informal norms that govern interpersonal relationships' (ibid.: 5).

Summarizing well a revived liberal legalism of the Parsonian school of sociology, he captured its twin emphasis on a relatively autonomous public sphere, governed by laws and the logic of bureaucracy, united with a consensual civic privatism, rooted in the socializing power of the nuclear family, through the mechanism of shared value orientations. In such formulations, we witness the idea of the total social system unifying town and countryside, linking the diversity of institutions and cultures, and connecting modernity with its past – directed by the interventionist state.

What we have to grasp here is that, over the last 50 years, the sociological theory of social control has been gradually recast as an account of the state as an institutional system for the reproduction of social values. Some, the radical critics, saw this negatively as the rise of Big Brother and others took the positive view that it was the shared values that were driving the ship. In its most liberal positive forms, the forms that emphasize the community end of the equation, for example in the currently popular work of Etzioni (1992), this normative functionalist version of social control could present itself as a kind of 'communitarianism' which celebrated the sociological centrality of certain fundamental human values (for example, family, community, freedom) and which stood against all forms of economism (whether Marxist- or Market-oriented). At the other end of the scale, when the valuable negativity of state-centredness was emphasized, it worked as an apology for the militarism, McCarthyism, and moral conservatism of post-war America: the 'Voice of America' whose mass-marketed, cheaply constructed and fully-sanitized values were transmitted to the globe via Korea, Vietnam and Donald Duck.

Normative functionalist versions of social control theory, inspired notably by Parsons's work, were, in the 1940–60 period, to become the new norm and to set the new agenda for talking about social norms and societal self-regulation (see Sumner, 1994: 161–9; and Melossi, 1990: 134–8). There was also a critical-liberal version of this, most notably expressed in Lemert's work, and that of the labelling perspective which flourished in the 1960s – and we will return to that later in this chapter. But first we must observe the contours of the post-war theory of social control for it would not be unjust to see it as the sociological technicians' fantasy of the new, international, world order of American imperialism, and, as such, of enduring relevance for the present and the foreseeable future.

The turn in the analysis of social control after the Second World War is interesting. It was marked as early as 1941 by an article written by Hollingshead; soon after one in 1940 by Wirth despairing the rise of propaganda and ideology amidst sustained cultural division (see Sumner, 1994: 91–100). Wirth's essay ended one era – the remarkable decade of the 1930s – with the conclusion that the era demanded, namely that any notion of social deviance was mitigated by the ideological character of thought and that there was no genuine moral unity to found a consensualist theory of the social control of deviance. Hollingshead's article, a year later, marked the beginning of the new era – the age of American imperialism – with the argument that social control worked through the organization of behaviours and that such organization could only be rooted in a 'system of reciprocal values and usages inherent in a culture' (1941: 221).

Ignoring and implicitly rejecting Park's corporatist-assimilationist model of social control in a multicultural society and its importance to the whole Chicagoan project, Hollingshead stressed that the essence of social control was not the formal mechanisms of control, or even the informal norms structuring personality, but the organization of the society as a whole binding its parts into 'a more or less coherent unity' (1941: 220). Society, in this sense, 'from the viewpoint of social control is a vast, multiform, organized system of appeals, sanctions, prescriptions, usages and structures focused upon directing the behavior of its members into culturally defined norms' (ibid.). Society as a system. What would transform the great melting pot from a pluralistic chaos into an efficient, functioning (fighting), machine was the organization of coherent links between values, mores, roles, ideologies and institutions. And, very quickly, what was wished for was whisked into being as a declared reality, exactly as in Disney's *Fantasia* (1940) or Stalin's abolition of class by decree in 1936. As Wirth was later to articulate in a Presidential address to the American Sociological Association in 1948, this organization of links between values, roles, norms and institutions depended upon producing a consensus, particularly through the mass media, which commanded people's loyalty. Propaganda was by now a 'good' thing, its value in the war being undoubted, and Wirth declared, in an address entitled 'Consensus and mass communication', that mass media output was a major source of economic and political power (see Sumner, 1994: 161–4). The constructable consensus was limited, because of continuing moral and cultural diversity, but there was a lowest common denominator of basic system needs or organizational coherence – the teamwork which the military bureaucracies needed to win a world war – and it was those lowest common denominator needs which politics since the Second World War has fed upon and never risen much above. System efficiency meant aiming low politically; the depoliticization and apathy that resulted in the 1980s and 1990s is a direct result.

As Wirth saw it, the task was one of 'mobilizing human action to prevent the suicide of civilization' suggested by the atomic bomb and the Holocaust. The post-war notion of social control was thus constructed as a bulwark against a repetition of the horrors of the 1939–45 War. It was not now a concept aimed at assimilation; it was a concept in the service of an institutionally rigorous, organized, social system. As Cuber argued (1940), an institutionally organized society could withstand the effects of diversity, deviance and divergence. What mattered now was the integrity of the system of roles and institutions which was the backbone and strength of society – its structure. Value dissensus on moral matters, for example, was tolerable, but there had to be a value consensus on 'the system of subordination-superordination and the perquisites of position' (1940: 486).

Social control was now a technical instrument in the hands of the managerialist systems analyst and was analysed accordingly within sociology for its effectiveness in sustaining core system-values and procedures. That idea was at the heart of sociological theorizing about social control from 1945 and remained so up to the 1980s, when the evangelical revival of the 'traditional' moral values of the silent majority demanded a different theorization or even the abandonment of the idea of social control. And, of course, understood in this, historical, way, it was an idea which was in no way contradicted by the liberalism and radicalism of late 1960s' 'labelling theory': decriminalizing marijuana use, for example, was quite arguable in a society which was founded upon functional acceptance of the core system values and procedures of corporate, militaristic managerialism rather than upon a more demanding moral code.

The long-standing dream of rooting a system of societal regulation in the shared norms and practices of a unified everyday life of a unified people was turned into a theoretical reality – albeit a very shrunken, functional one – by structural-functionalist sociologists operating within the amnesiac, anodyne, operationalist and business-like world of post-Holocaust, post-*Fantasia* America. In effect, they also became apologists for the post-1945 domination of societies all over the world by the military-financial-industrial complexes of American imperialism. At best, inspired by the need for organization during the war and teamwork to sustain the reconstruction after it, they simply forgot the world of recalcitrant social conflicts around class, gender and ethnicity, deep moral-political doubts about the viability and value of capitalism, and the babble of multiple discourses so bemoaned by Wirth (1936) – and, without much ado, left it behind in the 1930s. Social control was now to become the procedural and technocratic reduction of the desired normative consensus that had never actually happened and which had previously been the goal of earlier social control theory. It was to be a parody of the Parkian assimilationist project, a bureaucratized rule by fantasy, or, more prosaically, regulation by administrative decree in a fully televised world of spectacle, propaganda and mass-manufactured myth.

Even in the work of a relatively liberal sociologist like Lemert, this new approach to social control brought a focus on regulatory technique rather than on the substance of moral concepts (see Lemert, 1942). For him, decreasing social deviance was now a technical question, an issue of calibration: 'If an agency of control identifies with modal norms it automatically decreases deviation' (1942: 752). Power, Lemert implied, simply had to make some allowances for customary behaviour and to refrain from unnecessary regulation and criminalization (see Sumner, 1994: 153–4). It was a question of rational, technical, calculation as to where to pitch the level of social control exercised by official regulatory agencies in relation to typical social behaviour or norms. We should notice that now the word norm had come to mean what actually goes on out there as a matter of fact. It was losing its connection with older ideas of what was natural or right; although there were still several sociologists of law at that time arguing for a natural law theory of social control (see Pound, 1942; Fuller, 1942; Fuller and Myers, 1942). Parsons had started the ball rolling in 1937 by defining a norm as a 'verbal description of the concrete course of action thus regarded as desirable, combined with an injunction to make certain future actions conform to this course' (1937: 75). This ambiguous formulation was explicitly developed to distinguish his conception of norms from ethical-legal conceptions, and Parsons's discussion of it, in relation to military efficiency, clearly indicated that it was intended to be partly ethical or customary – although this aspect appears not to be vital – and partly functional as a necessity for system effectiveness. This definition, when matched with Wirth's scepticism of 1940 about the possibility of substantive normative consensus and Merton's realism (see Merton, 1938) in advocating a pragmatic limitation to the ideals of the American Dream (to prevent high expectations and crime as a result of their frustration), suggests strongly that normative regulation was now unequivocally becoming system management. The prioritization of popular moral values, notably liberty, community and the 'welfare of the common man', was disappearing and was being replaced by the scientific rationalist's sense of what was good for the social system. Social control was becoming less of a principled part of the social-democratic political project in the age of ideology and more of a technical arm of the apolitical welfare state in the era of social reconstruction. That was the key turn in the theory of social control which occurred between 1937 and 1951.

In the work of Talcott Parsons, social control was to become a feature of the social system. It referred to those 'processes in the social system which tend to counteract the deviant tendencies' (Parsons,

1951: 297). From then on, social control was to be defined in structural-functionalist sociology as a response to deviant behaviour.
Deviance and social control became inseparable twins in a discourse
about societal equilibrium. When institutions, roles and values were
interlocked in harmonious interdependence, every aspect of the social
system became, effectively, an agency of social control. Suffused with
the fundamental values of the society, every role and every institution
became a force for socialization into conventional norms; conversely,
every instance of individual waywardness, aberration, resentment or
resistance became an instance of social deviation. It was a sociological picture which produced what Wrong (1961) called 'an
oversocialized conception of man'. It led sociologists to talk a language of system, order and structure. No longer a rational regulation
of free-market capitalism, social control was now the systemic necessity of the welfare-warfare state. Assimilation into multiculturalism
had been replaced by socialization into a single homogeneous culture
of cybernetic functionality. The utopia had changed. The social demo-
crat Roosevelt had died and the general Eisenhower had taken over:
Amerika, the Land of the Free, was on the march and the bland began
to lead the bland.

   In *The Social System*, Parsons is crystal clear: social control 'must
always be stated relative to a given state of equilibrium of the system
or sub-system' (1951: 297–8). Social control became an adjustment
to system strains: a generic term for the kinds of answers Merton's
question had begged.

   This movement in the theory of social control was systematically
expressed at length by LaPiere in his *Theory of Social Control* of 1954.
Rejecting various theories of collective unity, including those of Hegel
and Hitler, LaPiere argued that culture, and its transmission, was only
a partial explanation of social behaviour, and that social order would
be non-existent if it was based solely on the transmission of cultural
norms. Thus, appeals to traditional moral values held little water with
the technicians of social control who saw any 'natural' socialization
process as essentially fallible and, therefore, not reliable for systemic
purposes. Faulty socialization, if culture was all and system was
absent, would have produced a highly criminal and unstable society.
Glossing over, but no doubt mindful of, the fact that up to 1940 there
was a lot of evidence for that portrayal of the USA, LaPiere con-
tended that what produced the predominant order in society was the
'corrective' to 'errors of socialization' (1954: 30), namely social control. Social control was thus theorized as the system-corrective to
cultural-transmission errors. It had been clearly and inextricably
linked to the concept of social deviance – and was to remain in such
bad company right up to the present day.

Social deviance and social control were, in this discourse, simply two sides of the same coin. The former was produced by the failure of the latter (see Parsons, 1951: Chapter 7; and Sumner, 1994: Chapter 7) and the latter was evidenced by the outbreak of the former. During the 1950s, the two concepts were twinned and linked in a discursive moment focusing on the explanation of juvenile delinquency in relation to system harmony, 'rebels without a cause' in Bell's phraseology (see LaPiere 1954: 28–30; also Bell, 1960: Chapter 7; and Sumner, 1994: Chapter 7); an ideological moment which served to map the weaknesses of the post-war social system. In this ideology, delinquents were rebels without justification in a welfare state based on the end of ideology, 'one-nation' consensus, and full employment, and were thus social deviants who needed correction or social control. Social control had now become a morally minimalist yet all-embracing concept to describe all kinds of practical system-management, rather than an active, dynamic ideal of social policy; its job was to describe and assess the effectiveness of state and community responses to social deviance, not to theorize the moral-ethical basis upon which one might achieve social regulation based on normative principles.

LaPiere went on to argue that social control forces deviant individuals to 'conform outwardly' to social norms (1954: 56). Social control was no longer a grand ideal of social democracy but rather an instrument for superficial harmony; it had in this sense become rather shallow and a little pessimistic. It stood for the maintenance of appearances and brushing social contradictions under the carpet – something we became familiar with in the Parsonian era.

Typically, the most common and most effective form of social control, for LaPiere (drawing on Weber), was that exercised by the individual's status group (for example, a community), but it was closely followed by the individual's institutional affiliations. He noted the multiplicity of status groups in the modern city, the high degree of tolerance towards breaches of group norms, or social deviance, and the likelihood of hierarchical structuration within groups. He went on to argue that social control was very important in the maintenance of morale within status groups, drawing tellingly on examples concerning troops in the war. This social control, LaPiere observed, often takes the form of rituals, ceremonies, myths, legends and argot. Of course, the greater the group morale, the less the need for social control but the greater likelihood of it being effective; the weaker the group morale, the greater the need for social control and the smaller likelihood of its success. All of which might suggest that social control was a little redundant: spontaneous group solidarity works best to bind groups and where social control is externally applied to such solidaristic groups it often backfires, causing resentment and resistance.

LaPiere resists this logic, however, and somewhat severely observes that if a group has high morale this does not mean that all its members 'conscientiously and consistently fulfill their status obligations' (1954: 218).

Following closely LaPiere's argumentation in this way reveals the kind of standard he and his generation of conservative sociologists were looking for after the Second World War – perhaps as a hangover from the disciplinary needs of war, they wanted more than lowest common denominator system efficiency. In this period of McCarthyism, all kinds of minor faults were taken as representative of a much higher deviation, as subversion from the goals of corporate, military America; status group tolerance was low.

In fairness, it should be made clear that LaPiere also recognizes that norm-upholders or law enforcers often act more out of their own self-interest than out of altruistic commitment to principle. However, it would have been more logical for him then to conclude that not only does social control not work well, since it is not necessary to sustain solidaristic groups and backfires when applied to oppositional or fractious ones, but also it is mainly brought into being for selfish reasons rather than for the sustenance of the group. Social control as a 'corrective', in LaPiere's work, was beginning to sound like the heavy hand of the over-fastidious nanny state or, perhaps, like an arm of political correctness wielded for sectional gain rather than general regulation.

In LaPiere's analysis, we also see again that the social control of deviance can take many forms ranging from mass extermination to gossip. As in Ross's work, it covered a vast range of phenomena. Always, it seems to be juxtaposed to the idea of the free-wheeling, biological, somewhat idiosyncratic and sometimes deviant individual. Always it seems like an over-extension of the Durkheimian metaphor of social constraint; the idea of the social as an organized constraint on egocentric behaviour. By the late 1950s, its usage in American sociology had settled into a comfortable reification of a multiplicity of very different ways in which organizations effectively regulate individuals' conduct. Moreover, this variety of ways of effecting some kind of patterned outcome became generalized as a system of institutions and techniques unified by a shared value-orientation. In the deep truth of this theory, the state was not really at the centre of this system of social control – that role was played by shared values; the state was a collection of institutions which adhered to those values and attempted to order the society accordingly. The state was thus concealed. The other great myth entailed here was that American society had arrived at a normative consensus. Of course, it had not and was still a great melting pot divided severely by class, ethnicity and gender.

The understanding of social control arrived at by Parsons, LaPiere, and other normative functionalist sociologists was discussed by Black (1984). His overview essay effectively confirms our reading of the history of the concept. Social control, he said, had by the early 1960s come to refer 'broadly to virtually all of the human practices and arrangements that contribute to social order and, in particular, that influence people to conform' (ibid.: 4). However, he argued, since that time the concept had developed a narrower meaning as the ways in which 'people define and respond to deviant behavior' (ibid.: 5). Social control had, after the mid-1960s, become purely a conception of the reaction to deviance (see Clark and Gibbs, 1965; Black, 1976). Unfortunately, this is a common misconception in sociological theory, reflecting sociologists' tendency to teach the field to students as an accumulating body of knowledge developed by one separate, hermetically sealed school of thought after another in nice, neat, consecutive order. So, labelling theory is always held to follow, as a corrective, upon normative functionalism. In fact, at least in the case of the concept of social control, our brief history shows that things were not so simple. The reality is that, following the seeds of thought planted by Hollingshead and developed by Lemert, Parsons and LaPiere, the concept of social control had been defined in terms of actual social-systemic or socially organized responses to deviant behaviour. The blunderbuss approach which included everything and anything as social control had not been superseded, it was simply twinned with the equally all-encompassing idea that social deviance is everywhere. Just because 1960s' sociologists focused on the dynamics of the regulatory process does not mean that there was a fundamental shift in the overall theoretical framework. In fact, such 'radical' sociology was well within the frame of an approach which emphasized the systematic intertwining of deviance and social control. All that is solid in Black's claim is that the re-emergence of the liberal-critical wing of American sociology in the mid-1960s brought about a sharp focus on the exact purposes, interests and ideologies of the specific groups engaged in the organized censuring of social deviance.

Black sensitively notes that 'the concept of social control may also seem to have penal or even coercive connotations' which he did not intend to import into his discussion, and adds 'there does not seem to be any word or phrase that adequately captures the wide range of phenomena to which the concept of social control is meant to refer' (1984: 5). He openly considered alternatives such as 'dispute settlement', conflict management', 'social ordering' and 'reglementation', but was clearly not happy with any of them and retained social control. Such hesitation and discomfort in the use of theoretical vocabulary is a clear indicator of a major conceptual problem or even crisis within the operations of what Kuhn called normal science. Accompanied by variable or irregular use of that concept, it indexes the fact that the time is ripe for an overhaul of the concept in question. By the time Black was writing that was certainly the case with social control, and the incoherence, infinity and flexibility of his version of the concept illustrates this. By the early 1980s, the concept of social deviance had reached a similar crisis; the theoretical framework which had produced the two concepts and their interlinkage was strained beyond its limits in trying to retain an explanatory grasp of the events and trends of the 1960s and 1970s.

Gibbs' work on the concept of social control in the 1960s attempted to rescue it from the lack of specificity problem. Indeed, his article with Clark began by observing that systematic attention to the field of social control had 'long since withered away' and that a reformulation of the concept might breathe 'new life' into the field (Clark and Gibbs, 1965: 398). The subject matter of the concept had become 'vague and impossibly broad' (ibid.: 399).

While Clark and Gibbs acknowledged in 1965 that 'contentless rubrics' fall out of common usage, and that this was a healthy thing for a discipline, they felt that delimitation of the concept of social control could produce a useful 'resurrection' of the concept. They thus delimited its usage to 'social reactions to behavior defined as deviant' (ibid.: 401) which, on my analysis, simply amounted to ratifying an existing tendency. Unfortunately, the weakness of this rescue attempt is fairly obvious. First, it seems odd to exclude all efforts to sustain conformity, such as those within institutionalized religion and education, and, second, if what was deviant was unclear then the whole edifice falls down. Moreover, Clark and Gibbs were simply rehearsing old errors or blind spots when they admit to being unconcerned with the actual content of norms (ibid.: 402), and thus confess their reinforcement of non-normative or amoral systems thinking. In many ways, the so-called labelling theory of the 1960s was amoral in exactly these ways. It opposed excessive stigma, unnecessary criminalization and heavy-handed policing but never attempted to explain why such regulatory severity was felt necessary, morally, economically and politically (Gouldner's famous critique of Becker represents another version of this same point; see Gouldner, 1975; and Sumner, 1994: 253–5).

In later writings, Gibbs worried aloud and at great length about the infinity of social control when defined as a response to deviance (Gibbs, 1981 and 1982). His redefinition of social control as a manipulation of others' behaviour was, on his own admission, 'ponderous' and not susceptible to easy comprehension (1981: 78). However, his work did emphasize the fact noted by Lemert (1972) that social control had become a very passive, as well as infinite, concept within sociology. It supposed a large amount of automation: socialization, when it worked, involved the 'acquisition' of norms and skills and was not very conscious or deliberate, and when socialization failed then social control of the ensuing deviance occurred as a matter of course. In this way, social control had little specificity or analytic 'bite'. It was an impersonal force immediately alerted to action by an alarm bell which was triggered automatically when socialization failed; just as detectives always catch their villains in television crime stories. Sociologists, whether functionalist, interactionist or Marxist, as Gibbs rightly noted, were curiously disinclined to investigate what types of social control succeeded under which social conditions. By the 1980s, social control was just a 'fire brigade' which societies threw at their fires: in the functionalist version that was a good thing; within 'labelling theory' it was overdone; and in Marxist work it was a bad thing (unless the society was a socialist one, in which case it was functional for order and self-protection). Gibbs's book of 1981 made the nonsense of this very clear. Moreover, it began to disentangle social control from deviance. For, if social control was manipulation it required no deviance to warrant it; and if law was social control of this kind, then it had no need of normative content or legitimating content any more (see Gibbs, 1982). With social control being defined even by the more conservative sociologists as manipulation, there was a blurring of the lines between the conservative, liberal and radical positions on social control in the West – none of them could envisage any consistent moral principles guiding, binding or structuring the substance of law or codes of ethics. All was becoming discourse: a mythic narrative with all the coherence and concreteness of patterns in the night sky, rooted in a great ubiquitous power beyond our grasp and signifying little for our own ethical practice. The 1980s, as we know from our own direct experience of state politics, was a time when the divorce of law from morality was apparently complete. The postmodern and the postconventional was upon us.

## Radical views of social control

Liberal and radical sociology in the 1950s, following the example of C. Wright Mills, had developed an alternative view of social control. In this view, there was no healthy plurality of thought which arrived at the same point to celebrate and institutionalize certain values. Rather there were several universes of discourse, revealing widely varying ideological preferences, whose languages reflected the reality of the unequal distribution of power and wealth. In this much tougher world of exploitation and oppression, what passed as social control was, in

fact, the coercive and propagandistic practices of the rich and powerful to sustain their position of strength. What was societally defined as
crime and deviance reflected 'the norms of independent middle-class
persons verbally living out Protestant ideals in the small towns of
America' (Mills, 1943, quoted in Lefton et al., 1968: 23). Moreover,
'traditional' morality and 'basic' values were mocked most by those
who preached them loudest – the corruption and sleaze throughout
the economic and political élites constituted a 'higher immorality'
(Mills, 1956 and 1967; see Sumner, 1994: 157–61). Social control was
thus characterized as political or moral 'enterprise', engaged in or
advocated by 'interest groups', 'élites', empire-building bureaucracies,
'moral entrepreneurs' or 'symbolic crusaders', whose efforts reflected
their own interests, ideologies and prejudices. It was social in that it
was part of society but it did not reflect any general moral consensus.
It was, in short, the sectional regulation of the subordinate.

Lemert had contributed substantially to this view. His seminal
paper of 1948 had suggested that social deviance was ubiquitous simply because of the pluralism of values in the USA. In *Social Pathology*
(1951), he outlined the nonsensicality of seeing crime as individual
psychopathology when even 'presidents of the United States have
appointed members of criminally corrupt political machines to high
offices' (1951: 20). And, in *Human Deviance, Social Problems and
Social Control* (1967), he had developed the theory of secondary deviation which posited that social control creates as much deviance as it
deters. Social control, from Lemert's perspective, had become all too
caught up in the 'struggle' of groups 'to maintain their position in a
hegemony of power relations' (1951: 56). Becker's analysis of the
Marijuana Tax Act reinforced this view, and subsequent studies by
Gusfield (1957, 1963) added that 'moral crusades' for legislative
reform were symbolic movements which extended the ideologies and
interests of their protagonists. Matza (1969) tentatively linked it all up
to 'Leviathan', without actually analysing the political economy of the
American state.

Clearly, this was a view of social control as part of the political
process, as part of the competition for power and the struggle for domination. Allied, as it was, to the theory of deviance as a social or
collective transaction between rule-makers and rule-breakers, and allied
to its intrinsic view of deviance as that which is labelled as such by
agencies of social control, this became the view of social control from
'labelling theory' – a view which could well be described as sceptical of
the roots, values and effects of social control as supposed in conventional, structural-functionalist sociology. Social control was clearly
becoming a very vacuous sociological concept by 1970; it appeared to be
better studied from the standpoint of economics, politics or cultural

studies – as an icon of economic imperatives, political strategy or cultural symbolism – for it had little integrity of its own. Within this liberal-radical analysis, its kernel as a social-system management device was being displaced by an idea of its susceptibility to non-systemic, non-rational, 'external' and self-interested determinants. In passing, I want to comment that the inner logic of organizations may not win over hearts and minds as an exciting justification for social control but, equally, such situational logistics had never been a mere invention either – the radical evacuation of the 'inner' content of social control during the 1960s was a key moment and left it with little to withstand subsequent charges of anarchism, relativism or hypocrisy. Nevertheless, the radical-liberal critics' point was a very strong one: lowest common denominator system-monitoring could hardly exist outside of the social contexts which give it meaning and purpose, nor indeed did such a form of social control emerge from nowhere in a historical sense.

So much has been written about the labelling perspective on deviance and social control that it is unnecessary to rehearse it here (see Pfohl, 1985: Chapter 9; Sumner, 1994: Chapter 9). What should be emphasized is that the perspective secured the tight link between the two concepts: deviance did not exist outside of its establishment through the labels of social control. Moreover, it rendered the social aspect of social control very doubtful – the 'social' became a misnomer as its partisanship was portrayed as an effect of economic, political or cultural conditions. Social control was becoming, for liberals as well as conservatives in sociology, a manipulation of power and ideology. Given that view, the emancipation of the suppressed humanity contained within stigmatized and excluded deviant groups depended upon the abolition, removal or minimization of all forms of social control. Given also that most sociologists were content to leave 'good' socialization to the exigencies of informal and unplanned life within families and communities, it meant that, by the 1970s and the arrival of the 'new' criminology, social control was not only a weak concept but was actually under attack as a useless extra level of regulation which caused only pain and assisted the rich and powerful.

The emergence of the 'new' criminology, the socio-legal studies movement, critical sociology of law and neo-Marxist cultural studies all accelerated the demise of social control as a concept with any substantial following. Social control by the time of the 1980s was seen by many as 'a mode of social domination, a form of oppression or tyranny' (Pfohl, 1985: 375). It was routinely taken to stand for the expression of authoritarian power and ideological bias; to stand for something distinctly 'social' and not at all 'natural' or healthy; to express the dubious conceptions of rationalistic and scientistic social policy now seen as destructive of human societies; and, perhaps above all, to represent the intervention of the state in the affairs of the people. It had become a theoretical icon of a lack of democracy. The wheel had turned full circle. Far from being a restraint on power, an expression of popular values and the basis of welfare-state social democracy, it had become a piece of technicians' jargon deployed by Superpower sociology – and that of Japan, Germany and the countries of the South-East Asian 'economic miracle' – to express the necessity of impersonal, value-free, unpopular, authoritative, technically rational system-management. It had become the vacant look, the blank stare, behind which hid the animated machinations of serious business and big power.

I will return to the radical critiques of the concept of social control in Chapter 6 of this volume. Only a few salient points need be made here. The central criticism of the post-war, American sociological concept of social control which emerged throughout the 1970s was that it was 'social control without history and politics, a concept severed from its original organic connection in the project of classical sociology' (Cohen and Scull, 1983: 6). In short, it meant that social control was a cloak for class control (Mayer, 1983; Stedman Jones, 1983), gender domination (Smart and Smart, 1978) and institutionalized racism (Hall et al., 1978). From the account presented in this chapter, that point is clearly very valid but, as Cohen and Scull also suggest, when it was taken to extremes, all state policies, and even moral or ethical codes, became forms of social control – with the unfortunate result that even ameliorative welfare policies were taken to conceal the hidden hand of capital and to avoid dealing with 'the real issue'. At the extreme then, all attempts at regulation became social control and thus damaging to the interests of the people – even if the people supported the regulation. Social control became a 'boo' word, synonymous with irrationality, destruction, pain and authority. Little surprise that a Left always looking below the surface for a threat or conspiracy was left behind for a number of years by the aggressive, moral-majoritarian politics of the New Right! So many had decried social control, scorned concepts of rights, and dismissed ideas of morality that resistance to the New Right was bereft of its historical legacy from Rossian and Parkian sociology. What sociological concepts had the Left to use? None. The historic tools had all been abandoned in a wave of anarchistic, cool, politically correct, nihilism. Today, these tendencies still survive, only they would now deploy Foucault to justify the supposition that because all knowledge is power-laden there can be no common sense, no agreed morality, no agreed truths, and no reasonableness.

The complexity and internal contradictions of the Left critique of social control from 1968 onwards was well understood, explored and exemplified in Cohen's *Visions of Social Control* (1985). Describing the term social control as a 'Mickey Mouse concept' (Cohen, 1985: 2), referring to any social process which induced conformity or to the coercive effects of state and social policy, Cohen's text confirms my view that the concept had lost any 'resonant or clear meaning'. He himself defined the category as referring to 'the organized ways in which society responds to behaviour and people it regards as deviant, problematic, worrying, threatening, troublesome or undesirable in some way or another' (ibid.: 1), which did not help matters much. Towards the end of what is a very loose, caring, sensitive, even tortured, and openly schizoid discourse, it becomes clear that Cohen believes that it is a 'cultural universal' that societies will have exclusionary forms of social control to clarify moral boundaries and reinforce social solidarity (ibid.: 233). Resuming the Durkheimian mantle, which he donned with such distinction in his formulation of the concept of moral panics in an earlier book (1973), Cohen concluded that exclusionary social control was ultimately more satisfying psychologically for populations. Blaming scapegoats left people feeling purified and solidified. Characterizing deviants as unacceptably different people, through ritualized degradation ceremonies or relentlessly mindless caricaturing in the mass media, functions better for social integration, he argued, than inclusionary social control. 'Exclusionary social control is symbolically much richer' (1985: 233), besides, as Cohen suggests, a commitment to inclusionary liberalism does encompass the comforting thought that if all else fails we still have the exclusionary mechanisms: failing *Neighbours* and neighbourhood watch, we still have the army. We fear chaos too much and domination too little. Control is always 'mother's little helper', a drug which we reach for in times of insecurity; as such, it can never work and can only be a means to more control. It becomes addiction.

By 1985 then, social control had come full circle. It was a Mickey Mouse concept in the full postmodern sense. That is to say, it was a fiction which served effectively within a field of fictions. Without Minnie Mouse and Donald Duck, Mickey was merely an interesting drawing of a mouse. Few accepted by the end of the 1980s that social control stood for real restraint or real order. Most saw it as counterproductive and partisan. Not at all social in that it was not democratic, but fully social in the sense that societies of the twentieth century needed it to feed their fantasies and comfort their insecurities. The control fix was real and few could live with the 'wisdom of insecurity' (Watts, 1992); so the question for the year 2000 is whether social control will continue to be the opium of the people or whether opium will again become the social control of the people.

# 2

# The New Order in Spain and an Hispanic Perspective on the History and Meaning of Social Control

*Roberto Bergalli*

It is well known that the introduction and application of the categories of sociological thought in the Latin American cultural field of social sciences have been guided to a great extent by the development of sociological thought in the North American cultural field. This has happened with particular emphasis in the more specialized areas of that sociology.

Before going into the specific matter of social control with respect to the Spanish-speaking world, however, we should explain why this relationship of dependence has emerged between modes of sociological knowledge in social formations very distant, in terms of structures, cultures and political systems, from those in which the pertinent forms of sociological knowledge were produced. Actually, as in any form of knowledge production, perhaps even more so in the area of social sciences, the processes of hegemony have sharpened the effects of dependence generated in the field of economic and political relations. And, at the stage reached in this relationship, in both Spain and Latin America – even despite their many differences – no one can deny such dependence upon the United States of America and the countries of what is now the European Union: the main protagonists of the present phenomenon of *globalization* or *internationalization* of an economy to which the whole planet is subjected.

When we talk about dependence, naturally we are not making reference to that concept as used within the framework of the populist nationalisms or pro-development nationalisms which constituted the axes guiding critical thought in Latin American social sciences until the mid-1960's (Cardoso, 1976: 94 ff.). What we are referring to is the kind of dependence that emerged as a consequence of the new era of internationalization of capital, which started with the neo-liberal policies of the aftermath of the first great energy crisis of 1973; a certain kind of dependence, one which underwent further transformation after the fall of the Berlin Wall and Soviet communism, in which the interests of social classes that until then seemed opposed (national bourgeoisies and imperialist bourgeoisies) are now allied.

If we admit this dependence in the production of knowledge, it is possible to state consequently that the importation of the concept of social control into Spanish and Latin American thought is fairly recent. However, such importation seems not to be guided by the first historical stage of the concept in American sociology, as defined by Sumner in Chapter 1, in which it constituted an important element for the construction of hegemony in relation to persuasion, consensus, reason, negotiation, commitment, informality, participation and awareness. On the contrary, the importation of the concept into Spanish and Latin American social thought has been more closely linked to the view which relates the idea of social control to that kind of social regulation centralized in and by the state, as the main instrument for the production of social order (Horwitz, 1990: 1).

### The sociological concept of social control in Spain

In the Spanish case, as a consequence of the retardation brought about by a long period of cultural obscurantism imposed by Franco's dictatorship, the social sciences only manifested a reception of the concept, first, with the circulation of the translations of the American structural-functionalists who made it fashionable (although there was a first edition in Spanish of Parsons's *Social System* in 1959, it was in fact the second edition of this translation in 1976 which had an authentic circulation), and, secondly, after the democratic system was established and the first works by sociologists who had spent their formative years in the North American academic world appeared (for example, E. Lamo de Espinosa who, in his volume *Delitos sin víctimas* (1989) makes varied use of the idea of social control in order to explain behaviour that, in view of the social change already openly manifest in Spain, began to be defined as deviant (see also Espinosa, 1980).

In this way, deviant behaviour becomes a category in Spanish sociological thought. However, from the beginning of the 1980s, there already existed in Spain a certain type of work which, taking into account the degraded conditions of mentally ill patients and analysing the similarities between mad people and dangerous delinquents that had been established by Spanish psychiatry since the nineteenth century, started considering madness as a kind of deviant behaviour (Alvarez Uría, 1983). In that period, there already existed a strong warning, well known in Spain, against the importation into Latin cultures of what came to be known as 'an ideology of change' (Basaglia and Basaglia-Ongaro, 1974), which had originated in foreign cultural environments. But, the lack of answers from psychopathology to the question of 'abnormal' personalities allowed for these to continue to be included in clinical symptomatology, within a classical positivist nosography. The mistakes that stemmed from traditional classifications – because within German medical culture psychopaths were still being defined as 'people who suffer and make others suffer' (Basaglia and Basaglia-Ongaro, 1974) – had managed to confuse the terms of the problem in Spain also, by means of a much more explicit value judgement such as that of *deviant behaviour*.

## The concept of social control in Latin America

Even though Latin American social sciences developed before Spanish ones, the use of the term social control was not widespread, at least not until the beginning of the 1980s (Bergalli, 1980). In any case, its use became restricted to the more specific discipline of criminology, in which the application of the idea of social control began with a much more political projection than it would have had in other cultural contexts. This could be explained by two different types of motives: one closely linked with the reception of a sociological point of view on the study of criminality; the other related to the political commitment of certain Latin American intellectuals interested in crime control issues which developed in relation to the situations of acute social injustice and severe violations of human rights that were apparent throughout the continent during the 1970s. In this period, in which the military dictatorships were particularly aggressive towards the deprived social sectors, authoritarian governments became a distinctive feature of the time (Brazil, Chile, Argentina, Uruguay – in the southern cone of Latin America – and the Central American countries were exponents of this type of regime). Therefore, traditional studies of crime, absolutely dominated by criminal law and biological criminology, which until that period had not been able to explain the extension of the penal system to control social behaviours, were displaced by socio-political approaches. This latter group, understandably, before analysing crime and criminality, concentrated on studies of the penal system and the expansive forms of its control over its traditional clientele, which, on clear empirical evidence, has always come from the weakest social groups (as is also demonstrably the case in more industrialized societies).

In this way, it was difficult for these intellectuals to keep the label of 'criminologists' as was likewise the case for the classical field of criminology with which they were concerned. In fact, according to the criticism made at the time (Bergalli, 1983: 200), a criminologist is someone who only emerges within official circles – that is, within those institutions which exercise penal control (police, justice administration, prison, juvenile institutions, etc.). However, those who are interested in the interpretation of political and socio-economic processes, trying to explain the phenomena of criminality that they generate, trying to be consistent with the democratic and appropriate forms of control which protect the majority of citizens from discriminatory use of the penal system, will no longer be called criminologists. They will be scholars with backgrounds in different areas of social science who will seek to build a social control model framed within a specific political theory which, above all, must be critical of the methods used by the traditional penal systems.

Thus, at the beginning of the 1980s a movement emerged, stimulated by a small number of scholars who took the first steps towards the construction of what came to be known as *a critical theory of social control in Latin America* (Bergalli, 1983: 202–5). This movement generated intensive empirical work, based upon three large categories of conduct which could be attributed to individuals as well as to the big multinational corporations that produced and are continuing to produce great social harm (although until then they had escaped the control of the traditional penal systems). These categories were:

1  those behaviours which affect the health and the human life of the whole community;
2  those in the area of high-level administrative corruption which affect the national heritage or damage the economy; and
3  those which affect the social heritage through threatening the environment or safety at work and through the adulteration of food products.

This empirical research confirmed the belief that social control must constitute a form of social regulation centralized by and around the state; by which token, the concept seems to have followed a similar direction to the one which Sumner attributes to the field of North American sociological culture during the New Deal and the birth of social democracy in the middle of the present century. This belief was reinforced when the state, in the more restricted forms it has been acquiring in Latin America under neo-liberal policies driven by projects of domination which exclude certain social sectors, brought about the deregulation of the markets with the subsequent monopolistic concentration of capital.

It is likewise important to emphasize that, despite the intense use of the idea of social control that was launched by this critical Latin American movement, a substantial contradiction also emerged within its bosom. In fact, although at first the main representatives of that movement linked their reflections to the philosophy of Latin American liberation (for example, Aniyar de Castro, 1981; Bergalli, 1982) – thus connecting the idea of social control with that of domination or, in their case, with the Gramscian concept of hegemony – there was also a divergent strand which had the intention of delineating what was at that time called the *typus* of penal control from its *genus* of social control (Bergalli, 1984), without losing sight of the fact that the former, while requiring specific study, answers to the strategy established by the latter. Confronted with the position of maintaining methodological unity in the investigations of both forms of control, and in order to convert what was called *the criminology of liberation* into a critical theory of social control (both formal, as constituted by the institutions of political society, and informal, as constituted by the institutions of civil society: Aniyar de Castro, 1981), the divergent strand aimed at an historical-epistemological revision of Latin American criminology which would, at the same time as contributing to a political theory that was specific to Latin America and within the framework of a global theory of society, also allow research to differentiate the specificity of the phenomena of criminalization. These differences opened up a heated debate, in which various positions were presented and, although this is neither the place nor the moment to discuss them (a summary can be found in del Olmo, 1987), they established the widespread use of social control in the discourse of Latin American studies of crime and society. This fact can be seen in 'readers' which have tried to present such studies from earlier years in Latin America (Aniyar de Castro, 1990; Birbeck and Martínez Rincones, 1992)

Later, once the concept of social control had been established within the study of regulation of criminality and a period of revision had started regarding the effects with which authoritarianism had impregnated various aspects of Latin American culture, the application of the concept was expanded within the social sciences. However, up until recently, there has not been research of an interdisciplinary nature. A collection of works of this kind has tried to show how phenomena such as urbanization, social issues, labour movements, the strong influence of immigrant cultures, racism as an oligarchic ideology, hygienism as a form of social moralization, positivism, military power, or university crises have constituted aspects of Latin American society through which a specific strategy of social control has been elaborated (Bergalli and Mari, 1989).

Nowadays, to analyse the uses of the concept of social control in order to understand the reality of Latin America, it would be necessary to study all those aspects which are influenced by the phenomenon of globalization or internationalization of the economy. Latin American countries are at present subordinated to two tendencies oriented towards improving their growth and their participation in the world market. On one hand, through fiscal and economic policies, constant adjustment programmes (belt-tightening programmes) are carried out which completely restrict social interventions. On the other hand, Latin American economies have played a peripheral role in international markets, as producers of raw materials, but as a consequence of globalization they are forced to seek integration. In this way, Mexico has decided to integrate with Canada and the USA through the North American Free Trade Association (NAFTA); in the South, Brazil, Uruguay and Argentina are attempting to set up the *Mercado del Cono Sur* (MERCOSUR). Despite the fact that both integrative initiatives have very different dynamics, it is not possible at present to make a final assessment. But neither of them (see CEPAL-ONU, 1994) have produced the increase in growth rates needed to eliminate conditions that increasingly keep large sectors of Latin American societies in extreme poverty, nor have they helped to prevent unemployment and underemployment remaining at unacceptable levels.

Bearing in mind this situation of the Latin American economies, it is important to take into account the conduct of democracy as a system of government. In this sense, Mexico, Peru and Argentina show the extent to which the mere fulfilment of the rules of formal democracy is insufficient to give material content to the political system and to transform it into a substantial democracy. But, at the same time, the continuity of the PRI as the political party in power in Mexico over the last 70 years, the election through popular vote of Alberto Fujimori as President of Peru, after reaching power through a coup d'état, and Carlos Menem's re-election in Argentina despite the corruption he facilitated within the political system, are clear examples of the most evident political manipulation. Faced with this picture of Latin American socio-political reality, the question of social control is resolved as a demand for respect for human rights, starting with the rights to life, employment and housing – which are the ones most assaulted by social injustice.

### The political-economic meaning of social control in Spain

Returning to the Spanish application of the concept of social control, it is worth noting that, after its appearance in the field of social science, it became a strong part of penal/juridical culture. This ratifies the idea that was sketched out before the more expressive form of the presence of the state in the field of punitive intervention constituted, for certain orientations, the essence of social control. Such an idea seems to reveal an adoption of functionalistic approaches to law, in the sense that emerges from both Luhmanian developments occurring in German penal law (see Luhmann, 1972, 1983, 1987) and less theoretical penal studies (Jakobs, 1991 (1983); Hassemer, 1986), since, from a systems standpoint, the power to reduce social complexity is assigned to the normative institutionalization of the expectations of behaviour that penal law selectively ensures through punishment – the most suitable mechanism for this purpose. This was expressed in several contributions made by distinguished experts in penal law, also characterized by their progressive positions and a marked *rapprochement* towards social sciences, following a line similar to that developed in German jurisprudence (Muñoz Conde, 1985; Bustos Ramirez, 1987; Mir Puig, 1982). Nevertheless, despite this approach, the conception apparent in those contributions does not avoid the faith in penal law as the axis of any strategy of social control; or, and this is the same thing, they accept that the penal system should become the most frequently used instrument of social control.

A first impression which may be gained from such contributions is that, on the one hand, in adopting the approach of functional structuralism, they affirm the incompatibility of autonomously elaborated juridical valuations with social guidelines or social values, since the self-reflexive character that law acquires in that approach is well known. Secondly, however, the supposed involvement with the social sciences which these contributions should have revealed is fallacious, because what these studies really achieve is the removal of all possibility of conceiving of social control as the best way to build consensus; although by conceiving of social control as *tough* control, they keep their perception of the social as something imposed and as the only way to maintain social order.

Meanwhile, what happened in Spain after the death of Franco and what subsequently became known as the process or transition towards democracy – quite distinct social situations – have, together with an expansive penal system, demonstrably acted as regulators of existence or, even, as moments of truly imposed socialization.

On this level, we should not forget the influence of the Spanish entry into the European Community and, subsequently, Spain's adaptation to the forms of social organization or cultural rules which have enabled the creation of the European Union. All this, although it might have meant a qualitative leap forward in the material conditions of a good proportion of the Spanish population, has also had negative consequences for other sectors of Spanish society. Data from the labour market or the social security system clearly indicate that the welfare which the social aspect of the Spanish state seeks to distribute on the basis of the 1978 Constitution has become a regulatory instrument of social behaviour.

In fact, it is generally established that, after consolidating the democratic system and incorporating a good proportion of Spanish society into a 'European' style of life, there was a rise in the level of social demands with no possibility of satisfying them entirely. This process began after 1986 during the PSOE's[1] second term of government, a term which changed its Marxistic propositions for social transformation towards those of a social-democratic nature, obviously much closer to the programmes of European parties affiliated to the Socialist International. With this, the consumerist aims of Spanish citizens became similar to those of their European peers, although their aspirations for greater distribution of the national revenue were limited. Within these restrictions, the kind of economic infrastructure produced by the economic incorporation of Spain into Europe had a decisive influence. Thus, many of the activities that had been the basis of Spanish industrial production in the last period of Franco's government (mining, the metal industry, shipyards) had to be changed when confronted with demands from the European Union to restrict production and keep it within fixed quotas from Brussels. The same occurred with agricultural production (milk, vegetables and fruit) which had always constituted the largest source of Spanish wealth, a big source of income for many, and a sector for the employment of land labourers and workers in derivative industries (particularly preserves). The fishing industry was even more badly affected; despite the Spanish having traditionally been consumers and exporters of fish and seafood, within a few years they had to restrict their consumption and exports to comply with EU Directives.

In this way, over a short period of time, the state of the labour market in Spain changed substantially. The adoption of sophisticated technology, understandably, also had a decisive influence on this process; technology resulting from the invasion of the Spanish economy by multinationals created a demand for skilled workers, at the time of the expulsion of labour from other, traditional, industries. Both processes – labour expulsion and a more demanding selection of workers – generated a radical transformation in the relations between capital and labour, one in which the socialist government played a very ambiguous role. At times it supported the demands of the *Confederación de Empresarios* (CEOE)[2] and, at others, those of the unions: *Comisiones Obreras* (CC.OO.) and *Unión General de Trabajadores* (UGT).

This brief overview of the social and economic transformations in Spain over the last 15 years aims to give only an insight into the profound change experienced by Spanish society, once the dark period of Franco's government had been overcome. On the one hand, the adoption of new social values and goals has provided different life-options to the Spanish, since the transition to democracy offered them entry to a welfare society. On the other hand, although the reform of the economic structure was carried out following the directives imposed by the process of European union, the serious restrictions on social policies generated by the globalization of the world economy have obliged Spain to postpone the satisfaction of important current demands by its citizens, despite their already having made great efforts and sacrifices. The lack of fulfilment of some constitutional principles of the welfare state, set out in the Spanish Constitution of 1978, is nothing more than a consequence of the late Spanish entry into the group of European social-democratic countries and cultures. How this situation has influenced matters of social peace and order is a subject which, I think, is very closely linked to the issue of social control strategies and for this reason I will attempt an explanation of the matter.

There is no doubt, as I have said earlier, that the Spanish incorporation within the group of European social democracies has meant a significant improvement, both in social relations between the Spanish people and in the relations between civilian society and the state. The supercession of Franco's long rule has not been easy after 40 years of authoritarian political centralism, extremely brutal repression with its sequel of deaths and exile, and moral conservatism. The division between the two Spains – the so-called 'black Spain' of fascism and the democratic Spain (a division that has even deeper roots) – had been reinforced by the Civil War (1936–9), although the sympathizers of the Second Republic who survived the struggle had either to go into exile or suffer the consequences of prison or internal segregation. For this reason, when Franco died there were serious doubts about the possibility of establishing a harmonious relationship between the two Spains. However, the process initiated with the installation of the constitutional monarchy, under Juan Carlos I, and the first democratic government, led by Adolfo Suárez, opened a new period of reconciliation which aimed at healing the wounds opened by the Civil War.

In this way, the serenity demonstrated by the Partido Comunista Español (PCE) and the more democratic conservative parties, together with the active participation of the Unions (CC.OO. and UGT) and the CEOE, made it possible to celebrate in 1977 what came to be known as the *Pactos de la Moncloa*, which established a social peace with the aim of building an economic model of democratic development. In this accord, the foundations were laid permitting the subsequent discussion and passing of the Spanish Constitution (December 1978).

## The transition to democracy and the frustration of consensual social control

In the manner described above, the process of transition towards democracy was based on a broad consensus within the democratic political parties. This beginning was to require – bearing in mind how much had happened on the path from the strongest form of Franco's policies towards a system of liberties supported and upheld by democratic political options – the setting up of strategies of social control expressing, and strengthened by, the social will of the majority. By this I mean that the democratic convergence built up in Spain should have also generated a widespread consensus as to how to establish a social order, involving even those sectors that were most reluctant in relation to the Organization of what is known as *El Estado de las Autonomías* (the State of the Autonomies), as ratified in the Constitution of 1978 (Art. 2). In this sense, the concept of social control that should be used in analysing the kind of system that emerges in Spain after the consolidation of the constitutional monarchy will also enable us to understand the historical phenomenon of the composition of a nation-state from a number of different nationalities. This assertion, which may seem rather like a rigmarole or a play on words, actually encapsulates the 'secret' of the constitutional development of Spain as a democratic constitutional-state (Art. 1.1, Spanish Constitution); although, even for this purpose, it has not been possible to resolve the old disputes between what are now known as the 'historic' Autonomies and the central power of the state, that is, Madrid, embodied at present in the figure of the Crown.[3]

This is a matter which, in effect, runs through the whole history of the social entity called Spain, and which played a decisive role at the time of settling the state-form of the Autonomies. However, what really matters when considering the form and development of a certain strategy of social control is, in this case, to show how the integration of these historic communities has been achieved within the organizational process of the Spanish state, and to what extent this process has generated, and is still generating, resistance – in some cases in the form of armed violence.

The will of certain Spanish regions, specifically Catalunya, the Basque Country and to a much lesser extent Galicia, towards autonomous organization, which had its first expression in the Constitution of the Second Republic in 1931 (the Project for a Federal Constitution of 1873 had different roots), was reborn with increased strength in the last few years of Franco's government and has lately been reinforced by the decentralizing trend that is pervasive throughout Europe. Whatever the reasons for this phenomenon – they are too complex to be described or analysed here and are not exclusive to Spain – it is a fact that its existence had such relevance that, at the time of the death of Franco in November 1975, it was necessary to deal with it immediately once the Law for Political Reform had been passed and before the drafting of the 1978 Constitution. The clear will to peace, expressed 40 years after the Civil War by the successors to both sides of that conflict, brought to light the need to provide a transition towards democracy that took as its starting foundation a state which, above all, integrated those regions which because of either cultural identity or opposition to the central power had 'lost' the war. Due to this, in the period preceding the drafting of the 1978 Constitution, a number of autonomous provisional governments were conceded to the interested territories by means of decrees/laws from Adolfo Suarez's government. This process began with the restoration of the *Generalitat* (or Government) of Catalunya on 29 September 1977 and led to the expansion of the system throughout Spain, still totally organized in pre-autonomy fashion when the Constitution came into force (6 December 1978).

The organizational framework for what came to be known as the State of the Autonomies was outlined in this Constitution of 1978 in terms of a system based on the free initiative of the concerned territories, as much for entry to autonomy as for the determination of its contents, within the limits of the Constitution (de Otto, 1987: 244). This constitutional possibility of entry to autonomy was immediately seized upon so that, as mentioned earlier, it was given concrete form in the Statutes of the Basque Country, Catalonia and Galicia. This initiative to autonomy was immediately followed by Andalusia and the other regions, in many cases with the aim of achieving the same levels of autonomy as the first three regions have stipulated in their respective Statues: that is, with the distinct power of self-government, in so far as each Statute established the competences which each autonomous Community wanted to assume among all those that were not exclusive to the central state (Arts 148 and 149, Spanish Constitution). Such a situation reflected, on the one hand, the different weight that each of the regions had in the drawing of the new political map of Spain, thus augmenting the old tensions between the centre of Spain – now embodied in the state government based in Madrid and the Crown itself – and the regions. But, on the other hand, it also made explicit the desire of many territories which, due to political neglect or historic delay in their development, saw in the process towards autonomy an opportunity for integration into a more organic form of growth.

Nevertheless, as we have already pointed out, the organizational process of the State of the Autonomies has not been peaceful. In some communities, particularly Catalunya and the Basque Country, important social sectors were reluctant to accept this kind of integration with Spain.

Strong cultural traditions and different forms of economic development enabled certain groups – those who had very much led internal resistance, particularly during the last stage of Franco's dictatorship – to adopt the radical position of not accepting integration with Spain. Such groups had, at one point, positions close to those supported by political parties of nationalist extraction: that is, aimed at safeguarding the cultural or national identity of the Autonomous Community.[4] A principal element, always the defining characteristic of these positions, has been the language; both Catalan in Catalunya and Euskera in the Basque Country, although protected under the bilingualism established in the Constitution ('Castilian is the official Spanish language of the State . . .' and 'The other Spanish languages will also be official in the respective Autonomous Communities according to the Statutes', Arts 3.1 and 2, Spanish Constitution) and the respective Autonomy Statues, have been the subjects of dispute and conflict which have always been taken advantage of by radical groups and nationalist parties.

The radicalization which I referred to earlier turned into violent demonstrations and expressions of dissidence, both in Catalunya and the Basque Country, during the process of fixing the constitutional form of the 'State of the Autonomies'. In one and then another community, radical groups plunged themselves into the practice of armed violence, which in the case of ETA (*Euskadi ta Askatasuna* or Basque Homeland and Freedom) presented itself as a continuation of the resistance against Franco. This allowed ETA to maintain some legitimacy and a sufficient social basis, at least in the first stages of the transition towards democracy, to receive great popular support.

### The penal control of terrorism in Spain

The forms of reaction expressed by the young democratic state and the law of Spain towards armed violence, particularly that of a nationalist-devolutionist kind, were no different from those effected by other European countries in the 1970s to deal with the same phenomenon, although the latter had other political or ideological origins (as in the Federal Republic of Germany, France or Italy). Such forms of reaction were simply an authoritarian exaggeration, within the framework of the rule of law, which can only be explained as the result of an atmosphere of panic. This panic which prevailed in continental Europe through at least a decade, 1975–85, not only affected political actors and legal figures, but also swamped the media and public opinion. It is estimated that, during what is known as the *warme Herbst* (hot autumn) of 1977 in the Federal Republic of Germany, at least half the attention that the government devoted to public matters was to the kidnapping of the president of German businessmen, Hans Schleyer, who was subsequently assassinated by the armed group known by the name of Baader-Meinhoff (Trenz and Zaitch, 1995). Exactly the same can be said about the *autunno caldo* of 1978 in Italy, because of the kidnapping and subsequent assassination by the *Brigate Rose* of the distinguished politician Aldo Moro, who at the time represented the axis of the talks between the *Democrazia Cristiana* and the *Partito Comunista Italiano* which could have led to the latter's incorporation into the Italian government. In the same way in Spain, immediately after Franco's death in November 1975, at a time when there was widespread belief that the strengthening of the constitutional monarchy and the parliamentary democratic system could constitute the foundation for a transition process that appeared very difficult, the armed groups of independentist nationalism displayed unusual violence.

It can be stated without doubt that the armed struggle, or contemporary Spanish terrorism, is marked by a constant: the presence of the organization ETA. The importance of this presence can be confirmed not only by the existence, duration and consequences of the armed activities of this organization, of which there exist abundant statistical studies and qualitative analyses (see Clark, 1990; García San Pedro, 1993), but also by the repercussions of its activities in political life, both in Spain and, in particular, in the Basque Country.

The history of ETA is inserted, however, in a complex mosaic of armed movements which, from the origins of the organization at the end of the 1950s – that is, at the peak of Franco's dictatorship – has gradually come to condition criminal justice policy towards terrorism and, consequently, to determine the Spanish strategies of social control so affected by the presence of this intrinsically political phenomenon. Such armed movements have been studied from the point of view of their political nature or origin and of their aims. Broadly, they can be classified as 'anarchist groups', 'Marxist groups' or 'independence groups' (García San Pedro, 1993: 159–91). Among the 'anarchist groups' the better known were, from 1962 when the 'Group of the 1st of May' first appeared: the 'Group of International Revolutionary Action', the 'Autonomous Combat Groups', and the 'Groups of Autonomous Internationalists', which were formed by scattered members who came from dissolved anarchist organizations. Among the 'Marxist groups', which were breakaways from the Communist Party of Spain, we find the 'Anti-fascist and Patriotic Revolutionary Front', the armed wing of the PCEml (the Marxist-Leninist Spanish Communist Party) which in 1973 became the 'Armed Front of the PCE-ml', and the 'Groups of Anti-fascist Resistance of the First of October' coming out of the Spanish Marxist-Leninists' Organization – all of which are still active to a certain extent. Finally, among the 'independence groups' one should differentiate between the Basque independence movement – within which, as observed earlier, ETA has been and still is a dominant group – and the Catalan independence movements, among which the *Front Nacional de Catalunya* (FNC) constituted a general core or axis and played an important role in the emergence and subsequent development of contemporary armed groups, among which *Terra Lliure* stands out. The latter was formed in 1979 and, without a strong ideological discourse (such as that of ETA in its different factions), sustained constant activity until at least 1985 (Fernández Calvet, 1986) after which it dissolved and its members joined the different Catalan nationalist parties, particularly the *Esquerra Republicana de Catalunya* (ERC).

It is precisely through the penal treatment of the armed struggle or terrorism in the post-constitutional era that we can appreciate the change in Spain from a strategy of social control that, during Franco's days was characterized by its harshness and its hard repressive character, encompassing capital punishment, torture and all sorts of measures – both with and without legislative backing. In effect, with the passing of the Constitution of 1978 and the affirmation of the rule of law, whatever consequences applied in the case of acts classified as terrorism obviously had to comply with constitutional principles and guarantees. However, as has been fully confirmed by research (Arroyo Zapatero, 1981; Bueno Arús, 1986; García Valdés, 1991; Lamarca Pérez, 1985; Muñagorri Laguía, 1985; Serrano-Piedecasas, 1988; Terradillos Basoco, 1988), the treatment of terrorism in the criminal justice system has been carried out, even when the rule of law was in full operation, by means of special legislation: legislation which has always been characterized as 'exceptional', and in violation of the framework of guarantees laid out by the 1978 Spanish Constitution for the running of the system of criminal justice (*penal control*).

Such exceptional status has been confirmed, in the first place, in substantive laws (that is, in the creation of truly penal norms) such as the Organic Law of 4 May 1981, which modified and added certain articles to the Penal and Military Justice Codes, and the Organic Law of 1984 that did not modify these codes but was kept as a 'special' law. The distinctive feature of the latter was that it extended the jurisdiction of criminal justice, enlarging extra-territorially the application of penal norms, expanding in general the punitive response, and introducing the figure of *arrepentido* (repentance) as a 'reward' option in the strategy towards terrorism. The exceptional character of the legislation to control terrorism has also been verified in the area of criminal procedure, especially that which regulates police intervention and the initiation of the criminal justice process. The first fact that emphasized this character was the extension of the jurisdiction of a sole tribunal – such as the *Audencia Nacional*, based in Madrid – for the trial of acts of terrorism, regardless of where in Spain they were committed. At the same time, the aforementioned laws established cautionary measures with regard to arrest and detention which increased the power of the police and lengthened the periods of detention and prison with respect to 'ordinary' crime. These laws also limited the rights of defence, increased police powers in house searches and interrogation of detainees, and restricted the right of the media to inform. Finally, the exceptional status of anti-terrorism measures was also illustrated in relation to prisons. In fact, the situation of detention, prisoners on remand, and the completion of custodial sentences for those condemned for acts of terrorism, has been characterized in the post-constitutional period by the notion of dangerousness held by its authors, by the most severe imprisonment measures (in comparison with common crime), and by confinement in top-security prisons (a wide-ranging and detailed study of all these exceptional characteristics of the penal treatment of terrorism can be found in Serrano-Piedecasas, 1988).

The most serious and long-lasting aspect of this exceptional legislation created for the control of acts of terrorism, however, is constituted by the penetration of many of its features into the legislation against common crime and routine criminal justice practice. This situation, which again has been confirmed by the studies referred to above, is not unique or exclusive to Spain. A similar situation was common in Europe in the 1970s and has not only characterized the control of emerging phenomena such as terrorism, but also of drug-trafficking, organized crime and even political corruption from a standpoint which justifies their treatment as appropriate to situations requiring resort to exceptional means. It is alleged that the rule of law is not prepared for this kind of situation, that ordinary legal instruments are insufficient, and that, in political-legal terms, the resolution must be to have recourse to the old idea of *Notfall* (emergency) or *Ausnahmezustand* (state of emergency) to control exceptional situations, to respond to the *necesitas* as a basic element in the satisfaction of political obligation (Bergalli, in Serrano-Piedecasas, 1988). That is, if the link exception–authority, synthesized by Carl Schmitt in the political formula of the *Diktatur* (explained in the first edition of his *Die Diktatur*, 1921), had a meaning in the typical project of the modern state, and was regularly satisfied by the rule of law, which involves the monopoly of legitimate violence, then that link should have an entirely different meaning in the political project of the contemporary world: that of the globalization of the economy, the disappearance of welfare, and the shattering of the principles of sovereignty (understood from a technical standpoint as a monopoly that is legally linked to legitimate violence). In conclusion, the primacy of political reason or *raison d'État* over legal reason has become the guiding principle for the penal control of those acts which, although considered as terrorist, are the expression of political dissidence, despite the social harm they may cause.

The generalization of a kind of penal treatment of phenomena that endanger a system of political domination extended throughout Europe, and known as social-democratic, has been considered inherent to a *culture of emergency* (for the Italian case, see Ferrajoli, 1989; and for the Spanish case, see Bergalli, in Serrano-Piedecasas, 1988). Rather than trying to analyse here the issues related to the elaboration of a specific culture, it would be appropriate to point out something which perhaps, because it is very obvious, should not be mentioned here, but which is important to bear in mind: namely, that it is necessary to study in depth those infrastructural conditions which have brought about a modification of certain norms and guidelines in the politics of social control in one of the areas at the heart of European capitalism. This fact is supported by the idea, which seems to be more accepted in all branches of cultural anthropology, that, whereas the concept of the cultural takes its essence from what is supra-individual (Kroeber), the rejection of the premise of a unilinear cultural evolution common to all societies should also be recognized (Boas, Malinowski and his functionalist school). In this way, since moving beyond the historic school of Tylor, the scientific concept of culture has displaced the crystallization of the heritage of static societies closed to external influence. The search for cultural universals, which had its most illustrious exponents in Clark Wissler, with his elaboration of a 'universal cultural schema', Bronislaw Malinowski, with his table of 'universal institutional types', and G.P. Murdock, with his elaboration of a series of 'common denominators of culture', has fallen into disuse since the demonstration of cultural relativism and the non-existence of a *consensus gentium* or consensus of all humanity (Geertz, 1973). Thus, it is possible to think that the conditions of coherence and orientation of a culture, through which individuals inserted into the structure of a historically determined society organize their experience and guide their behaviour, can undergo rapid alteration because of the intrusion of external elements. These remarks, though very schematic, summarize the essential anthropological elements which enable us to recognize the existence of a *culture of emergency* in some European countries. In Spain, as a result of the development of an unprecedented level of social conflict and the influence of situations common to the more open Europe – both products of the tension between the poles of disorganized capitalism – there has been a change in infrastructural conditions which developed into more or less marked levels of cultural incoherence or, if we accept this analysis, into triggers of a specific culture.

This is the stage at which we find ourselves in Spain at the time of the legislation of what is known as the 'Penal Code of Democracy'. The replacement of the Penal Code of 1944 implemented by Franco was an unavoidable duty for Spanish democracy. Although that Code was subsequently reformed, both during Franco's days and in the period of transition towards democracy, this piece of penal legislation was, until its replacement, a completely outdated instrument. Social change in Spain has been as radical in the last 15 years as the transformation of its economic structure which, despite being of a financial-speculative rather than productive nature, has allowed the country's entry into the world of post-industrial societies. Similarly, even though its political society (and its instruments of state) suffer from a lack of the growth that would enable it to fulfil the demands made by civilian society, the replacement of the old Penal Code was an obligatory task. Many opinions have been offered on the Bill which has recently been passed in the Spanish parliament, some positive and others less so. In general, all these opinions have concentrated on the fact that the Penal Code is the main form of expression of a strategy of social control, with which the idea of social regulation centralized in and by the state would be maintained in Spain, as the main instrument for the production of social order.[5] But, what we should also say here is that, even if a new Penal Code is passed in accordance with the social and economic transformation of Spain, this new piece of criminal justice legislation will require a radical change in the application of the criminal law. The Spanish penal system as a whole should be viewed as the ultimate object of this reform. It is those policies that deal with crime, and thus the 'toughest' expression of social control, that most require democratic change (Bergalli, 1991).

## Notes

This chapter was translated by Jacqueline Vitali and Colin Sumner.

1   Partido Socialista Obrero Español. The socialist party of the Spanish worker: similar to the British Labour Party.

2   The confederation of industrialists.

3   It is convenient here to emphasize that the process of configuring the State of the Autonomies in Spain was not simple. Nevertheless, from the beginning there was a recognition of those Autonomous Communities, Catalonia, the Basque Country, Galicia and Andalusia, which – before the measures of the Constitution – had positively plebiscited their Autonomy Statutes (Art. 148.2, Spanish Constitution). Subsequently, the territories which conjoined specific characteristics (bordering provinces with historic,

cultural and economic affinity, and constituting a province with historic regional organization or the island territories: Art. 143.1, Spanish Constitution) also had the opportunity to form specific Autonomies, although, in some cases, these processes were artificial. Thus, the State of the Spanish Autonomies is, at present, constituted by 17 Autonomous Communities.

4   The term 'nation' is used in the Constitution ('The constitution establishes the indissoluble unity of the Spanish nation, a common and indivisible fatherland (*patria* – CS) of all the Spanish people . . .', Art. 2) and some Statutes of Autonomy in different form.

5   It should be noted that during the parliamentary debate about the Penal Code the *Partido Popular* promised a reform or even abrogation of the Code. The 'Penal Code of Democracy', given the recent electoral success of the *Partido Popular*, is thus unstable and its future remains in the hands of the politicians.

# 3

# State and Social Control *à la Fin de Siècle*: from the New World to the Constitution of the New Europe

*Dario Melossi*

In this chapter I aim to take stock of developments in social control during the century that is coming to an end and to shed light on their relevance for the process of European unification. In particular, I intend to show that ideas about how to construct and theorize social order, first developed at the dawn of the century within the pioneering American experience of the Progressive Era, are still relevant today and are especially important for the construction of a European democratic polity. These ideas involve the rejection of the notion of the state and the emergence of a concept of social control; an emergence strictly linked to the coming to maturity of a democratic form of polity.[1] This relationship of control and democracy is a further theme in the chapter; a seemingly recurring paradox.

In particular, I claim that, together with the advent of a democratic society – that is, of a society where the fundamental rights of the working masses were recognized and were made to a certain extent enforceable – the nature and direction of processes of social control changed deeply. Whereas the control of the main structure of social relations in pre-democratic times was exercised largely by means of coercion and was organized around the figure of Leviathan, after the democratic turn – which took place at different times in different societies – social control started to be characterized more and more as *social control of the production of meanings* and the 'myth of the state' began to lose its force and appeal. This 'epochal' change took place first in the United States of America around the period of Roosevelt's New Deal. The Pragmatists and the Chicago social scientists in particular provided intellectual testimony to such change. In Europe it took hold only after the defeat of Fascism in World War II and the subsequent economic recovery, but did not really unfold until the breakdown of the Soviet Union and, therefore, the end of the Cold War. I suggest that its main intellectual testimony can be found in the works of Michel Foucault.

The concept of social control I am referring to is obviously neither the criminologists' social control, such as Hirschi's or Gibbs's, which is a mixture of Durkheim, Freud, early Chicago School, Parsons and professional managerialism, according to which social control is essentially a restraint on deviance (Melossi 1994b), nor a pragmatic concept embodying a political and social project.[2] It is rather a *theoretical* concept, which first developed within the era of American Progressivism, and is best represented in George Herbert Mead's sociology and social psychology (see Mead, 1964 (1918, 1925, 1934)). It is, in other words, a notion of social control as constitutive of forms of social order and disorder (so that, in my view, a rejection of the theory of social control cannot be motivated on the grounds of a rejection of the concept of deviance).[3]

### The state and its subjects

It is my contention that concepts such as the state and social control are not at all 'innocent' but are actually used in order to construct social order. This is particularly clear in the case of the theory of the state, of course, the main social function of which has been to make the state 'live' in the sense that the people who *are* the state – the members of its organs, etc. – find in such a theory reasons justifying, to themselves and others, their being and doing what they are and do. These theoretical practices are not mere 'descriptions'. This is a way of 'doing things with words' that goes radically beyond that pointed out by J.L. Austin (1955) and speech act theory in general.

These concepts are, therefore, historically grounded, and are strictly linked to the main patterns of the societies in which they were produced and are to 'serve'. A sure 'sign that a society has entered into the secure possession of a new concept is that a new vocabulary will be developed, in terms of which the concept can then be publicly articulated and discussed' (Skinner 1978, II: 352). Skinner adds that at the end of the sixteenth century, 'the term "state" began to be freely used for the first time in a recognisably modern sense' (ibid.). At first, in *The Prince's* crucial semantic oscillation, Machiavelli (1977 (1513)) wrote of 'the state of the prince', meaning the sum of the resources that the prince could count on – wealth, men, land, etc. However, this sum of resources slowly ended up being simply an appendage of the prince and acquired a personality of its own, becoming the State of the prince. Once it acquired these characteristics it was quickly reified and became an abstract *persona*, for instance in Hobbesian theory. 'Leviathan', Hobbes wrote, is 'a COMMONWEALTH, or STATE, in Latin CIVITAS, which is but *an artificial man*; though of greater stature and strength than the natural, for whose protection and defence was intended' (1962 (1651): 19). This 'automaton' built 'by the art of man' (ibid.) therefore acquired certain characteristics: he came to represent authority, personality, social unity, patriarchality (see Pateman's *The Sexual Contract*, 1988).

The theories of the social contract have certainly known many versions but they all seem to coalesce in the image of a multitude of atomized and rational individuals who chose to come to a contractual agreement with everybody else: an agreement, the object of which was the founding of a state. Individuals and state are the two polarities of political and legal science. In fact, at the basis of the theory of the social contract, there is both a concept of the state and a concept of the 'free' subjects of the contract. Starting in the nineteenth century, however, a subterranean history developed underpinning that of the social contract, a history which has unfolded around the idea that subjects of rights do not come, so to speak, ready-made but have to be produced. From Marxism, to Meadian interactionism, to Foucauldism, other cultural traditions have explored these alternative venues in different ways. For instance, Marx in *Capital* made a distinction, which is crucial to his theory, between a 'sphere of circulation' and a 'sphere of production' (1977 (1867): 176). When Marx turns from discussing the labour market, within that sphere of circulation which is in fact 'a very Eden of the innate rights of man' (ibid.), to inquiring into the process of production of surplus value and turns, therefore, to 'the hidden abode of production', the 'physiognomy of our dramatis personae' suddenly changes:

> He, who before was the money-owner, now strides in front as capitalist; the possessor of labour-power follows as his labourer. The one with an air of importance, smirking, intent on business; the other, timid and holding back, like one who is bringing his own hide to market and has nothing to expect but – a hiding. (ibid.: 176)[4]

A certain literature of the 1970s (Foucault, 1977 (1975); Melossi and Pavarini, 1981 (1977); etc.) spelled out an implication of Marx's analysis: that not only in the sphere of production of 'normal' goods, but also in all the ramifications of the production of subjects of rights (of 'human capital') did authoritarianism reign supreme. Such a critical standpoint was necessarily connected to a critique of the theories of the social contract. The main point of such a critique is, in a nutshell, the idea that something like the process of 'authorization' that is portrayed in the myth of the social contract, also goes on *within* the process of production of the self of each participant to the contract – a process of 'self-authorization' to which those 'states' and 'societies', that individuals are supposed to have formed in freely partaking of the social contract, do not seem to be at all foreign. Our 'acceptance' of the social contract, in other words, is actually predicated on social control: individuals are not originals but are embedded in a network of social relations that are at the same time constraining and resource-supplying (Giddens, 1984). In different ways, Marx, Durkheim, Nietzsche, Freud and Mead all developed this very point (Melossi, 1990).

In fact, the more a society became social contractual, therefore tendentially democratic (Tinland, 1985), the more it became important to provide individual subjects with ways in which they could attain that free rational level that was necessary in order to perform, politically and otherwise.

**Paradoxes of democracy**

In a comparative dimension that I find insightful and helpful, this relationship of democracy and control, which I would call the first 'paradox of democracy', has been addressed by the Mexican writer, Octavio Paz, in a 1979 essay, 'Mexico and the United States'. There Paz dealt with some of the issues tackled by Weber in his classic *The Protestant Ethic and the Spirit of Capitalism* (1958 (1904–5)). Now, it is rather well known that one of the intellectual sources of Weber's masterpiece was an essay by legal theorist and friend Georg Jellinek on North American Protestant sects and the Declaration of the Rights of Men (1901 (1895)). It was the freedom sought by the Protestant sects that were leaving Europe and the equality of rights that was practiced within the sects, Jellinek claimed, that are at the roots of our modern concept of human rights; comparison between Catholicism and Protestantism can, therefore, be instructive.

Whereas Catholicism rewards loyalty to the *political* authority of the Church, which represents the mediating power between the community of believers and the divinity, Protestantism rewards the direct relationship of the believer to the divinity, therefore emphasizing *moral* commitment. The former focuses on the external elements of control, the latter on the internal ones. The former emphasizes oral and visual communication, as in the sensual baroque Churches; the latter emphasizes individual reading of the Bible and, therefore, rationalism. In the Feuerbachian language of the young Marx:

> Luther, without question, overcame servitude through devotion but only by substituting servitude through *conviction*. He shattered the faith in authority by restoring the authority of faith. He transformed the priests into laymen by turning laymen into priests. He liberated man from external religiosity by making religiosity the innermost essence of man. He liberated the body from its chains because he fettered the heart with chains . . . It was no longer a question, thereafter, of the layman's struggle against the priest outside himself, but of his struggle against his *own internal priest*, against his own *priestly nature*. (Marx, 1964 (1844): 52–3)

Could Freud have said it better, had he only had a feeling for historicity? In any case, according to Octavio Paz, these two basic attitudes would have brought, to the conquest of the New World, two very different political styles and two different ways of dealing with the indigenous populations. Paradoxically, the authoritarian Spanish/Mexican style would have produced an inclusionary type of civilization, whereas the democratic English/American style would have been exclusionary. Whereas the Spanish conquistadores did not assume that homage should be paid to a principle of equality, the New England colonists did. The Spaniards were, therefore, content with eliminating the Indian leadership and proceeding to 'integrate' the rest through conversion – placing them at the bottom of the social pyramid, as quasi-forced labour. The more demanding North Americans could not afford to integrate the Indians within their social contract; in a tendentially equalitarian society based on rationality and self-control, the Indians were too different. There could be no 'rational conversation' with them. The result was extermination and isolated 'reservations' for the few survivors.

This was not, however, the only paradox of democracy. In case human beings who had not been civilized or who had lost their civilization were still similar enough to the members of the religious covenant to be accepted, at least as potential members,[5] then it was necessary to arrange those trappings of taming and training that could actually introduce them into a conversation with their fellow men – the very prerequisite for democracy. The American belief in the goodness of punishment – as represented, for instance, in the project of the penitentiary – had this very origin, as Thomas Dumm has brilliantly shown in his Foucauldian analysis of the origins of the penitentiary in American democracy. His analysis takes off from Tocqueville's first analyses of both democracy and the penitentiary (Tocqueville, 1961 (1835); Beaumont and Tocqueville, 1833):

> I argue . . . that the emergence of the penitentiary in the United States was a project *constitutive* of liberal democracy. That is, the penitentiary system formed the epistemological project of liberal democracy, creating conditions of knowledge of self and other that were to shape the political subject required for liberal and democratic values to be realized in practice. The American project, a system of self-rule, involved not only the establishment of representative government with an extensive suffrage, but also the establishment of institutions which would encourage the internalization of liberal democratic values, the creation of individuals who would learn how to rule their selves. (Dumm, 1987: 6)

Democratization was, therefore, accompanied by the creation of institutional practices such as those invented by Jeremy Bentham in England, and then made famous two centuries later by Michel

Foucault, in the *Panopticon*. At the same time, the science of those institutions was produced: a knowledge that designated society as an object of inquiry that comes *before* and *separately from* politics, that is, at the very root of politics. Society, together with a wealth of social institutions, became the focus of analysis and indeed the focus of new sciences – the *social* sciences. Especially in France, the continuous revolutions of the nineteenth century were a sign that politics, together with the accompanying idea of the social contract, was unable to guarantee an orderly society. These revolutions in France (and not only there) showed that politics alone was unable to guarantee order. Politics had to be superseded by a discipline that would look at the very roots of social behaviour, its 'pre-political' roots: sociology.

Indeed, authors at the turn of the century were obsessed with *the crowd* and the problem of its control. From Gustave Le Bon (1960 (1892)) and Scipio Sighele (1985 (1891)) to the much more sophisticated Robert Ezra Park (1972 (1904)), the question was how to control the masses that had irrupted into the social and political arena. This was one of the deepest signs of modernity, because once the rural masses were no longer hegemonized by the Church and its religious discourse – a process that had started with the Protestant Reformation and even earlier, in Northern and Central Italy, with the 'heretic' movements – the question became how to 'manage' them or, even better, how to orient them in a direction that was *useful* and not destructive. The answer that had traditionally been fashioned by political theory, the state, started to sound very inadequate. Already Marx had struck a powerful blow against the pretensions of the state and especially of Hegel's theory of the state to represent real social unity and universality (Marx 1844 (1964)). Moreover, Kelsen later criticized any sociological concept of the state because, he claimed, there is no way to give a definition of the state independent from a juridical definition (Kelsen, 1924; Melossi, 1990: 72–82). After encountering Freud's psychoanalysis, in the exceptional Austrian intellectual climate of those years, Kelsen went on to find in the state a hypostatization of a power figure, a fatherly figure, along the lines of Freud's writings about mass-psychology (1955 (1921)): the state was nothing but an abstract representation of the father, strictly connected to the figure of the leader. A democratic state was, therefore, a contradiction in terms for Kelsen. A democratic state was a stateless society, one in which the brothers reign (but not the sisters, as Carole Pateman was later to observe (1988)).

In the centre of the 'civilized' world of those years, in France, another answer to the question about social order was becoming readily available, one that foreshadowed the future developments on the other side of the Atlantic. One of the founding fathers of sociology, Emile Durkheim, in a lesser-known work, the Bordeaux lectures on the *Physique des Moers et du Droit* (Lectures on the Physics of Customs and Law, 1898–1900), established a connection between democracy, communication and the 'strength' of the state. Probably influenced by the twin development in France of a bourgeois world together with communication and democracy, he claimed that a democratic state is actually a much stronger state than an authoritarian one because it is a state which is able to 'organize' and, therefore, direct and orient – that is, 'rationalize' – opinion. He then proceeded to attribute to the state the role that, a few years later, sociologists and philosophers at Chicago would attribute to social reform.[6]

### The emergence of social control

It was in fact in the American experience that, at the beginning of the twentieth century, the notion of the state was to be 'disrupted': first in the pioneering work by American political scientist Arthur Bentley (1908), then by many other American political and social scientists (Passerin D'Entréves, 1967: 59–65). Many were the influences that brought about that result. There were specific cultural traditions, such as Lockeanism, that is, a way of constructing the social contract that endowed the individual with a sovereignty of rights that would never be given up entirely and that connected with the British tradition of common law as a type of historical natural law. There was, of course, the influence of Federalism and the idea of the original character of American states' rights. What seems to me, however, to have been of particular importance was the difficulty, within the American culture of those years, of thinking the European concept of the state as something meaningful, in spite of the position of many American political scientists:

> American political science was, since its inception under the aegis of Francis Lieber at the University of Carolina and later at Columbia College, and until World War I, dominated by the German idea of the state – the state whose origin is in history, whose nature is organic, whose essence is unity, whose function is the exercise of its sovereign will in law, and whose ultimate end is the moral perfection of mankind. (Fries, 1973: 391)

However, against the social diffusion of such a view stood the reality that so many Americans' experience had been shaped by the attempt to rid themselves of Europe, and all that Europe represented to sons and daughters of (former European) peasants, unemployed workers, persecuted political and union organizers, penniless artisans and *déclassés* of all kinds; a representation that was often connected with a bureaucratic, authoritarian, corrupt and inefficient machinery pompously called 'the state' by schoolteachers, law professors and professional revolutionaries of all sorts. Moreover, the images conjured up in that concept were ones of authority and unity that, quite clearly in American social reality, were in no way 'given' but had instead to be *built* through action, and established on the ground of consensus and persuasion.

In addressing the reality of immigration, Park and the other Chicago sociologists tried to come to terms with the problem of communication, that is, of how to co-ordinate the action of millions of men and women coming from different countries, believing in different religions, speaking different languages and yet who had to work together, with the efficiency, energy and motivation that their capitalist bosses desired. The only political environment where this could have happened was one characterized by a *democratic social organization* like the one that Charles H. Cooley, George Herbert Mead and John Dewey, among others, were able to prefigure (see Melossi, 1990:114–24).

That is why I claim that the special conditions of the period between the Progressive Era and the New Deal set the agenda for the development of a theory of social control, rather than imposed specific political solutions. The problem of social control imposed itself, so to speak, and became 'the central problem of sociology' (Park and Burgess, 1969 (1921): 42). What Chicago sociologists actually saw – either through direct political involvement, for instance in the fundamental experience of Jane Addams' Hull House (Deegan, 1988; and Shalin, 1988), through literary representation (Cappetti, 1993) or through social research – was the construction of order ('material' and 'intellectual') through communication and social interaction. The scientific elaboration of such insight suggested, in turn, that social reality could be modified or reformed in a much more efficient manner through manipulation of meaningful symbols than through the traditional weaponry of the state, that is, law and coercion. This position is summed up nicely in Thomas and Znaniecki's famous 'methodological note', introducing their classic work, *The Polish Peasant in Europe and America*:

> The oldest but most persistent form of social technique is that of 'ordering-and-forbidding' – that is, meeting a crisis by an arbitrary act of will decreeing the disappearance of the undesirable or the appearance of the desirable phenomena, and using arbitrary physical action to enforce the decree. This method corresponds exactly to the magical phase of natural technique. In both, the essential means of bringing a determined effect is more or less consciously thought to reside in the act of will itself by which the effect is decreed as desirable and of which the action is merely an indispensable vehicle or instrument; in both, the process by which the cause (act of will and physical action) is supposed to bring its effect to realization remains out of reach of investigation; in both, finally, if the result is not

attained, some new act of will with new material accessories is introduced, instead of trying to find and remove the perturbing cause. A good instance of this in the social field is the typical legislative procedure of today. (1958 (1918–20): 3)

Certainly, this orientation could not be separated from a social style that thrived on the triumph of economism and economic production. As Gramsci wrote in *Americanismo e Fordismo*, in the United States 'hegemony was born out of the factory and need[ed], in order to be exercised, no more than a small number of professional brokers of politics and ideology' (1975 (1929–35): 2146).

However, '[t]he process of communication', Mead rejoined (1934: 259), 'is one which is more universal than that of the universal religion or universal economic process in that it is one that serves them both'. In fact, it is in the pages of George Herbert Mead's essays that we can find the most developed version of this project: in his idea that social control meant being able to take the role of the other, an idea that brought him to a crucial identification of social control and self-control. In anticipating and 'rehearsing' what the response of the other is going to be to my conduct, I exercise self-control, but in so doing, I have to assume the standpoint of the other – so, in effect, the other controls me. In my effort to make myself understood, social control is at the same time a constraint and a resource. Social and self-control are collective achievements that take place in the field of social interaction (Mead, 1964 (1925)). The Hegelian-trained Mead spoke of a *Phenomenology of Mind* (Joas, 1985 (1980): 232): the Polish peasant who had left his rural hamlet, travelled by carriage to the Baltic Sea and embarked on a ship that would take him to Ellis Island; who then lived in the bustle of immigrant quarters in Manhattan or Chicago and worked in a factory in which most co-workers were unable to understand his language;[7] who went through a veritable linguistic, psychological and cultural journey, inhabiting wider and wider circles of meaning, and discovering at every new transition a new vocabulary and a new form of social life. As the young C. Wright Mills was to write, developing Meadian themes, 'back of a vocabulary lie sets of collective action' (Mills 1963a (1939): 433).

For the whole period of most intense social conflict, between the 1880s and the turning point of 1937, free speech and the related First Amendment freedom of assembly and association, were severely limited thanks to an attitude held by American political élites that could not easily abandon a coercive mode and embrace democracy as the preferred means of dealing with social conflicts, especially in the workplace (Kairys, 1982). The changes in the jurisprudence of the Supreme Court on these issues, which took the form of the eventual prevailing of previous dissenting opinions by such luminaries as Oliver

Wendell Holmes and Louis Brandeis, opened the way to acceptance of fringe and marginal groups in American life, in the same way and at the same time that workers' organizations became respected partners within the political and economic leadership of the New Deal. It was only at this point that the scenario of social control finally changed in favour of an alternative which had certainly been long simmering on the back burner.

## Social control of meaning

The control of the 'social object' through control of language rather than through coercion, became paramount, as the acute perception of the young C. Wright Mills was able to capture in 1940 (1963a (1939); 1963b (1940)). The selling of products and of the American way of life, the 'good life', through a skilfully elaborated art of advertising was fully developed by then, as Stuart Ewen shows in his analysis of the origins of the advertising industry (1976). The entertainment and recreation industries had also been powerfully centralized and streamlined, so that both production and distribution of ideological products could unfold within a hegemonic perspective, at least as far as the masses were concerned (Cohen, 1990). And broadcasting, of course, was the scene of a battle from which the basic structures of the American mass media were to emerge (McChesney, 1993).

The complex of these apparatuses came to constitute a kind of so-called 'virtual reality' that, in becoming a powerful means of social organization, was to represent also the conflicts and fissures of social reality. This was already quite clear in the advertising industry, for instance, which in proposing the image of the 'good life' – the 'American way' – was actively siding in favour of a consumerist culture against the old Protestant Ethic style. In fact, the new media became active propagandists of a complex social change that was to break with the traditional authority structure of the past in favour of a democracy of consumption where the moral command of self-indulgence was opposed to the morality of sacrifice. The apostles of the culture of consumption were to start an intense recycling programme of the worst commonplaces of Bohemian romanticism, the spokepersons of which had inveighed against the traditional values of authority, family and sacrifice throughout the nineteenth century. These 'new' and 'transgressive' values were to be bought, lock, stock and barrel, by the industry of image-selling and increasingly transformed into a new discourse of social control. We have witnessed an acceleration of this process in recent times with the commercialization of the 1960s counter-culture, pioneered in the 1970s by such skilful artist-entrepreneurs as Andy Warhol.

For instance, in a recent analysis of the origins of television soap operas in the 1950s, Ksenija Vidmar (1994) has shown that, beyond the myth of the harmonious, conservative 1950s, the representation of early soap operas on American television had to deal with the transformations in the American family brought about by economic change and war, and the very different roles that men and women found themselves in when compared to the 'ideal nuclear family' (see also Spigel, 1992). If then, on the one hand, 'soaps' were supposed to reaffirm traditional values, often such reaffirmation was betrayed in the very unfolding of the visual and textual narrative which was becoming the vehicle for the emergence of a sort of 'social unconscious'.

That much social control is supported today by mass media, however, does not mean that there is currently a greater 'fragmentation' and 'indeterminacy' of meaning than in the past. It is not even that clear that there is a 'greater complexity', if we take into account that the increasing centralization and standardization of the mass media is probably contributing to reduce the *diversity* of message-production – as witnessed, for instance, by linguists' preoccupation with the linguistic forms, dialects and whole languages that are fast disappearing. In fact, in the actual interaction of everyday life, 'fixations' of meanings that are cogent and powerful, even if somewhat contingent, do happen and are strongly connected to the operation of mass media of communication.

## Postmodernist goes to war, does not find it

A good case in support of the above point was the Gulf War and the media treatment of it, especially in the United States. A polemic has been going on for some time now around the articles that Jean Baudrillard wrote at the time of the Gulf War, first predicting that the war would not happen on 4 January 1991, 12 days before the war actually broke out, then denying that it was happening and that it had happened (Baudrillard, 1991; Norris, 1992; Merrin, 1994). Baudrillard's argument runs after the media events and predictably shifts from a concept of the war as not happening because 'virtual', to a nostalgic concept of the war as not happened because not fitting the stereotypical image of *la belle guerre*, nineteenth-century style. What I personally found embarassing and annoying in Baudrillard's articles on the war is not only the silly, Paris-centric provincialism of his anti-Arab and anti-American stereotyping, or the echo-effect of a prose mimicking and amplifying the previous day's press commonplaces, but that Baudrillard's leitmotif in these articles seems very consistent with the perceptible underlying agenda of the mass media's mobilization during that time – that is, the obliteration of the sense that a war was actually happening, was controversial and was bloody.

As the linguist George Lakoff noted, metaphors were extensively used by the media in order to construe the morality tale to tell the American people (Lakoff, 1991). The war was smoothly presented as being almost like army manoeuvres. The bombings were 'surgical strikes', our belief in which was supposed to be enhanced by video-game-like presentations. The attack was a reaction against Iraqi atrocities, some of which turned out to be highly dubious, such as the story about Kuwaiti babies being thrown out of their incubators. Iraqi civilian deaths were 'collateral damage'. The rallies against the war – very large, especially in San Francisco – were downplayed, particularly nationally and internationally. Even the rusty old tool of censorship was used, both by the American Government and by the big networks themselves. First of all, there were strong restrictions on the media in the field, through the creation of the infamous 'press pools' assembled and escorted by the military themselves. Added to this, the very networks were timid in presenting materials that might have caused government or the military any embarassment (Gitlin, 1991). It even got to the point where a demographer, who had released to the press estimates of the Iraqi deaths which were deemed 'too high', was fired from the US Census Bureau (*San Francisco Chronicle*, 14 April 1992).

This censorship was not the least reason why we saw so little of the war on television, by the way, as Baudrillard complains in his articles. So, far from not happening, the 'virtual' instruments on which the military, the political élites and the media relied were used in order to manage and shape reality – a reality of which, of course, élites generally seem to know, or at least seem to think they know, more than we do. In short, the issue as I see it is not the 'virtual' transformations of reality; it is, rather, the 'real' consequences of representation. A revealing study by communication scholars Lewis, Jhally and Morgan about the relationship between the media, public opinion and public knowledge, carried out a few weeks into the war, found that 'the public are not generally ignorant – rather, they are *selectively misinformed*' (1991: 5). In particular, they found that heavy television-watching was not only associated with higher support for the war but, a bit more surprisingly, with greater ignorance about the war and its circumstances.

In short, the attitudes of the élites to the whole business were essentially realistic, very modernist indeed, and in line with the old principle of total mobilization of human beings, things, values, moralities and gods in pursuit of *Staatsräson*! How could a critical outlook play a different game, without taking the chance of becoming the apologist of élites' convenient picture of reality? 'Who then, besides the Arab masses, is still able to believe in and get excited about [the war]?', the sociologist rhetorically asks (Baudrillard, 1991: 23–4). Indeed. Given that the bombs were falling on 'the Arab masses' and not on French sociologists' Left Bank desks, the former showed a reasonable inclination to get excited about the whole business. The latter, watching the bombs fall on the CNN news coverage, saw only a boring 'virtual' war. What depth of insight. What epochal vision!

There is an issue at stake here, however, that is a bit more substantial than this; the very concept of our social reality is involved here. The 'fragmentary', 'undetermined' reading of postmodernism (whatever may hide under this label, this seems to be the 'common opinion' about postmodernist readings) appears to drive towards a sort of existential despair where, according to temperament, one can either choose orgiastic pleasure or commit suicide. Both 'choices' are functional, however, to the idea of letting the drivers do their job, without disturbing them too much. The least real, the furthest away, the most virtual their job appears, the best for them.

In the era of a world of production that increasingly happens in the rarefied field of information – whether it is information to do production, to do information, to do art, to do sex or whatever – the complex soft- and hardware operations that are linked to the management of information are obviously hidden from the scrutiny of 'the many', who are left to deal with their misery, their consumption and their sins (all carefully administered by their superiors) in exactly the same way in which the mysteries of the Church protected élites from the inappropriate gaze of peasants in medieval Europe. The very technological format of the process of production is today, therefore, also the best protective screen of that process, hidden behind the cryptic nature of electronic information systems. What would a member of the élite desire more than that? Only a philosopher explaining to the masses that even the little bit of atrocity and roguery they think they have seen has actually not happened. Dorothy Smith has written of

> the complex organization of the media, of formal administrative process, of the 'scientific' media of research methodologies, professional journals and the like. These bring into being a universe of facts, images, data, findings, models, etc. etc. which stand in for and are treated as reality . . . The character of ideological practice . . . is more now than a reflection of reality. It is a form of reality in becoming a form of action as well as representing a reality beyond itself. (Smith, 1976: 53–4)

This is the point: so called 'virtual' reality is by no means less than real. On the contrary, it is a particularly meaningful and powerful form of reality.

## Democracy and the 'tyranny of the majority'

Fascism, communism, and mass democracy competed for supremacy throughout the twentieth century. In a sense, they competed on the same terrain because they were all *mass* societies trying to come to terms with the irruption of masses on to the political scene. 'Democracy' turned out to be superior because it was able to provide the highest degree of mobilization, from the perspective of élites, and the highest degree of freedom, from the perspective of the person in the masses. Fascism and communism were primitive forms – because their propaganda was one and the same thing as the image of the state. The ideal situation is, instead, one in which everybody shares similar thoughts not because he or she is coerced or even openly pressured, but because he or she freely so 'chooses' – because there is no discrepancy between the desire of the ruler and the desire of the ruled.

This is the process which North American political and intellectual élites and especially élites in the field of advertising, telecommunications and the entertainment industry have been working on, in a plural, competitive, conflictual and 'free' manner, throughout this century. At the same time, the political and legal system has given legitimacy and credibility to such a process by setting up the conditions of a strict separation between cultural control and political control – a separation that may be overcome now, for example in the United States, not by sleight of hand but only by the exercise of hegemony – that is, by that capacity of aggregation and construction of consensus that Tocqueville had already in 1835 (1961) decried as 'the tyranny of the majority'.

The tyranny of the majority, however, may be such only in a metaphorical or, at most, sociological sense, not in a strict legal or political sense. The observance of the separation between cultural and political control is, therefore, a powerful support of social control in the sense that without it the system would not be credible. This is the ultimate paradox of democracy in mass society, the paradox that has been fine-tuned throughout the twentieth century: only that type of social control, that type of 'fixation of the social object', which appears to be the result of the 'free' and 'unconstrained' interplay of the human agencies involved is actual, effective, social control. Social control that is somehow darkened by the doubt that it may be directed by the power of political intervention is immediately tainted with the suspicion of undemocraticness and, therefore, loses its legitimacy, and thus its power.

A good case in point seems to me to be the recent Italian case of Silvio Berlusconi, the telecommunications and retail industry tycoon who became Prime Minister of Italy for a short period in 1994–5 thanks to his control of the private broadcasting system, which gave him a substantial advantage in the elections of March 1994 (Ricolfi, 1994). Mr Berlusconi, as Prime Minister, proceeded to gain political control of public telecommunications. It seems to me that his main weakness is probably to be found exactly in the reach and extension of his powers, which is very difficult not to conceive of as a dramatic case of a 'conflict of interests'. This, before being a legal and a constitutional problem, is a political problem, because such a situation can only project a shadow of suspicion on the otherwise routinized work of the mass production of meanings. The state of affairs so created can be easily portrayed by Mr Berlusconi's political adversaries as somewhat pre-democratic – more similar to a Bunny Club version of the Ministries of Propaganda of Fascist Italy or the Third Reich than to the anodyne and market-oriented character of giant American television networks (of course, the fact that Mr Berlusconi's main political ally is the 'post-Fascist' *Alleanza nazionale* political party, does nothing to allay those fears).

### Social control through crime?

It should be noted that the so-called 'intractability' of many social problems – the fact that it seems to be very difficult to establish a rational and reasonably efficient discourse about 'crime', for instance – has also to do with the fact that the amount of social control which is to be found in the public management of the *images* of social problems is probably much higher than that to be found in the proposed *solutions*. This is, of course, an old truism of sociology, first announced clearly by Durkheim (1938 (1895)), who claimed that crime is functional to the definition – and redefinition, as Kai Erikson was to add (1966) – of the social boundaries between what is allowed and what is prohibited. The awesome way in which today's society, and especially its mass media, delves into the representation of crime and crime stories, whether 'real' or 'fictional', amounts to a giant daily re-proposition of a 'gazette of morality', fine-tuning the conflict and debate about the boundaries of prohibition and permission at a specific time and a specific place (Melossi, 1993). Those who are the protagonists of such drama, the 'criminals', are therefore usefully and socially processed in this representation. The main function of this representation is not so much the control of the 'criminals', but rather the control of those who are outside of the boundaries of the criminal justice system and whose daily lives need to be regulated in order to secure their ongoing contribution to production and civil life – that is, to a given social order. Without criminals, the much more strategically important system of social control of the generality of citizens, of 'good' citizens, would not be possible (that is, 'illegalities' have to be managed, processed and produced as 'crime' or 'delinquency', as Foucault explained in the most insightful and least known section of *Discipline and Punish* (1977 (1975): 257–92).

Whereas it is true that is very difficult to build a 'rational discourse' on the question of crime and punishment – indeed the increase of punishment in the United States over the last 20 years may hardly be accounted for on rational grounds (Melossi, 1993) – it is also true, for instance, that had such discourse established itself it would have been substantially harder for a Republican presidential candidate to use the image of the big, black, bad man, Willie Horton, going out of the 'revolving door' of the Massachusetts criminal justice system under Governor Dukakis to terrify an innocent white, middle-class, suburban family (an advertisement that figured prominently in George Bush's victorious 1988 campaign against Michael Dukakis – whose partner happened to be, lest we forget, the black leader Jesse Jackson).

The fact is that in a society obsessed with anxieties, in which many traditional identities having to do with class, politics, ethnicity and gender are rapidly declining, the criminal presents respectable society with the gift of ideological, if not social and economic, recomposition:

> The criminal does not seriously endanger the structure of society by his destructive activities, and on the other hand he is responsible for a sense of solidarity, aroused among those whose attention would be otherwise centered upon interests quite divergent from those of each other. (Mead, 1964 (1918): 227)

It has been noted that the increasing social fragmentation of 'postindustrial' (Bell, 1973) or 'risk' society (Beck, 1994) has been destroying self-identifications based on traditional concepts of class and politics. Immigrants and the underclass in the United States and Europe today are a labour-market result of such changes, but are sometimes identified as 'the cause' nevertheless. They become, therefore, the instrument of a typical ideological procedure through which a social recomposition of the (lower) middle class is effected symbolically. So, while the once-industrial working class, deeply disorganized and fragmented, experiences a demoralization, and a loss of security, values and sense of self-worth and identity that may certainly result in anomie and crime, the 'illegalities' so produced are instantly co-opted and put under check as 'useful delinquencies' (Foucault, 1975), through the work of recomposition of a symbolic moral universe. Criminologists' 'official' social control, therefore, plays a subordinate role *vis-à-vis* the broader type of social control that I have tried to address throughout this chapter (on this, more generally, see Melossi, 1994b).

### State, social control and the 'European Constitution'

After World War II, Europe was divided between two super powers: the United States, powerful in its Western part, and the Union of Soviet Socialist Republics in its Eastern part. Certainly in the Western part, many of the features of the kind of democratic mass society which had been developing in the United States – including its system of social control – took hold. However, there too democracy was somewhat limited. For instance, in countries where strong political Lefts were present, those Lefts were not actually allowed to reach a steering position in government. Accordingly, the old myths of the state and of a coercive system of social control were still very present. In the East, of course, such questions were not even asked. Almost from the very beginning, however, a slow process of thawing started, helped both by the relaxing of hostility between the two blocs and by growing internal developments in Western societies, in which increasing consumerism, advertising and technical potential for telecommunications were all quickly happening. It was, however, only with the fall of the Berlin Wall in 1989 and the concomitant implosion of the Soviet Union that, finally, the kind of social model that had been growing in the United States over the course of the twentieth century could be exported to Europe – and grafted onto the body of each original European culture, often extremely different from the American one.

It seems to me that, in the work of Michel Foucault, one can read the announcement of this turn of events. To the faster and faster changing Europe of the 1970s, Foucault explained – first in *Discipline and Punish* (1975 (1977)) and then especially in *La volonté de savoir* (the introduction to the planned history of sexuality, 1978 (1976)) – that power shows first and foremost a constitutive and not merely censorious quality, and that the notion of the state is but an obstacle in thinking about power relationships. Such a message, on the fringes throughout the 1970s and 1980s, acquired its full disruptive weight with the breakdown of the Soviet Union in 1989 and the consequent renewed possibilities of democratic development within both Eastern and Western Europe. In the new situation, freed at least in part from nuclear blackmail, the dynamics of democracy could accelerate and the question of the creation of consensus, of a public opinion, could occupy centre-stage once again. The current battle raging over control of mass telecommunications, within each European country and across Europe, may be understood only against that historical backdrop. Now, Europe also may be run by the power of the image rather than the power of the tank.

Of course, a crucial complication in the European case, as well as a powerful impulse to speeding up the whole process, is that at the same time a process of not only economic but also political unification is under way; so the state-concept is under attack and a new form of social control is being prepared, not only because of long-term structural developments but also because of ongoing political transformations.

Actually, progressive European Federalism between the two World Wars had already identified in the doctrine of the state, with all its accompanying elements, one of the most reactionary features of Europe and one of the causes of recurring European conflicts and miseries (see Silvio Trentin's *Stato, Nazione, Federalismo*, 1945, and Altiero Spinelli and Ernesto Rossi's *Il Manifesto di Ventotene*, 1941 (1991)). This tradition has been revived recently in the elaboration of those who, for the first time, have merged the issue of European federalism with that of federalism within what used to be the individual, European nation-state, like the Basque legal theorist Gurutz Jáuregui Bereciartu:

> Human collectivities have created diverse structures for organizing themselves in response to the social, economic, and other necessities of the moment. The nation-state appeared as the juridico-political structure that was adequate for a determinate type of society . . . Today it is abundantly clear that the existence of the nation-state is increasingly less synonymous with independence. At present, the nation-states lack meaning. I refer to those already constituted as much as to those that wish to be. The present national problem in Europe regards not the creation of new states but the disappearance of the existing ones, a disintegration that, in fact, should be accompanied by . . . social and economic transformations. (Jáuregui Bereciartu, 1986: 164)

In fact, the search for a new way of political being in Europe is slowly bringing to the surface an obfuscation, if not an obsolescence, of the role of the old nineteenth-century nation-states, and the emergence of new entities, carrying a national or quasi-national identity but not necessarily aspiring to statehood. The principles of subsidiarity and proportionality adopted in the Project of European Constitution[8] seem to suggest that faculties and powers that traditionally resided with states, are being redistributed among different political subjects, the European Union and the Regions. However, the old state-centered ideology is still present today both with those who think in terms of a 'Europe of Fatherlands', as it is typical of most European conservative forces, and with those who would like to project the sinister shadow of a centralized, 'Napoleonic' Euro-state onto the new European polity.

In fact, a clear contradiction exists between the effort of building a political union and that of respecting the principle of sovereignty of the old nation-states, one which very few really want to question openly. This is quite clear in the cited Project of a European Constitution. The principle of subsidiarity is proclaimed loudly (Art. 10) but concerns only the individual nation-states, not the national-regional entities that are constituted within each state and which should also take advantage of the subsidiarity principle – with significant consequences inside each state for its relationship to its internal regions. Citizenship is attributed only to citizens of the member nation-states (Art. 3) and more courageous proposals such as the one of Italian Europarliamentarian Renzo Imbeni (PDS), to recognize frankly a concept of European citizenship independent of individual national citizenships (Imbeni 1994) – a citizenship, therefore, that could have been extended to individuals from non-member states – was so distorted in the course of discussion that Imbeni himself decided to vote against it in the end. Europe once again bowed before the claims of the old state-national sovereignties.

Indeed, the issue of citizenship, and the related question of immigration, are a sort of acid-test for social control in the Europe of the late 1990s. In the same way that the social control of crime is a dependent variable of the much broader issue of social control, so in Europe today the social control of immigration, that is becoming central to European policies in more ways than one (Waever, Buzan, Kelstrup and Lemaitre, 1993; Pastore, 1993), is strictly related to the concept of social control that is going to prevail in Europe – that is, to the kind of social and political *constitution* that will ultimately obtain.

Elsewhere I have recalled Kai Erikson's theory of deviance (1966), according to which a community publicly debates its cultural, moral and legal boundaries through the notoriety of famous cases of deviance (Melossi, 1994a). It seems to me that immigrants from outside the European Union perform a very similar role, whereby the talk about immigrants' criminal and cultural deviance, with which European mass media are replete (Van Dijk, 1993; Ter Wal, 1991), is not only a vehicle for controlling immigrants' behaviour but is also a vehicle for intra-European debate about the existence, nature and essential characteristics of a European identity that appears to be very problematic (Schlesinger, 1992). Will the constitution of Europe go in the direction of a democratic and federalist society held together by loyalty to a 'constitutional patriotism', as Habermas seems to suggest on the left (1994 (1992)), or will it take the direction of a new European Empire, as Alain de Benoist (1993–4 (1991)) seems to suggest on the right? We already know from our reflections on Paz's essay that it is not at all sure which one of the two models would be more inclusionary, even if we may have a rather good idea of which one would probably be more democratic (the problem being of course that, as we have seen, those two qualities do not go necessarily hand in hand!).

These political-legal-constitutional backdrops are connected to the even broader problem that a 'European public sphere' does not really exist, given the traditional connection between nation and democracy (Habermas, 1994). And yet the existence of such a sphere is essential to the making of a European democracy. Only within it, may a process of cultural identification develop which is strictly connected to the question of democracy or, to be more precise, to the so-called 'deficit' of democracy in Europe today. As Guenther Schaefner has noted, the making of European law is still shaped on the model of a treaty among sovereign nations rather than on the model of a constitutional organism (Schaefner, 1991: 686–7). At the same time, no European institution is really equipped, *de jure* and *de facto*, to provide democratic control and legitimation. Not the national parliaments, too far from Brussels to check effectively on the intricate European bureaucracy. Not the European Parliament, because of its limited powers, but also for a more substantive political reason: namely that for a parliament truly to be recognized as the expression of the political will of the people, such will has to be constituted at the level of the parliament itself, as should the political parties that make up such a parliament. However, there is no 'European public opinion' and there are no 'European political parties'. Whereas bureaucratic decision making in Europe is becoming more and more unified and centralized, the formation of democratic opinion is not, and political debate is still by and large going on at the old-national level and not at the European level. There is no 'European public sphere' and so there is no European democracy. In Habermas's terms, the present condition of Europe brings to the fore the tension between systemic (that is, economic and administrative) integration and socio-political integration (Habermas, 1994: 28).

### Conclusion

We have to conclude, therefore, that the system in place today is an autocratic government based on contacts among the various European governments, a system that is offensive to feelings of national popular sovereignty without actually constituting a European popular sovereignty. Those who wish to overcome such a situation are working toward the creation of a European Constitution, of a federal, political and electoral system and, especially, of the European 'public sphere' that would have to accompany such a complex legal and political change. We have seen how democracy, as a political form, is complementary to a high degree of development of social communication. Certainly, the creation of a common economy is also necessary. *Le doux commerce*, however, is not enough and we should not forget

Mead's warning about the pre-eminence of communicative interaction over economic interaction (it goes without saying that it is not possible to think of a European identity and culture without asking the question about a tendentially common European language).

In fact, developments in the field of the mass media of communication have a special impact on the process of European unification because the only level at which a 'European public sphere' is currently being constituted is that of European newspapers and satellite television channels, where ironically, substantial American interests and inputs are at stake (one has only to reflect that the only actual worldwide 'public sphere' of sorts is beamed from Atlanta, Georgia). A process of European democratization will not only have to mean the extension of the actual legislative powers of the European Parliament; it is quite likely that the European Parliament will also have to confront the situation within each national member-state, and within Europe as a whole, concerning the actual implementation of the principle of freedom of speech. It is highly doubtful that a true implementation of such a principle could be confined to the current radical *laissez-faire* interpretation without considering the problem of protecting a *plural access* to the tools by which freedom of speech is actually exercised. According to American jurist Archibald Cox (1986), for instance, such access is today seriously endangered by the growth of governments' near-monopoly of information on security matters, by the concentration of private control of the mass media and the growing influence of political advertising. Consequently, critical legal theorists are today questioning the supposedly 'harmless' nature of free speech, and are using arguments similar to those of J.L. Austin's philosophy in order to show that speech is never really 'free' or 'unconsequential' and there is, therefore, a legitimate public interest in regulating it (Fish, 1994; MacKinnon, 1993; it is no accident that in the recent Italian political debate, discussed above, Mr Berlusconi's coalition appealed to the principle of free speech in order to defend its quasi-monopolistic control of private telecommunications in Italy).

In conclusion, it should not come as a big surprise that in the Europe of the 1990s the non-existence, or very limited existence, of a European identity corresponds to the non-existence, or very limited existence, of a European environment of communication, and to the non-existence, or very limited existence, of a European democracy. The process of creation of a European democracy cannot be separated from the processes of European communication, unification and self-identification.

The drafting of a European Constitution should be found at the crossroads of all these processes. However, because also of the formalist conceptions of law that still prevail in Europe, a consciousness of the fact that the making of a common European culture has to interact with the creation of a collective sense of rights, and of a common legal culture, seems to be missing. Social control and law are strictly linked – long before any functional relationship – at the linguistic and cultural levels, because the creation of a common culture is strongly intertwined with the creation of a common law. A common language and culture must find in a Constitution the repository of their values, their hopes, their programmes – and the Constitution must find its life in a common language and culture. In summary, whereas we can see that the question of the state is quickly disappearing behind us, the question of a democratic regulation of actually existing processes of social control is what this new *fin de siècle* seems to be placing squarely in front of us, and is what we are asked to contend with.

## Notes

I would like to thank all those who contributed in various ways to the development of the ideas presented in this chapter, though the ultimate responsibility is, of course, mine alone: Roberto Bergalli who organized the Colloquium at the University of Barcelona where these ideas were first presented; the students of the 1994–5 Master's course in Sociology of Law of the International Institute for the Sociology of Law, Oñati, Euskadi, Spain, who were exposed to, and actively debated, some of the theses discussed here; and last, but certainly not least, Colin Sumner and his students and colleagues at the Institute of Criminology, University of Cambridge, who asked many important and useful questions on the occasion of my visit on 30 January 1995.

*Dario Melossi*
*University of Bologna*

1   I should note that the ideas presented here are an effort at summing up and developing 'in the direction of Europe' the main ideas of my *The State of Social Control: A Sociological Study of Concepts of State and Social Control in the Making of Democracy* (Melossi, 1990).

2   If one would wish to find a criminological reference point, one would have to look in the direction of the pluralist and conflictual criminology of Sutherland, Lemert, and Becker, all of whom would agree – in different ways – that 'deviance' is a product of social control. However, the notion of social control that I have developed throughout this chapter is a concept inherently connected to society's order, therefore to social theory, and not to specific aspects of society, hence specific subdisciplines of sociology.

3   This seems to be a point where my analysis departs from that of Colin Sumner (1994).

4   It should be noted that nothing that has happened since the epochal 'fall of the wall' in 1989, may be taken to contradict this crucial junction in Marx's argument. Quite the contrary. Those very events suggest, if nothing else, that there is no place, in reality or imagination, or even in the past, where our labourer would find good grounds for being less 'timid' and suspicious.

5   Judgements about such similarity may be surprising and historically relative. For instance, Daniel Cohn-Bendit and Thomas Schmid, in their *Heimat Babylon* (1994

(1992)) quote from a pamphlet by Benjamin Franklin, *Observations Concerning the Increase of Mankind and the Peopling of our Countries* (1751), where Franklin warns against the immigration of 'dark races' to Pennsylvania. Nothing particularly new, it would seem; except that for Franklin, the dark races were 'the Spaniards, the Italians, the French, the Russians, and the Swedes . . . Also Germans are dark, except for the Saxons who, together with the English, make up most of the white people on earth. I would like to see their number increase [among the immigrants]' (Cohn-Bendit and Schmid, 1994: 96, my translation). Some of these races have definitely been 'bleached' in the meantime!

6    It is interesting to note that also Gramsci developed the Hegelian concept of the state, namely the concept of the ethical state. Gramsci, however, gave it an insightful realistic twist by seeing the state as the result of the work of intellectuals dealing with moral and cultural matters. Gramsci's ethical state proceeded from the bottom of social reality instead of being deduced from the top of abstraction. Passerin d'Entrèves notes how also Croce expressed a 'sceptical' view on the notion of the state in 'Elementi di politica' (1925) (Passerin d'Entrèves, 1967: 65).

7    For instance, when the famous strike in the textile industry of Lawrence, MA, broke out in January 1912, about 15 different ethnic groups worked there (the largest one being Italian).

8    In 1994, the European Parliament examined and discussed a project for a European Constitution (Oreja, 1994), elaborated within the Committee on Institutional Affairs. It decided to defer further discussion to its successor, the Parliament elected in 1994, with a view to submitting a proposal to the intergovernmental conference of 1996 (Resolution on the Constitution of the European Union, A3-0064/94, 10 February 1994).

# 4

# Controlling Social Panic: Questions and Answers about Security in Italy at the End of the Millennium

*Massimo Pavarini*

That I am a 'critical criminologist' derives from the social definition attributed to me by the scientific community in the light of what I have written and declared in some 22 years of academic activity. Little, indeed nothing, indicates that 'critical criminologist' is a semantically equivocal epithet that I would be pleased not to have inscribed on my tombstone.

Since the beginning of the 1970s I have followed with intellectual and even emotional intensity the international discussion that has been carried on since the early years of that decade within the restricted circle that is 'critical criminology'. For better or for worse, I have made my own contribution in the debate. Without any false humility, I consider that contribution to have been rather modest; I have to confess, however, that on the whole the debate itself seems to me to have been a rather modest one. I read in H. Simon (1991: 174–4) that in a lifetime one is hardly ever confronted by stark alternatives, in the sense that life is not a maze where at each turning we are forced to choose one way or another, right or left. Life is more like a game of chess which is not won or lost with just one right or wrong move but by a whole series of moves that only hindsight will show to have been right or wrong. Life is a series of continuous, albeit slight, adjustments, none of which are ever perceived as innovative or a changing of tack from the previous course. We always believe we are travelling along a straight path; indeed, it is our declared intention to proceed unerringly forward, first one foot, then the other. But with each step, we very probably shift just slightly and imperceptibly from that straight course. And so, after many steps – as many as may be taken in more than 20 years – we may well find ourselves travelling in a radically different direction. Convinced we were moving in the original direction, we now realize that we are going a totally different way. Little wonder at the resulting disarray and the soul-searching question: how could this have happened?

This is just how I would describe my own journey within critical criminology. In my approach to criminal justice issues I have never been aware of taking any sharp turns away from the views that emerged from the discussions during the mid-1970s among a group of my friends, the founders of the journal *La Questione Criminale*. And yet, many of my current positions undoubtedly differ from the extreme opinions held then, as indeed they differ, often radically, from the viewpoints expressed today by many of those friends and colleagues with whom I once unconditionally shared the same ideas.

The reflections that follow focus on what most concerns me today, both from a scientific and political viewpoint. My scientific and political commitment over the last few years, in favour of policies to ensure crime prevention and security for society's citizens and to develop a policy of social control, would be defined in Italy as 'democratic' and in the English-speaking world as 'left-wing'. In order to make myself understood beyond the political lexicon used in Italy, I would liken my current position to that of certain 'old' British friends, and as part of 'New' Left Realism. My opinions radically diverge from theirs, however, on several crucial issues.

In this chapter, I would like to give a theoretical account of my 'visions of social control', with specific reference to the situation in Italy at the close of the millennium, aided by the experience I have gained by descending from the ivory tower of academia and 'getting my hands dirty' with social control policies.

## The crisis in criminological creeds and its effect on criminal policy in Italy

The current criminological debate bewails the fact that criminological theories of the last 50 years are increasingly fraught with dissent as we approach the new millennium (Nelken, 1994).

Criminological knowledge is the direct offspring of the great Enlightenment theories (Lyotard, 1984), which gave rise to a number of 'strong ideas' on criminal issues. One cardinal belief is the idea of state, which blithely simplifies the whole question of the relation between criminal law and individual freedoms. Another theory is underpinned by the paradigm of social control (van Krieken, 1991: 1–25), and considers the issue of criminal deviance in terms of social engineering policies. Both these traditions have been enlisted to champion alternately authoritarian and progressive political beliefs: the first has supported the ideology of an authoritarian state, but also the liberalist *garantismo* movement in favour of civil law concepts such as 'due process' and 'checks and balances'; the second has been invoked by advocates of an advanced social state, but also by the harbingers of the worst Orwellian nightmares. Every formulation of social control has always produced its mirror image (Cohen, 1985). These criminological creeds have fallen foul of modern times. The advent of postmodern approaches, even in criminology (Cohen, 1990; Smart, 1990; Hunt, 1991; Brodeur, 1993: 73–121), is a clear demonstration of the ongoing crisis. The vicissitudes of criminal policy in Italy today are indicative of this upheaval. In fact this current crisis has especially undermined the culture and policies of social control as advocated by left-wing parties – in other words, the political and cultural forces that most identified with traditional Marxist thinking. A look at the criminal question in Italy over the last 20 years clearly shows the dominant influence of left-wing penal policies. With moderate and conservative parties reluctant to commit themselves on criminal policy issues, it was the Left in Italy, with its Marxist cultural background, which made the decisive thrust both in shaping penal policies during the emergency situation of the mid-1970s against 'left-' and 'right-wing' terrorism, and in formulating the prison and penal procedure reform laws. It was again the Left in Italy which sanctioned the introduction of special procedures to combat organized crime (Neppi Modona and Violante, 1978).

Apart from any specific tactical reasons,[1] I believe that the Italian Left's insistence on criminal policies is explained by its entrenched commitment to the idea of the state and hence its understandable tendency to conceive any reform of the state in terms of changes in the law, including criminal law, rather than changes in society through social movements and community action.

This general trend seems offset by what the Italian political lexicon calls the *garantista* school, in other words, that liberal legal tradition in favour of procedural and other guarantees. Although a minority movement, *garantismo* is espoused by several intellectuals and legal professionals active in left-wing politics. These advocates of legal guarantees may seem in radical contrast to the left-wing political forces sustaining the criminal policy clampdown mentioned before. In fact, the *garantista* school is in favour of a drastic reduction of the sphere of criminal offence, calling for 'minimum criminal law' (Baratta, 1985b: 443–73; Ferrajoli, 1985: 493–524). Their call to narrow the scope of criminal law and curtail the whole system of penal justice is not just defensive but highly constructive. Indeed, while the Left majority favours more criminal law, this minority, 'legal guarantees', school has come out in favour of less criminal law.

Luigi Ferrajoli (1989), the most articulate and profound advocate of the *garantista* school, asks a searching question: what alternatives to legal provisions should the social state of the future adopt? In so far as current illegality in Italy derives in part from the forms of its past and present legal system, which is undermined by such a degree of uncertainty in law as to encourage criminality, Ferrajoli (1994) urges reducing the sphere of criminal justice as an essential, albeit partial, step towards restoring a state of legality. His thesis is simple: before entering into the merits of the items to be enshrined in the new forms of legality – that is, what interests should enjoy penal protection, etc. – we must understand that an acceptable level of legality will come about only by reducing the legal definitions of illegality.[2]

Despite their radical divergence, both those who want to extend the scope of criminal law and those who want to curb penality project the image of the Italian Left as a champion of criminal justice, since both trust that more or less criminal justice simply depends on bringing in legislation to penalize or de-criminalize.

Further confirmation that traditional criminology is floundering on the slippery slope of criminal policies comes from the abolitionist camp (Hulsman and Bernat de Celis, 1982; Christie, 1981; Bianchi, 1996: 1–11; Mathiesen, 1984; Scheerer, 1983: 525–41), whose theories have been accredited in countries that have made the most coherent effort to implement democratization through social control strategies.

The abolitionist approach (for a critique, see Pavarini, 1985: 525–53) holds that criminality is simply a fictitious construction, as is the very idea of the state, and therefore neither criminology nor criminal policy will ever be able to hold effectively in check that which is artificially defined as falling within the sphere of penality. In fact, the abolitionists maintain that the system of criminal justice is merely a tool to bolster an artificial order set up by the social state in order to monopolize the repressive resources (Sgubbi, 1990). A monopoly is created by bringing into existence an artificial system defining what is penally protected, where that which is penally protected belongs exclusively to the sphere of criminal law since it exists only by definition of that very criminal law (Savelsberg, 1987: 529–41; Delmas-Marty, 1985). Doing away with the penal justice system is, therefore, tantamount to ridding civil society of the impediment which has presented it from seeking and finding solutions to its problems.

Over and above their radically divergent views, advocates of repression, the *garantista* proponents and abolitionists alike all forget one crucial point: that determining the criterion with which to choose what deserves penal punishment and what may be otherwise resolved (in other words, choosing to do away with penal protection) is a matter for society to decide. This implies that the whole question of reducing the penal sphere is not a matter to be pursued exclusively by paring formal criminal law to a minimum or by abolishing it altogether. Rather, the conditions must be created within society for a *de facto* minimum or non-existent penal justice system.

It follows that the new conditions of legality in a future social state must be sought in political, social, cultural and economic strategies which, much more than legal norms, will meet society's demands for security without involving the criminal justice system (Downes, 1988; Melossi, 1993: 259–79). In other words, the scope of de-penalization and criminal abolition must be determined not so much by rewriting the laws but by ensuring social conditions able to provide alternative answers to the problems that are currently the exclusive terrain of criminal justice.

## A paradox at the end of the millennium: social panic, a punitive vocabulary and the privatization of security

The growing social demand for security against crime reflects subjective feelings of insecurity, regardless of whether this sense of insecurity is or is not well founded and the result of an objective state of diminished security (Balkin, 1979: 343–7). This growing demand for security manifests itself as a protest against the institutional and public offering of social defence (Conklin, 1975). Institutional and public efforts to provide safeguards against criminality are perceived as being unable to meet the social demand for security; again, whether this is actually the case is another matter. This phenomenon, usually manifested by widespread social panic, is an indication of disproportionate social unease; anxieties exaggerated out of all proportion.

There are many expressions used to describe the failure of public security: the rise in crime, which in turn has become more sophisticated and thus more threatening; the ineffectual measures applied to combat criminal deviancy; the inability of the social state to ensure law and order; the obsolescence of the mechanisms of informal social control (Brown, 1990). An unfulfilled need for social security generates a social demand for security. The risk today is that this demand will be met in two ways: (a) by attributing greater importance to criminal law in a pernicious circuit of self-referral and self-enhancement that legitimizes the penal system itself (Dershowitz, 1976) in a manner that is prevalently symbolic (Baratta, 1984: 5–30; 1985a: 247–68); and (b) by allowing the security of society to become increasingly a matter for the private, or rather the non-institutional, non-public sphere. The crisis of the social state has coincided with the emergence of security as a burning political issue. Indeed, public security from crime is a typical issue of the post-welfare era. This is no temporal coincidence: there is a structural link.

Of scientific interest is that the emergence at the close of the millennium of this obsession with security has given rise to two opposing consequences: the first, privatization of the 'security' commodity, that is, objective security; the second, increasingly widespread manifestations of collective feelings of insecurity, that is, subjective security. The real or presumed failure of the welfare state's social control system to guarantee the 'public good' and security against crime is denounced from a neo-liberal pulpit. Since the state is no longer able to guarantee its citizens basic security, then civil society has the right to appropriate (or better, re-appropriate) this, making security a commodity to be purchased on the private security market. Private security has thus become a big business prospect both today and for the future, since all forms of social wealth acquire greater value when augmented with a security investment: the price of real estate, the prestige of service and catering firms, the reliability of a business, the appeal of a service (be it a taxi ride or a hotel stay), etc. Any form of private consumption may be enhanced with a private security investment. The high cost of the private security offering determines, however, unequal distribution of social security, dangerously exacerbating the social risks of victimization depending on the individual's ability to afford access to the private security resource.

Looking ahead, the most likely effect is a strong tendency towards re-feudalization of social relations.[3] As security becomes a commodity on the private market, we will see a process of overt public sublimation of subjective insecurities, which will become a tradeable asset on the political scene. Widespread feelings of insecurity due to the perceived threat of crime in fact tend to present themselves as social demands for greater security; these demands increasingly become a public value to be negotiated to the advantage of those political luminaries offering symbolic representations of security. Alongside private market trading in material security, we will witness the development of a parallel market dealing in symbolic security.

Political hegemony will thus increasingly focus on the following trade-off: electoral consensus in exchange for symbolic representations of security. In so far as the symbolic production of security is by and large provided by criminal law, it follows that the social demands for security are founded on demands for greater penality, which will be increasingly met by political offerings of wider-ranging criminal justice. While security as a material value is subject to free-market exchange, the symbolic security resource enjoys a monopoly since the penal resource is, by its very nature, public.

The privatization of security on the one hand and the widespread public acknowledgement of insecurity on the other, thus become part of a closed, self-referential circuit (Luhmann, 1983). In so far as the private security market is unable to meet the widespread security requirement – or at least is unable to satisfy the needs of the economically disadvantaged – it will in turn produce subjective insecurities.

And vice versa: since the public offering of a symbolic dimension of penality cannot produce material security, it will induce higher private consumption of security. In other words, greater penal repression will go hand in hand with greater recourse to the private security market.

The process of self-referral mentioned above will lead to a new strategy of social control in a post-welfare society: the social control of panic and security. There are two metaphors that aptly describe this new vision of social control: first, a gallows on the virtual public square that is the television screen, indicating the sensationalist mass-media denunciation of the enemy within and broadcast over television channels specializing in capital executions or criminal trial hearings; and, second, widespread consumption of security technology, the ownership of which becomes the new status symbol denoting wealth. Right-wing cultures have little difficulty in responding to the social demands for security by exasperating both its symbolic representations and the technocratic-liberal characteristics offered by the penal justice system (Feeley and Simon, 1992: 449–74).

On reflection, it is clear that social insecurity from criminality is the product of a social construction in which the actual crime risk plays a relatively marginal role (Robert, 1990: 313–30; Duprez, 1991: 275–92). Nevertheless, we must take people's fear seriously, since social panic over criminality is increasingly becoming a catch-all concept, in which the most diverse subjective and collective insecurities become unlikely bedfellows (Lagrange, 1992: 1–29).

### Society's demand for security and social control policies in Italy today

In recent years the Italian situation has offered an interesting example of the relation between society's demand for security and social control policy. There are two features that make the social control of security in Italy unique. First is the historical fact that the appearance of security as an issue in Italy came about a decade later than in other European countries.[4] Second is another historical fact: security became a burning issue very swiftly in the early 1990s in the midst of a political rather than an economic crisis; it was not so much the social state that was failing, rather the political and institutional foundations of the First Republic.

Let me proceed in an orderly fashion to explain the intricate change of perspective that has taken place. Until the end of the 1980s, criminal policy in Italy was anomalous to that of other Western countries. We must note something which is often overlooked in criminological debate and which I have had occasion elsewhere to examine in detail (Pavarini, 1994c: 49–61): over the last 20 years Italy has recorded some of the lowest levels of penal repression in Europe (Council of Europe, 1990: 6), as a consequence of little social demand for punishment. This is the striking feature of the Italian situation. The social demand for penality was inordinately muted for a very long time.

Social conflicts and strife were not channelled into commensurately vociferous social demands for penality, nor did they give rise to widespread sentiments of insecurity. There are many complex reasons why the socio-economic cycle in Italy failed to produce changes in the punitive lexicon at a social level and a call to raise the threshold of punishment (Melossi, 1988: 13–18; 1990). Complex, too, are the reasons why collective sentiments of insecurity for many years failed to appear. The explanation may be sought in the specific political and cultural history of Italy where, unlike other countries, collective sentiments of insecurity found expression as a political demand for change and greater democratic participation. In other words, social communication through the medium of political language encouraged a social construct of unease and conflict that went beyond the moral confines of guilt and punishment.

The correctness of this hypothesis is in part confirmed by the current situation: the present crisis of the politico-cultural model has seen the rise of both widespread moral indignation advocating the 'sword of justice' as the only remedy for all ills, and a social demand for security. From the end of the 1980s, the situation changed radically, both in terms of levels of repression (ISTAT, 1993) and private consumption of security (Alvazzi De Frate, Zvekic and Van Dijk, 1993).

In the three-year period, 1991–4, Italy's prison population doubled – an unprecedented rise in the whole history of incarceration in the country (Melossi, 1988: 13–18; Ministry of Justice, 1990). The first comparative study to be undertaken on social representations and reactions to crime indicates Italy as being the European country where fear of crime, especially street crime, is greatest (Van Dijk and Mayhew, 1993: 40). The same authors report Italy to be one of the largest consumers of private security within the European Community.

This rapid change points to several theoretical considerations:

1   The basic reasons that made social control anomalous in Italy in the recent past are the very same reasons that have created the anomalous situation today: they have simply produced opposite effects. This hypothesis may be expressed another way with the aid of Tamar Pitch's assessment (1989) of the change in the responsibility paradigm. The 'de-responsibilizing' paradigm that formerly dominated Italian culture has given way to one of individual responsibility. And the de-responsibilizing paradigm in Italian culture was for many years coupled with the paradigm of

political responsibility.[5] In fact, the social demand for security from crime was traditionally expressed as a political demand. But the political crisis and the resultant social malaise has led to the emergence of the very same demand being expressed outside the Italian political lexicon. The social demand for security is no longer expressed in the de-responsibilizing language of politics but is now couched in the eminently responsibilizing terms of a demand for penality.

2    The second consideration concerns the equivocal nature of the current social demand for security. The social unease and panic produced by the current political crisis in Italy has not, as we have said, been channelled into a social demand for a better future. It has led to the call for a better present 'immediately'. Since this social demand cannot be met, the result is a moralistic intransigence that foments righteous crusades to seek out scapegoats on whom to heap all the ills of society. Two Italian surveys on the social representations of the problems that most worry public opinion (DOXA, 1992; Eurisko, 1993) indicate that street crime is in first place, especially crime committed by young drug abusers, followed by political corruption, youth unemployment, the recession and pollution. More than 25 per cent of the sample interviewed indicated widespread drug addiction as the main cause of increased delinquency. This significant change in the paradigm of the social construction of the 'enemy within' is well illustrated by what the newspapers have labelled the *Mani Pulite* (Clean Hands) campaign of judicial repression of political corruption (Della Porta, 1992; Sapelli, 1994). The complex, intricate phenomenon of political corruption was for years tolerated in Italy as the inevitable cost of relations that had built up over time between the political party system and the Italian economy. Graft and corruption, it was thought, could be wiped out only by radical change in these relations. Socially, the phenomenon was perceived as being in formal contrast with the law, but certainly not to the extent of provoking a popular movement of moral indignation.

The current politico-institutional crisis, on the one hand, and the process of de-legitimization of the party system with no prospect of political change on the other, have brought about a new social construction of this same phenomenon of political corruption: the whole economic crisis is now seen as the sole responsibility of dishonest politicians in cahoots with Mafia criminals intent on sapping Italy's economy.

These changes in social representations are exemplified by the new social consensus now accorded to the fight against the Mafia. Here too, we are not dealing with a new form of crime – the Mafia existed well before the creation of Italy as a nation-state – nor has the Mafia become more threatening on account of more menacing behaviour (Gambetta, 1992). Today, however, the Mafia is socially perceived as more menacing, despite the fact that objectively it is no more threatening than before. The social representation of the Mafia as a threat has grown enormously, because the Mafia issue is now viewed from outside the political paradigm which formerly, while not providing a justification, did nonetheless mean that it was seen as an anthropological, cultural and social phenomenon. Stripped of this paradigm, the Mafia symbolizes 'evil': so, for the first time in Italy, the Mafia has become 'just' a criminal justice issue. The degree of legitimation which the penal justice system, the judicial machinery and the police currently enjoy in Italy is unprecedented in the entire history of the Italian Republic. A recent opinion poll (Eurisko, 1993) shows that the police forces – traditionally as feared as they were scorned by the Italian public – now meet with the approval of 88 per cent of the population for their anti-crime activities; similarly, the magistracy enjoys the support of 75 per cent of Italians.

The ambiguity of the social demand for security when expressed as a demand for greater penal repression lies in the fact that genuine exasperation over the injustices and illegality of the present are translated into the illusory language of 'law and order' to be imposed by penal repression. This widespread acceptance of repressive action legitimizes repression on many fronts. The consensus behind measures introduced to fight conspicuous crimes (political corruption and organized crime) spills over into an indiscriminate rise in the levels of penality.

The focal question revolves around the need to understand the politico-cultural reasons why the fear of criminality is increasingly being expressed in terms of social insecurity. Once this social construction has been understood, efforts must be made to couch the problem in language that will galvanize the collectivity to work towards ensuring the material conditions for social security.

3   The third observation more directly concerns the culture and policies of the Left in Italy today in the wake of the process discussed above. The general inability of political language to give expression to the new demands for social security finds the Left in Italy at a complete loss, with no solutions to offer. It is currently paying the price of failure to keep pace with cultural changes. With its political language emasculated, the Italian Left now appears culturally obsolete, unable to interpret and grasp the new social processes that have emerged. The social demands for security are uncritically equated with social demands for legality, to be met by penally

repressing crime. Fighting the good fight for a 'new legality' is thus no longer bound up with political and social change, but with instilling respect for formal law and compliance with the current rules of the game. The dangerous consequences of this spiral are obvious: first, affirming a 'new' legality is tantamount to bolstering current formal legality; and, second, affirming formal legality is often synonymous with a campaign for greater effectiveness of the state's repressive machinery.

The Italian Left seems to be suffering from having confused the social demand for security with a social demand for legality – and this latter with a social demand for greater and more effective repression. The result, as I indicated at the outset, is there for all to see: the political and cultural Left in Italy today is jointly responsible (with the other political parties) for encouraging social insecurity at a symbolic level, and hence for the call to reinstate legality through penal repression.

### The need for a 'realistic' approach to the current Italian situation

Given the social representations described in the previous paragraphs, I believe that it is wishful thinking to expect either that the symbolic resource offered by the criminal justice system may be done away with in the immediate future or that the privatization of security from crime may be curtailed without providing an alternative response to the social demands for security. This realistic position is convincing, whether or not one believes that the subjective feelings of social insecurity derive from objective conditions of insecurity related to crime or that the social panic has different roots.

We are faced with a Weberian hypothesis whereby scientific truth does not become translated immediately into a politically pursuable objective. In fact, I am convinced that recourse to penality, as a means of stabilizing the social system, the current sphere of action and the institutionalization of expectations, has nothing to do with whether penality is an effective means of solving society's problems. Similarly, a market ideology that increasingly legitimizes recourse to private resources to meet security requirements is hardly able to produce greater material conditions of enhanced security. The two strategies – more penal justice and more private security – are not only congruent but also mutually enhancing, despite their being fruitless.

The dangers inherent in the two processes just described take little imagination to see, nor does the difficulty of thwarting them effectively. Care must be exercised, however, not to fall ingenuously into the trap of two opposite, intellectually radical, and idealistic positions.

The first is that of placing absolute trust in an improved criminal justice system, whether it be a minimum penality, one that protects socially approved interests, or one that abolishes criminal justice altogether. This is not because the penal system should not be reformed or because we should not strive to reduce the system, even going so far as to abolish it, but because reforming or abolishing the criminal justice system will be a purely abstract exercise and will fail to bring about those significant transformations that will redefine the social confines of legality. The second mistake is to re-propose, albeit with embellishments, the traditional recipes for solving the crime issue: more social justice; more democracy; more social participation; more political commitment for a better, more just society which will perforce have less criminality and less fear of crime – or indeed enjoy no crime at all and a life free of fear. This is not because it is unreasonable to believe that a society that is more just, compact and democratic will not also be one that is objectively and subjectively safer from crime, but because the problems to be solved cannot be invoked as solutions to those same problems. In so far as the social construction of security is self-referential, the issue must be tackled on two fronts: (a) new ways of governing the material conditions producing security must be found; and (b) the means of governing the social reactions to collective feelings of insecurity must be identified.

In my view, the situation in Italy at the end of the millennium dispels any illusion that a definitive solution to the criminal question may be found. Nor do I believe tenable the lofty academic view that the criminal question is not a problem, or, at most, a false problem, and that Italy's real problems lie elsewhere. More realistically, and more modestly, I believe that we must work to bring crime down to levels compatible with our political and economic democracy, both in terms of the social damage it causes and the social reaction it engenders. In sum, this means 'getting one's hands dirty' and tackling social control policies. Navigating the treacherous Italian seas of political compromise means coming to terms with the positions of New Left Realism (Young, 1989; Young and Matthews, 1992a and 1992b) and their new proposals for prevention.

It is easy to condemn this movement out of hand, at least theoretically (Pitch, 1986: 469–88; de Leo, 1986: 453–69). I too have joined the detractors (Pavarini, 1994a: 43–62) when the so-called New Left Realism approach to the crime issue has been couched in hackneyed terms that merely offer an explanatory model of criminality. New Left Realism is not, nor can it be, an expression of a new theory of criminality and social control. It is truly 'realistic' if, right from the start, it declines to be a 'strong idea'. It is truly 'new' if it consciously accepts that only partial solutions may be proposed on the crime question and not '*the* solution to the crime problem'. The attribute 'left' is one that will have to be won in the field, however, by taking into the political arena what has so far inhabited the realms of technocratic and administrative ideology; if, in short, the criminal question can be confronted in terms of political and economic democracy – a project as ambitious as it is uncertain.

## Coming to terms with the ambiguity of prevention

A 'new' word has recently crept into criminological debate and criminal policies: prevention (Graham, 1990; Johnson, 1987). Unless qualified, the term prevention is extremely equivocal since it is used to indicate diverse concepts. Even qualified by adjectives like criminal, it still lends itself to a multitude of meanings. Let us start by clearing the field of what we do not mean today by 'the prevention of crime'. All modern criminal justice systems claim legitimacy from the fact that they have been brought into existence to prevent crime (Baratta, 1985a: 247–68). It is believed that the punishment of crime prevents further crime by deterring potential offenders from committing crime (general negative prevention). Crime prevention is also achieved because penal sanctions make it impossible for an offender sentenced for a crime to infringe the law further (special negative prevention). Prevention is also achieved because the punishment may consist in treatment intended to re-educate the criminal (special positive prevention) and also since the punishment has the function of producing social integration (general positive prevention). That the criminal justice system has succeeded in achieving, even partially, these preventive goals is highly doubtful. In the light of numerous empirical studies into whether the preventive aims of the penal system have been achieved and to what extent, I would say it does not (Pavarini, 1994b).

The penal system aims to defend society against crime by dissuasion and not prevention. This is true even when penal provisions do not entail inflicting punishment but rather consist in conflict mediation, and compensation for or settlement of interests violated by a criminal act. Even *ante delictum* preventive measures claim legitimacy as crime prevention measures. Of many types and of remote origin, such as limiting personal freedom or access to assets, preventive measures are *de facto* punishments meted out to those who are suspected of being socially dangerous, without, however, any crime being proved: punishment exacted without a crime or trial. The extremely authoritarian nature of these provisions aimed at guaranteeing law and order by disciplinary social acts unencumbered by the formal guarantees of the penal system is strongly denounced by 'liberal' opponents as repression camouflaged as prevention.

Criminal prevention found currency in the past during the discussion of social reforms. By the second half of the nineteenth century, the issue of preventing crime was already central to the principles underpinning progressive and revolutionary political movements. Indeed, polemic was often rife among those who thought crime would be solved with the advent of the new classless society and those who urged social reform policies as the only 'alternative' to the penal repression of crime. This debate concerns us (Garland, 1985; 1990), in the sense that all criminal policies of the social state, to varying degrees, still take their cue from the idea that crime is an 'effect' of social inequality and contradiction, and that only by removing or solving these issues will it be possible to prevent crime. In short, more social justice will lead to less crime.

It is easy to demonstrate how naïve the optimistic faith in the crime-preventing effects of social reforms is, as is the belief in a mechanical cause–effect relationship between social welfare, or the lack of it, and criminality. Unfortunately, both rich countries and developed welfare states often have higher crime rates as well as different types of criminality compared to emerging countries. In most Western countries, the increase in wealth and social development have not been accompanied by a fall in crime rates. Moreover, the collective sentiments of insecurity over crime do not seem positively influenced by the level of development of the social state.

Certainly, there is a relationship between social and economic policies, social malaise and crime, but it is not that linear relation so dear to the positivist school of the nineteenth century for which higher wages, less unemployment and more education equalled less crime and more social security. Thus, equating crime prevention with social development is insufficient to define 'new' prevention.

Having cleared the field of the 'other' preventions, it may be said that, today, 'new' prevention is internationally defined as that which is capable of actually curtailing the frequency of undesired, though not necessarily criminal, behaviour by adopting solutions other than those offered by the criminal justice system (Lab, 1988; Van Dijk and De Waard, 1991: 483–503).

There are three main features involved in this notion of criminal prevention: (a) reducing criminality; (b) not having recourse to the criminal justice system; (c) being able to verify empirically the aims achieved. This is a wide definition, embracing a multitude of concepts. Indeed, this understanding of prevention has produced a series of extremist or naïve interpretations.

One interpretation has been defined as 'situational technological prevention'. A neighbourhood or building complex can be made secure from crime by installing surveillance devices to deter crime or better to defend the inhabitants. This, however, in no way acts upon the cause of crime. There are a multitude of security-enhancing means: greater police surveillance, private policing systems, closed-circuit television, electronic surveillance, intrusion-alarm networks, etc. (Bone, 1989; Newman, 1972; Poyner, 1983). A neighbourhood or city block can easily be 'fortified' to resist assault from the outside. But such a system – provided, of course, we were prepared to pay the price for living in such maximum security social conditions – is only feasible in contained, physical, social spaces and for a limited time. A modern metropolis cannot be turned into a fortified city, protected against crime, and attention levels in the surveillance of an urban quarter cannot be protracted indefinitely without the very survival of that city, neighbourhood or block being seriously jeopardized.

Technologically based prevention is, therefore, both illusory and politically dangerous. It also denotes ingenuousness, since this sort of situational prevention renders one metropolitan area safer at the expense of surrounding areas which will subsequently have to bear the brunt of additional criminality. This sort of prevention is, moreover, counter-productive in that it augments collective feelings of insecurity: more control and surveillance may end by creating a greater precep-tion of previously hidden crime and bringing it to the attention of the community.

A completely different matter is prevention that appeals to social participation. A neighbourhood can be made safer from crime by gal-vanizing local inhabitants to exert widespread social control and to police their area (Greenberg, 1985; Hope and Shaw, 1988; Osborn and Bright, 1989; Skogan, 1990). The picture is now no longer that of the fortified city but of civil society coming together to form a network along which information passes swiftly and from which nothing escapes. The reference here is to a highly ambiguous notion of com-munity, as a group of people who at times share a common situation, at times the same interests or values (Nelken, 1985; 39–67).

There is a whole range of prevention strategies that come under the umbrella of this concept of prevention: the creation of 'neighbourhood watch' groups to police housing-blocks, schools, sports centres and parks; the organization of private self-defence squads, such as shop-keepers in a street coming together to curb attacks on their property; women grouping together to avert the risks of sexual violence and drug-pushing to minors in public or other places (Council of Europe, 1989).

I do not believe we should be prejudiced against these operations, although they must be very carefully examined on an individual basis. The risk that these spontaneous manifestations of prevention policies conceal unacceptable attempts by civil society to take repres-sive (and not preventive) functions into their own hands must never be underestimated. More importantly, however, recent participative prevention campaigns have proved fairly ineffectual in actually preventing crime. Or rather, this acutely focused social attention does succeed in restoring peace and quiet to a neighbourhood: preventing petty crime, vandalism and minor delinquency. These strategies do, however, produce one marked effect: although fairly ineffectual in preventing crime, participative prevention campaigns nevertheless produce social representations of greater security. In short, the community *feels* more secure from crime even though it probably is not.

Finally, new prevention policies have been envisaged as part of social action in its wider sense (Cooper, 1989; Findlay, Bright and Kevin, 1990; Scholte, 1989; Farrington, 1989; King, 1988). In Italy, the best known and most widely adopted social prevention action has been within the framework of social intervention and welfare schemes whose beneficiaries are often not specified nor are they identifiable. Any programme set up to improve the economic, cultural or general living standards of a disadvantaged community or restricted area like a neighbourhood is undoubtedly also a crime prevention measure. Providing housing and jobs for new immigrants certainly helps the social integration of these newcomers; investing in vocational training helps school-leavers enter the labour market; organizing recreational and sports activities may help to keep young people off the streets; actively promoting the integration of former prisoners may well help to offset the crime-inducing effects of prison. This is all very true, but the extent to which these prevention campaigns result in less criminality is something we will never know (Pavarini, 1992a: 32–49).

Unfortunately, the impossibility of verifying the preventive effects of this type of social action de-legitimizes the action itself. Even if prevention programmes probably do produce security, they are unlikely to produce collective feelings of security. Preventive strategies implemented in social states with economic problems often fail to meet with social consensus, as they do not appear to offer an immediate guarantee of social security.

Worldwide, most prevention policies are stymied by being overspecialized or overgeneralized. Situational prevention, being directed to 'virtual' criminals and deviants in an attempt to mould their conduct, becomes exclusively defensive with doubtful effects both in terms of prevention effectiveness and of any favourable, lasting repercussions on collective feelings of insecurity. Affirmative social prevention action, on the other hand, runs the risk of being 'offensive' but not targeted; attenuating but not resolving broad-based social malaise while incapable of providing proof of actually achieving crime prevention. What then can be done?

**Integrated prevention**

I believe that the now voluminous literature on prevention, although not providing firm solutions, does offer several valid discussion points. Let us review a few of the major ones.

It is generally agreed that crime prevention must be conducted at the 'local' level, with as decentralized a format as possible. The unit most recommended is the 'neighbourhood' (Council of Europe, 1987 and 1989; Lagrange and Zauberman, 1991: 233–55). The full significance of this choice should be examined, however. If this means admitting that 'top-down' preventive policies – such as a national prevention initiative – do not work, then we cannot but agree. But serious doubts would be raised if prevention action were to remain exclusively on a local scale. Of paramount importance is the relationship between the local and central dimension, for example, between a neighbourhood area and the local municipal or regional authorities (for Italy, see Pavarini, 1992b: 11–14 and 1993: 27–30; Ajmone, 1992: 29–32; Ajmone and Pavarini, 1992: 7–10; Pepa, 1994: 31–4; Creazzo, 1994: 27–30). Prevention should always be pursued at the local level which, however, is linked to a 'central pole' that finances, co-ordinates, adjusts and, in particular, lays down strategy guidelines and assesses the action's effectiveness.

Prevention action is effective to the extent that it mobilizes people and creates widespread social consensus. Our judgement must, however, be more cautiously extended if preventive action is always to be managed by the local community or groups of citizens. Advisedly, a few illusions should be entertained in this case. Everyone admits that, especially in modern urban conglomerations, one can no longer take for granted a general adherence to a set of commonly-held values – the core of any true 'community'. Indeed, it may even be argued that this sharing of values is not desirable.

Mobilization of the citizenry around prevention campaigns often has its roots in a negative element: fear of crime. And we know how often the alarmist representation of crime fails to coincide with reality. On occasion, indeed, social panic is strongest among those least at risk of falling victim to crime and, at times, where there is greatest risk, there may be less fear. Although collective panic over criminality should be taken into account, consensus for crime prevention action cannot be based only on this fear (Baratta, 1993: 9–14; Pitch, 1994: 23–6). A distinction must be made between prevention action aimed at reducing the crime risk, making cities safer, and intervention that succeeds in enhancing collective feelings of security, without actually achieving greater security.

Finally, let us come to the question of the police. Should the police – public and private forces alike – be involved in prevention policies? Before attempting an answer, I would like to give two value judgements: (a) present-day police forces, at least in Italy, are not equipped culturally or otherwise to take on the task of enforcing new prevention policies (Palidda, 1993); and (b) it would be unrealistic to contemplate instituting prevention without the involvement of – or, worse, in the face of – those forces officially entrusted with security, and law and order.

The primary objective must, therefore, be to allow the municipal and private law-enforcement bodies to acquire the professional skills and know-how required by crime prevention strategies. Much has been done, not always successfully, in other nations to institute integrated preventive action involving the police, social services and the general public. These experiences should be examined carefully and with an open mind while, of course, bearing in mind the specifics of the Italian situation. We can learn a great deal, I believe. The value of public security, if it is to remain such, must be conceived within a framework that does not permit monopoly.

Given the complex manner in which the issue of public security has developed within the social state, we cannot dismiss it merely as a matter of law and order, *ordre dans la rue*. The police, although essential to safeguarding the value of public security, are not sufficient since they cannot be its only guarantors, nor should they be. Safeguards of the public good, that is security, can only be assured by the concerted action of all those institutions that democratically, and hence at grass-roots level, legitimize the control of security. Only in this way will the governance of security be democratically and not bureaucratically legitimized.

By taking charge of local security, local democratic government institutions automatically become accountable for the value of public security in their jurisdiction – and this directly concerns the social services, which in Italy come under the local authorities. Called to tackle social malaise, the social services have for some time now been confronted with the implicit mandate of providing social safeguards and preventing deviancy. 'Confronted' is the operative word, since it expresses the inevitability as well as the difficulty of accepting accountability for social safeguards against deviancy and criminality. For example, social services workers have always seen prevention as the main aim of their work, in that tackling social malaise averts its negative social effects, which include deviancy and crime. At the same time, however, the general feeling among social services operators in Italy is that their preventive aim is achieved once they have provided, or tried to provide, a possible solution to the unsatisfied needs of those manifesting social unease. But when, as I fear often happens, this unease is not dispelled, the social demand for safeguards against the possible effects of social malaise goes unanswered. In other words, social safeguards against insecurity must go hand in hand with safeguards to avert social malaise (Pepa, 1992) – and this means also assuming responsibility for the demand for social control. Without any doubt, the new prevention policies require that the social services assume responsibility for this.

Finally, let me deal with the question of research. Prevention campaigns implemented at the local level must be able to avail themselves of local 'observatories' capable of pinpointing requirements and the social demands for security, as well as changes in attitude as prevention policies proceed. Feedback is, therefore, essential for any prevention initiative. In Italy, these observatories will have to be created from scratch.

The path is fraught with difficulties, however, not all of them economic: what type of observation and research should be carried out is just one of the controversial areas. First, can any local crime observatory really assess 'actual crime rates'? I doubt it. Certainly a local crime observatory could provide more than the raw crime data provided by police and judicial statistics which, as we know, tell us nothing about undetected crime and little about the workings of the crime repression system. Research on the victims of crime would certainly provide a different representation of criminality, less distanced from reality. It would, however, always be a subjective representation (Van Dijk, Matthew and Killias, 1990; Kaiser, Kury and Albrecht, 1991; Gatti, Fossa, Marugo and Materazzi, 1991: 363–85; Alvazzi de Frate, Zvekic and Van Dijk, 1993). Nonetheless, such research would provide a much wider representation than official statistics. There is the risk, however, of heightened social alarm once the findings are disclosed.

Similarly, opinion polls on security reflect an often contradictory range of security requirements: the demand of shopkeepers not to be robbed will most probably not coincide with the demands of a new, immigrant community to be protected against racist attacks.

As to the social representation that each of us have of security, is this a subjective representation of a real risk or simply the effect of greater or lesser vulnerability to mass media messages? Even though the fear of crime is highly subjective, research on what people fear most will not so much reflect public opinion on security as give a sum of individual fears (Smauss, 1980: 363–400).

Despite these pitfalls, surveys must be conducted. Most importantly, the in-depth information they provide must lead to suitable preventive action in the field. Better understanding of how public insecurity is constructed will enable positive action to be taken on these processes in order to produce greater security. Security can be built only gradually by means of an 'integrated' prevention policy.

Prevention policies, as we have seen, aim to change given material situations as well as less tangible cultural mores. In the first instance, the opportunities for deviant behaviour are curtailed or the opportunities for averting delinquency increased. In the second, prevention policies seek to encourage the development of social norms that encourage proactive security behaviour. Preventive action may thus be situational or directed at social development. Prevention is situational when the aim is to make it more difficult to commit crime or to make it easier for potential victims to defend themselves. It in no way tackles the underlying causes of deviant behaviour or victimization.

In medical terms, prevention can be primary, secondary or tertiary. In the case of prevention of delinquency in a given geographical area, primary prevention would be those policies that involve the community at large; secondary prevention, the prevention policies involving those directly concerned, either actively or passively, with delinquency; and tertiary prevention would be the prevention policies directed at deviants themselves, either active or passive.

Prevention action may be defined by its focus, since it may address (a) actual or potential delinquents, (b) given situations that encourage or potentially encourage deviancy, and (c) the real or potential victims of deviant behaviour. The combination of these three classifying criteria has been the subject of several preventive action projects (Van Dijk and De Waard, 1991: 483–503). An integrated prevention strategy is one in which these various aims are pursued in synergy. The aims are as follows:

● To identify social demands for security in their context, producing more realistic social representations of the threat of crime to society.
● To diversify the social and institutional reactions to criminality in the light of the social risk of victimization and the social costs of crime.
● To reinstate the political connotation and the concept of rational choices (namely, reinstatement of the damage-reduction paradigm) when dealing with many problems and conflicts which today elicit only emotional demands for penality dictated by fear.
● To devise policies which take greater account of the effects on the social environment, that is, which create awareness that any political choice will have a public security spin-off or fall-out.

# Notes

This chapter is a reflection on some aspects of an ongoing research project for which 60 per cent of the funds have been provided by the University of Bologna for the years 1992 and 1993. Stephanie Johnson translated the text.

*Massimo Pavarini*
*Professor of Penology, Faculty of Law, University of Bologna*

1   In the first place, the fact that the left-wing parties considered 'red terrorism' as a threat to the very survival of the democratic Left. Second, the fear that other criminal phenomena, such as 'black or right-wing terrorism' and the involvement of certain state-run institutions – as well as the links between the Mafia and the political system in power – might forever thwart the hopes of the Left alternating in government. For the parties of the democratic Left, the fight against these criminal acts was tantamount to a struggle for political survival. So, while certain government political forces opted for doubtful, indeed criminal, choices, the democratic Left opted to defend itself by enlisting the massive assistance of criminal law sanctions.

2   In Italy, de-criminalization is viewed as identifying the principle which is able to draw a distinction between what deserves penal protection and what may be protected outside the criminal justice system. In this political exercise of marking out what requires penal sanction, the paradigmatic reference in Italy has always been the fundamental rights enshrined in the Constitution (Bricola, 1973: 47–137).

3   An historical, and to some extent personal, digression: I live in an old town in Northern Italy, Bologna, renowned for many things: the oldest university in the world, incomparable cuisine, per capita income on a par with Sweden and, especially for visitors, a medieval town with a hundred towers. These phallic, and today rather ridiculous, constructions belonged to rich, patrician families and were built to protect the noble household and the populace living around the *palazzo*. Often as much as a hundred metres high, with a series of wooden balconies, the towers were vantage points from which the family's private police could 'survey' the surrounding area. Armed with the most deadly weapon of those times, the crossbow, these security forces could slay any intruder as he entered the little kingdom. These things came to mind while reading Davis's *City of Quartz* (1990, 1993).

4   The 'law and order' campaign and the spread of social panic over crime have also been studied by Italian criminologists (Grandi, Pavarini and Simondi, 1985) during the 1980s, but only to follow the example of authors from the English-speaking world. It was an imported debate since at that time 'law and order' was not a social issue in Italy.

5   The Italian saying 'It's raining . . . damn the thieving government' very aptly sums up how an abstract, impersonal entity is blamed for everything that is seen as socially evil, unjust, undesirable and frightening. The Italian political lexicon is a complex weave of two historic traditions: the Catholic matrix with its providential conception of history in which universal judgement has always outweighed individual judgement, and the Marxist matrix with its belief in the rebirth of society through revolution. Both these cultural traditions have encouraged the process whereby social expectations do not entail individual responsibility for society's ills.

# 5

# Social Control: a Defence and Reformulation

*Sebastian Scheerer and Henner Hess*

Social control in the widest sense has always been and will always be inextricably linked to the existence of the human animal. But while it can justly be regarded as a central, indispensable and omnipresent aspect of social life, from archaic groups all the way to the global village, theoretical efforts directed at the clarification of 'social control' as a concept began only a century ago and have often led to results that seemed to obscure rather than illuminate the objects of study, their history, contexts and perspectives. Hence we find it useful to take a fresh look at the main problems associated with the current use of the term, to attempt to develop a more adequate formulation of the concept, and to try and catch a glimpse of the control mechanisms that are most likely to shape life in the future.

## A much criticized concept . . .

The concept of social control – according to its inventor, Edward Alsworth Ross (1866–1951), 'a key that unlocks many doors' – is a child of the twentieth century. Ross first developed it in 1894 'while he sat in an alcove in the Stanford Library during Christmas recess' (Weinberg et al., 1969: xvii), then published a series of articles in the *American Journal of Sociology* (starting May, 1896), and in 1901 made 'Social Control' the title of his most successful book. His attempt to ascertain how people 'are brought to live closely together, and to associate their efforts with that degree of harmony we see about us' (Ross, 1901: 3) was greeted with enthusiasm by many of his colleagues and reform-minded followers. It is also true, though, that Ross himself was not a very systematic thinker and that his concept has remained one of the most elusive and under-theorized ones in the social sciences (for a more detailed account, see Sumner, Chapter 1, in this volume).

## Vagueness

The most frequently cited problem with 'social control' is the extreme vagueness of the term – a criticism that had been articulated by Hollingshead as early as 1941 and repeated ever since. According to

Stanley Cohen, social control has become 'a Mickey Mouse concept' that plays a different role in different places, and nowhere a clear one: 'Historians and political scientists restrict the concept to the repression of political opposition, while sociologists, psychologists and anthropologists invariably talk in broader and non-political terms. In everyday language, that concept has no resonant meaning at all' (Cohen, S., 1985: 2). While some scholars use the term in a historically specific way, namely 'in its true Chicagoan sense', involving 'the participation of informed and diverse publics in the construction of associations which are meaningful to those publics and which function to regulate the terrible consequences of unregulated capitalism' (Sumner, Chapter 6 in this volume, see also Melossi, 1990), others use a much more formal approach in which social control designates everything that contributes to the construction and reconstruction of social order (see Hess, 1983a). In addition, while some favour an emphatic, value-laden understanding of the term, in which the very concept of social control is inextricably linked to the vision of a new society which is regulated by itself rather than by state decree (see Sumner, Chapter 6 in this volume), others find it more promising to decontextualize the term from the socio-political messages it carried during the Progressive Era in the United States. While both approaches to a definition of social control do have their merits, it is also certainly true that the use of the term for two different things in the same criminological and sociological discourse requires constant attention if one wants to avoid equivocations and superfluous quarrels. Small wonder, therefore, that many scholars would probably subscribe to the historian John A. Mayer's (1983: 22) statement that the usage of the term social control had rendered it 'more productive of confusion than of meaningful analysis'.

Strange as it may sound, however, vagueness alone is not a sufficient reason to discard the analytical potential of a concept. As a matter of fact, vagueness even seems to be a characteristic trait of practically all central notions in the social sciences and beyond. Just ask a Nobel Prize winning economist about the exact meaning of the term 'money', a famous philosopher about 'truth', or an acclaimed surgeon about a definition of 'health', 'life' or 'death' and, chances are, you will harvest a good deal of embarrassment. In the social sciences, terms like 'structure' and 'social control' are of the same type and abstraction as the above mentioned concepts, and there is no reason why they should not share their paradoxical fate of being both indispensable and irritatingly elusive. While a theoretical clarification is urgently needed, social scientists might be comforted by the fact that they are not the only ones to face this problem, and that other disciplines are faring quite well by using and attempting to clarify their central notions instead of simply discarding them. In the social sciences, by the way, the term 'structure' started out being exceedingly vague. It was not abandoned though, but progressively clarified (see Giddens, 1984; Sewell, 1992). We do not see any reason why the term 'social control' should be treated any differently from the equally abstract and vague, but also equally important term 'structure'. Once rescued from being under-theorized, it would allow us to relate to all the problems of social order and would enable criminologists and sociologists of deviance to use it 'to describe and think about most if not all of their field's subject matter, thereby prompting recognition of conceptual and empirical relations that otherwise would go unnoticed'. It would, in other words, serve as a classical 'central notion' of the social sciences (Gibbs, 1989: ix).

*Stasis*
Another problem is the concept's awkwardness in relation to social change. Just like the term structure (see Sewell, 1992: 2), the term social control seems to empower what it designates, implicitly transforming into an overwhelming force what otherwise would show the complex and contradictory face of a social conflict. To many critics, therefore, using the term already implies an 'overestimate of the operation of social control' (Stedman Jones 1983: 47) and a far too rigid determinism of social life, resembling a command structure that by definition meets with no effective resistance (see Sack, 1993). The fact that Parsonian functionalism had absorbed 'social control' in the 1950s as 'a set of mechanisms to prevent the origin of strains or to preclude their expression in overt deviation' (Weinberg et al., 1969: li) did not exactly help to avoid such misconception, since this formulation laid all the emphasis on the capacity of social control to maintain a given order. All told, the centrality of the concept to Parsonian thinking rendered it anathema to all those who disliked positivism, functionalism, Parson's style of writing, and conservative politics. And that was, at least in the late 1960s and all of the 1970s, the large majority of sociologists, criminologists and academic professionals in the field of crime, deviance and rehabilitation. Scholars like Stuart Hall et al. (1978: 195), for example, were (and probably still are) convinced that the concept 'cannot designate the significant moments of shift and change'. Neither, they claim, does it 'differentiate adequately between different types of state or political regime', nor does it 'specify the kind of social formation which requires and establishes a particular kind of legal order'.

In spite of its popularity, this criticism is also far from convincing. To identify 'social control' with an emanation from an unrealistically unified and totalized source of power reveals nothing about the term but a lot about a given writer's blindness with regard to the actual complexity and diversity of social life. One just has to stay aware of the fact that social control complexes intersect and overlap, that there are competing sets of norms and values, and that each and every set of control mechanisms is bound to interfere with and to be relativized by many others. To recognize the necessary imperfection of social control is to understand that the processes of social control and of social change are not mutually exclusive, but completely interdependent. If Hall et al. (1978) also find it unsatisfactory that the term 'social control' does not differentiate between different types of state or political regime, one might feel justified to ask if they require the same from the term 'structure' – or, for that matter, from their own terms such as 'state', 'political regime', 'social formation' or 'legal order'. The right answer would be that the most general concepts are not designed to differentiate in themselves, but to allow for differentiations on lower levels of abstraction. The particular usefulness of terms like 'structure' and 'social control' lies in their potential to allow differentiations between, for example, the structure of feudal and that of capitalist societies as well as between the dominant means of social control in one society and in the other – including the detection of turning points from one kind of control to the other. In short: concepts like structure or social control are not made to designate moments of shift and change, but to allow for comparisons as well as for the detection of these moments.

*Law and state bias*
In its original version and during the first decades of its existence (including its functionalist understanding), the concept of social control was concerned with such pervasive and 'active' forces like public opinion, religion, traffic regulations and socialization. It was only in the 1960s that Clark and Gibbs (1965) advanced a reformulation of the concept that intentionally reduced its scope to 'reactions to deviance'. The argument they advanced at the time was not theoretical, but pragmatic. Their intention was to build a new specialized sociology, a field of study and research that was to be called 'the sociology of social control', modelled after such fields as the sociology of labour relations, of sports, of education, and the like. In Clark and Gibbs's own words, their definition represented 'first and foremost an attempt to give the field an independent and meaningful subject matter' (1965: 402). For this purpose they thought it unwise to use the broader concept of social control, since that would make it difficult to draw a clear line between the special branch of sociology they had in mind and all the rest of sociology. Since this proposal coincided with the growing popularity of the social reaction approaches to deviance

(labelling theory, stigmatization, secondary deviance, criticism of legal institutions and procedures) their reformulation became a great success, although, one must add, the amount of theoretical work invested in both the reformulation and its discussion were rather modest. But be that as it may, everybody in the field seemed to be happy with the new formulation, using it in their studies ever since. The narrow concept, therefore, gave rise to a whole body of literature that was mainly concerned with the juvenile justice system, the police, legislation, the courts and corrections. It was only then that the concept acquired its bias in favour of easy-to-see and easy-to-define institutions like the police, the law, courts and prisons.

The disadvantages of this procedure became clear when the sociology of deviance turned its attention to forms of control much more subtle than the law and the criminal justice system; when scholars like Michel Foucault revealed the paramount importance of the forces of 'normalization', and when feminist research showed that control over women's behaviour was not generally dependent on legal institutions and formal interventions, but rather on the genderized formation of desires, role models, and dreams – phenomena that are hard to reach with an analytical tool that normally only spotlights handcuffs, police interrogations, shotguns and correctional institutions. The definition that Clark and Gibbs had given to the term social control proved incapable of recognizing the relevant aspects of 'the complex and contradictory relationship of women to the state and law', as Chunn and Gavigan (1988: 110, 120) observed. But there is no reason to follow Chunn and Gavigan's advice to abandon the concept altogether. This would throw out the baby with the bathwater, since the unfitness of one definition of a term does not imply the unfitness of all definitions. In other words: to meet Chunn and Gavigan's justified requirements, it would be enough to reverse the step taken by Clark and Gibbs in the 1960s, and to re-open the concept for a broader understanding. Such a revised understanding of social control would have to incorporate 'active social controls' (Lemert) and the 'productive, pastoral' power (Foucault), since it could no longer deny their basic relevance. Or, as Dario Melossi says, 'Our desires, our moral choices, our identification with role models, images, heroes, are indeed the ways in which we are controlled' (Melossi, 1990: 170). We will show later on in our discussion what such a systematic reformulation could look like, and how it could serve as an analytical tool in the analysis of the very subtle proactive processes that produce conformity.

*Euphemism*

Some scholars argue that the term 'social control' is really less an analytical tool than a treacherous euphemism used to conceal the brutality of the fact that there are, for example, many countries in which 'social control' is being exercised by torture, public executions, massacres and the like. A pale term like social control does little to denounce such practices. It rather conceals than reveals them. They contend that one should be as explicit as possible rather than using innocent-sounding abstractions of a deceiving neutrality. It is for these reasons that Heinz Steinert (1995) and Fritz Sack (1993) argue for a replacement of the concept of social control by politically more meaningful terms such as 'social exclusion' or 'social discipline'. A closer look at the substitutes, though, reveals that they are more explicit simply because they are less abstract, designating specific types of social control instead of the totality of the production of conformity and the reaction to deviance. Social exclusion is just one class of reactions to deviance (the other being 'social inclusion', that is, intensified attempts to integrate the person in question), and it is hard to see how a concept that is part of a larger one should be able to replace the more abstract notion without damaging its theoretical potential. Similar problems arise when one considers a replacement of the term by 'social discipline', or '*Sozialdisziplinierung*' as Gerhard Oestreich (1969) had called the making of modern occidental man during the reign of European baroque monarchies. While it may be true that this period deserves more attention because of its vital importance for the formation of modern 'social characters', it is hard to see how such a specific term could ever serve the ends of a category like 'social control' (which, through its very level of abstraction, has to cover all historical phases and cultural peculiarities). Again, an analogy to the term 'structure' may be of help: while there is no way to deny that some social structures produce more violence (structural and other) than others, it would probably be counter-productive to ban the term 'structure' with the allegation that the term itself is a euphemism designed to conceal the brutality and loss of lives that some of these 'structures' engender.

*Sloppy use*
In spite of the concept's vagueness (or maybe because of it) there has been an inflationary tendency towards what David Rothman called 'sloppy use' of the concept in a flood of publications proclaiming that this or that movement or institutional reform served the ends of 'social control'. According to Rothman:

> To attach the label of 'social control' to these institutions and to let the matter rest there hardly represents an advance. Taken by itself, the label is often redundant: what else are prisons if not institutions for control? Or it is too encompassing: is not every institution, from the family to the office place, an institution of social control, either an agent of socialization (in

the Mead–Ross tradition) or an agency of coercion (in the Cloward–Piven tradition)? And social control by whom? For what purpose? And why in this form rather than in another? If once it was fashionable to think every process of social change could be explained by reference to 'status anxiety', one can detect signs of a new fashion, labelling every institution an institution of social control. (1983: 113–14)

While this criticism certainly fits the facts (especially for a tendency in the 1970s), it is not necessarily a good argument for the abandonment of the concept as such, but rather an admonition that should be directed to all students, scholars and researchers – one that applies not only to the theatrical misuse of the concept of social control, but also to that of 'power', 'structure', 'capitalism' and the like. Put in other words: if one were to give up every concept that has been subject to inflationary and sloppy use, the social sciences would instantly become speechless.

### . . . but nevertheless a key concept

Most arguments advanced against the usefulness of social control as a concept seem to rule out the possibility of saving it by yet another reformulation. Taken at face value, they seem to be directed against the very concept itself (that is, all possible meanings). But when examined more closely, they only apply to the unfortunate, albeit widespread definition invented by Clark and Gibbs in the mid-1960s, who indeed intended to narrow it down to 'reactions' to deviance. The bulk of criticism stops at this point, taking the Clark and Gibbs version of the term as the final point in the concept's history. Remarkably, nobody seems to deal with the possibility of elaborating a more consistent, theoretically more sound and more systematic reconstruction of the term. In our opinion, though, there is no reason to discard such a possibility a priori. After the pragmatic reformulation by Clark and Gibbs, it is now time to venture a systematic reconstruction of the concept. Such a revision should enable the concept to cover a theoretically (instead of only pragmatically) defined subject matter. It should allow for the investigation of proactive and subtle ways of shaping human behaviour. It should not make it seem an awkward exercise to deal with social change. And it should go without saying that it should be designed in a way that encourages analytical and discourages sloppy (that is, merely rhetorical) use.

In our opinion, the solution to the pressing conceptual problems of social control, therefore, does not lie in its abandonment, but in its theoretically sound, non-contradictory reformulation. The concept should be reconstructed at a high level of abstraction so it can serve as a central notion in criminology and the sociology of crime and deviance. Seen as a basic concept that sheds light on the regulation of behaviour and the dialectic between change and order, it will be comparable to terms like 'economy', 'structure', 'religion' or 'kinship'. 'Social control' will help in the analysis of all social contexts by focusing on their particular control mechanisms.

As we will propose to use it, the concept is ahistorical. This is not because we want to ignore historical differences, but because the notion of social control – just like that of 'kinship' – must be abstract enough to encompass all historical situations in order to make historical comparisons possible. Thus, 'social control' must be ahistorical as a general term in order to be useful as a tool in the analysis of all specific historical situations. Any concept that is 'historical' in the sense of being applicable only to one historical situation would, by definition, not be able to serve that universal purpose. Indeed, this argument has been acknowledged by the majority of social scientists who will try to work with the concept. When Black speaks of social control as 'all the practices by which people define and respond to deviant behavior' (Black, 1984: xi), and when Horwitz (1990: 1) sees social control as 'the aspect of society that protects the moral order of the group', they implicitly envisage such an ahistorical definition. If the study of social control is constituted by 'What people consider to be right and wrong and how they act when their notions of justice are violated' (Horwitz, 1990: 1), then social control is bound to occur in 'primitive' as well as the most 'advanced' societies, thus enabling the researcher to start her or his comparative studies from this central and ahistorical notion. The problems with Black's and Horwitz's notions are not that they are not universally applicable, but that they either lack precision or are biased in terms of focusing on 'morality'. As far as Black's definition is concerned, it makes one wonder if and how the prevention of deviant behaviour is to be included in the study of social control. And as far as Horwitz is concerned, just consider activities that only intend to protect the moral order of the group (but do not succeed); consider the question if social control only applies to a 'group' (and if one can justly consider 'society' to constitute merely another 'group'); and consider the possibility of a given group just 'protecting' or 'advancing' its 'interests' instead of a superior 'moral order' – does it not also exercise 'social control'?

Because of these and other doubts about Black's and Horwitz's definitions, we believe it to be useful to work out a new and more systematic definition. While the theoretical foundations of our own concept will become clearer in the course of the argument laid out in this chapter, our definition may already be spelled out here. We use the term 'social control' to refer to all social (and technical) arrangements, mechanisms, norms, belief systems, positive and negative sanctions that either aim at and/or result in the prevention of undesired behaviour or, if this has already occurred, respond to the undesired act in a way that tries to prevent its occurrence in the future (see Hess, 1983a).

This definition instantly evokes some questions and sceptical comments. Apart from its Germanic and/or Weberian phrasing, many may find it quite unsatisfactory that it does not indicate whose standards it is inclined to adopt when it speaks of 'undesired behaviour'. But, in the end, this turns out to be an advantage rather than a disadvantage of the concept, since it allows changes of perspective according to the different actors, norms and implementations involved. Obviously, most kinds of behaviour are the object of the most controversial attitudes, being admired by some, tolerated by many, and perhaps disliked, detested or even prosecuted and punished by others. The acts of vandalism that some soccer hooligans commit with great regularity are horrifying to victims and most bystanders, but are regarded as status-enhancing and, therefore, very 'desirable' by the vandals' best friends. The unspecific concept of social control allows us to look at the hooligan subculture and their specific way of internal (group) control as well as their attempts to control the actions of those surrounding them, but also to look at, let's say, police strategies to prevent or contain the hooligans' destructiveness.

As far as the vastness of the concept is concerned, it is true that it covers everything that intends to produce or maintain, or that results in the production or maintenance of, social order – be it socialization, education, the routine of political administration or the extraordinary violence of a military dictatorship, the subtle tradition of table manners, or the less subtle activity of the criminal justice system. And beyond all this, it also covers the decisions of a referee at a soccer match as well as the maintenance of religious beliefs during church ceremonies. Thus, the study of social control is, in a specific way, equivalent to the study of society in general, as Park argued (see Sumner, Chapter 1, in this volume), with 'in a specific way' meaning a specific perspective that is interested in the rules, the prevention of deviance from the rules, and the sanctions imposed ( or not imposed) on infractors. Sociologists have a lot to say, for instance, about a soccer match. They may analyse its entertainment value (which they are less likely to do), but they may also focus on the economic powers behind each team (which they are much more likely to do) or on the making of modern heroes and their function for everyday life. If they look at it from the perspective of social control they will concentrate on the rules of the game and their preventive and reactive enforcement, on infractions that go unnoticed and those that may have been noticed but go unpunished; or they may focus on the problems posed by crowd behaviour, on architectural designs that may be conducive to violent clashes or that may serve a preventive function; or they might interview the security personnel on their work situation and attitudes, and how they reflect on their interventions, or many other aspects. While all these social-control-related topics are extremely varied, they do share as their common denominator the interest in the making, maintenance and infraction of rules – and that is what any inquiry into social control is all about.

## Types, limits and ironies of social control

### The basic need for social control

It is a truism that all societies, including the most unjust, unequal, disorganized and anomic ones, manifest certain structured patterns of interaction and routine behaviour which we refer to in aggregate as 'social order'. Otherwise we would not call them societies. While the existence of a given social order used to be attributed to external and immutable forces, such as the will of a divinity or the laws of nature, modern thinkers have come to the conclusion that the social order is in effect a result of human activities, albeit under conditions that are not a product of the human will alone. Translated into sociological terminology we would say that the great discovery of modern thought was the fact that social order does not exist without permanent efforts at its reproduction, and that this reproduction of the social order is being achieved by what we refer to as the mechanisms of social control.

One of the first modern thinkers to advance this line of reasoning was Thomas Hobbes. For a man who had experienced the anomie of the religious wars in England, the problem of social order was of paramount importance. His question was how human beings could overcome the disastrous situation in which 'every man is Enemy to every man' and where life was 'nasty, brutish, and short'. It is generally agreed today that his very global recommendation of a centralized state power as 'a common Power to keep them all in awe' (Hobbes, 1909: 96) neglected some relevant alternatives, since there did and still do exist other forms of peaceful social organization. Before the advent of a state, mankind lived for thousands of years in what Max Weber called 'regulated anarchy', with kinship as the main ordering structure. Nevertheless, Hobbes's great achievement was the discovery that social order does not come upon human societies by divine will, the laws of nature or other outside powers, but that its creation and maintenance is an unavoidable and authentically political task. In other words: while Hobbes's 'condition of warre' is a virtual reality only, and while the monopolization of violence by a strong Leviathan is only one possibility of dealing with this virtual reality, he did point out the truly inescapable fact that all societies are endlessly confronted with the problem of upholding order.

The fundamental reason for this is anthropological: the fact that the human being, as a 'non-determined animal' (*'das nicht festgestellte Tier'*, as Nietzsche said), lacks other animals' built-in directives. For better or for worse, humans do not automatically follow their instincts, but rely on the construction and reproduction of cultural patterns in order to find individual and collective security (Gehlen, 1940). But cultural patterns (unlike instincts) can be transcended at any time and, therefore, both the individual and society have to live with the ever-present possibility of non-compliance and the disappointment of expectations.

While this basic contradiction between the individual fate of freedom and the social necessity of normativity will accompany human beings until their last day on earth, there also exists in all modern societies a second contradiction that necessitates the existence of agencies of social control. This second contradiction is not anthropological in essence, but of a much more recent historical origin. It is, put very simply, the contradiction between those with more and those with less social, economic and political power. Thus, the privileged are forced to control the underprivileged, lest the latter do away with privileges or, more probably, replace the former in their privileged positions. While the anthropologically founded contradiction between individual and society renders social control truly inescapable, the second contradiction is, in principle, limited to non-egalitarian societies, and therefore subject to relevant changes and even abolition. As a matter of fact, history is replete with attempts to overcome the problems of the class divide, to create egalitarian societies and thereby eliminate the non-anthropological need for social control – from Spartacus's slave revolt and the medieval heretics all the way to the socialist movements and Marxist revolutions of the twentieth century. Once established, though, the patterns of domination of one class, one race or one sex over the other have proven to be rather resistant to abolition. At best, collective efforts have succeeded in reducing the acuteness of some of these contradictions, as in the case of the anti-apartheid movement, the conquests of trade unions, civil rights groups and the feminist movement.

*Proactive control: the construction of conformity*
From Ross (1901) to Lemert (1967) social control was seen not only in terms of a reaction to deviance, but also, and even primarily, as something that actively produced conformity in the members of society. And while they repeatedly stressed both the influence of family education (socialization) and the power of public opinion over the

behaviour of individuals, this extremely important focus started to be neglected in the late 1960s, when the meaning of social control was narrowed down to the reactive side. It was only when feminists started to complain about the insufficiencies of a mere social reaction approach to the making of 'good girls' (Cain, 1989) that the deficiencies of the concept became apparent to some. Even that would not have helped to uproot the all-to-narrow concept of social control had it not been for the simultaneous shift of attention from punishments to the construction of conformity by means of discipline, stimulated by the writings of Michel Foucault and the new (and mostly French) social historians.

Conformity is constructed through a great number of means. These range from the most subtle seductions to overt violence, and from short-term interventions to long-lasting arrangements. As any glimpse at the history of church and state censorship, at wartime information policies, or an awareness of a dictator's watchful eye on press imports can show, simply to keep people uninformed used to be, and still is, a very frequent method used in the production of conformity. Bereft of essential knowledge about alternative perspectives – moral as well as political options – they, therefore, tend to conform to the standards provided by those who have the power either to withhold general education as such (keeping the majority of the population illiterate) or to make it difficult to get access to relevant (background) information.

While 'information management' in the widest sense of the term is still a favourite means of active social control, the global communication networks have definitely made it more difficult to isolate larger parts of the world population from relevant data. But this development is in itself very ambivalent since, not only does it promise more freedom of information, it simultaneously carries the danger of an inverted form of censorship through the exponential growth of 'information' (mostly trash) that may make people as disoriented as did traditional manipulation.

An important but widely neglected means of active social control is 'techno-prevention' through devices that simply do not allow the occurrence of certain undesired behaviours or behavioural effects. The architecture of public or private buildings, according to the principles of 'defensible space' (Oscar Newman, 1972), aims by design to reduce the occurrence of undesired entries; while fences that separate highway lanes or car ignitions that simply refuse to work as long as the driver has not put on his safety belt may not prevent road accidents, they do tend to minimize their consequences. This kind of active social control is one of the secrets of the astounding success of such phenomena as, for instance, McDonald's fast-food restaurants. As George Ritzer explains:

> Human workers, no matter how well they are programmed and controlled, can foul up the operation of the system. A slow or indolent worker can make the preparation and delivery of a Big Mac inefficient. A worker who refuses to follow the rules can leave the pickles or special sauce off a hamburger, thereby making for unpredictability. And a distracted worker can put too few fries in the box, making an order of large fries seem awfully skimpy. For these and other reasons, McDonald's is compelled to steadily replace human beings with non-human technologies, such as the soft-drink dispenser that shuts itself off when the glass is full, the french-fry machine that rings when the fries are crisp, the pre-programmed cash register that eliminates the need for the cashier to calculate prices and amounts, and perhaps at some future time, the robot capable of making hamburgers. (Experimental robots of this type already exist.) All of these technologies permit greater control over the human beings involved in the fast-food restaurant. (1993: 11)

Few scholars have paid attention to the dilemmas connected with this emerging pattern of social control. The liberal mode of social control respected individual freedom of choice and relied on the threat of sanctions against those people who were tempted to make a wrong choice. The new mode is one of a structurally imposed security-orientation and abolishes that freedom from the very beginning. Undoubtedly, the political and ethical issues related to this shift of emphasis will become more pressing in the next decades.

The fact that it does not take intentional acts by the enforcers of order and/or intentional submission to a personal command to have proactive control, or to produce conformity, will also be of growing relevance. As a matter of fact, the bulk of work in the process of producing conformity is not being done on the level of intentional action. In the field of housing policy, for instance, simple market forces are clearly sufficient in the exercise of a very rigid (and, in a way, efficient) system of keeping 'undesired' (that is, poorer) neighbours away from the well-to-do suburbs. While the 'invisible hand' (Adam Smith) of market forces has always played a certain role in the prevention of undesired behaviour, it is probably true that the relevance of 'the quiet force of economic relations' (Karl Marx) is on the increase. For example, while feudal lords still had to resort to the conspicuous force of visible coercion in order to extract the surplus production from their subjects, the very structure of today's labour market suffices to make the worker sell his labour-power to the capitalist, who can then harvest the surplus value without resort to spectacular action. Many theorists believe that increased commodification in present-day societies adds still another dimension to the ever-more subtle means of producing conformity. In their opinion (see Campbell, 1987), the ever-increasing numbers of once 'simple' commodities becoming 'romanticized' as symbols of life-styles, personal identity, adventure and excitement, are rapidly becoming the most alluring and influential agents in the shaping of people's motivations and actions: people are increasingly 'doing everything there is to be done' in order to be able to afford their 'dream car', their 'dream vacations', their 'dream house' and the like.

Evidently, it is much more efficient to make people want to do what they are supposed to do instead of having to stand behind them wielding the big stick of coercion. To transform an obligation into the subject's 'own will' often takes a lot of effort, but once achieved it often continues to work for a long time without any additional outside investment. While criminologists have traditionally overestimated the role of formal state interventions for behaviour control, it is now time to comprehend, as Dario Melossi (1990: 170) states, 'how positive motivations are instruments of power potentially much stronger than threats' (see also, Melossi, Chapter 3 in this volume, on proactive control through mass media). This kind of proactive control begins not with any reactions to deviance, but in the earliest (perinatal) phase of child-rearing. And while the primary object of every society's considerable investment in education and socialization is the contradiction between individual and society (making a 'social animal' out of the 'little savage'), all socialization also carries a political component that aims at the preventive control of potential disruptions emanating from the second basic contradiction in modern societies: the contradiction between those who are in politically privileged positions and those who are not. When children learn to salute the flag of their country, learn the national anthem etc., they are expected to internalize features of the political (and at the same time the economic) system's status quo that will make it easier for those in power to appeal to their identification and thereby make them conform to the given definitions of, for example, the national interest – even if that 'national interest' contradicts the individual's own interest. (For prevention as a method of proactive control to curtail the frequency of undesired behaviour, see also Pavarini, Chapter 4 in this volume.)

*Holes in the net: individual freedom and social change*
Of course, there never was and never will be such a thing as a perfect system of social control. But while that is a lamentable fact for past and future victims of crime (as well as those who, for other reasons, might be interested in the perfection of control over human behaviour), it is also certainly a positive and reassuring fact, since it implies the impossibility of ever establishing a long-lasting, completely totalitarian system of social control as imagined by George Orwell (in *1984*) or Aldous Huxley (in *Brave New World*). The necessary imperfection of social control is not only the best guarantee yet for the

survival of individual freedom, but also the very point in the concept of social control that makes sure it is compatible with social change.

The reasons for the essential imperfection of social control are numerous, with the most basic one being the essentially non-determined character of the human animal. The human character's inextinguishable capacity to transpose and extend learned schemas to new contexts, thereby creating new conditions with new possibilities out of the old elements, includes the freedom to transgress normative expectations and even neutralize internalized values for the sake of innovation action (see Sykes and Matza, 1957). Likewise, any effort of those in power to change the subjects' beliefs and resulting actions might completely fail, when the subjects stubbornly stick to their internalized norms and resist even the most brutal control measures (like the early Christians in Rome, Jehovah's Witnesses under Stalin, or some communists under Hitler). Therefore, the effect of any enactment of control attempts is never entirely predictable. A specific approach by a police psychologist to persuade a person threatening suicide not to jump can work with the majority of cases, but may even provoke the lethal jump in others. On a macro-level of social action, the complexity of conditions and interrelations transcends any notion of calculus and prediction. A soft diplomatic reaction to a regional claim for independence may, for instance, either help the challenged central government to restore confidence and undermine the rebels' support, or it could allow the secessionists to accumulate resources and build international support nets; similarly, while the adoption of a tough line of action may crush the revolt for good, it could equally provoke a rush of solidarity with the rebels leading to a sudden defeat of the central government. In the end, all teaching and drill of any knowledge and skill is polyvalent. A highly disciplined workforce may be the dream of every factory manager but, once unionized, such workers also tend to be highly disciplined union members and a source of constant headaches for managers.

> The form of the factory embodies and therefore teaches capitalist notions of property relations. But, as Marx points out, it can also teach the necessary social and collective character of production and thereby undermine the capitalist notion of private property. (Sewell, 1992: 19)

Alternatively, another essential reason for the unpredictability of outcomes of control attempts is the necessary multiplicity of social webs in which any individual is embedded. As Simmel ((1992) 1908: 305–44) pointed out, the individual lives her or his life at a crossing point where several reference groups intersect and overlap. While non-identical role expectations and normative orders may cause stress in the individual on the one hand – imposing a segmented existence – this plurality of normative embeddings also serves as a reliable source of freedom, since it allows the individual to balance one requirement against another, to shift allegiances and to increase his or her radius of action. Even the young child is already embedded in different normative systems with mutually contradicting influences, beginning with the conflicts between the mother's policy with regard to television and the consumption of sweets and that of an auntie or grandma. Later on, the parental norms are challenged by those of the peer group, and soon it becomes apparent that there are numerous difficulties and ambivalences in the determination of 'proper behaviour' as well as in the legitimation of institutions. On a larger scale, the Christian religion, for instance, was as useful a vehicle for the legitimation of the feudal lords' interests as it was for the legitimation of the egalitarian revolts of poor heretics in the late Middle Ages and early Modernity.

In present-day societies there is no single (religious) schema that can be exploited by contradictory interpretations, but there are normally various (secular) schemas that oppose each other and leave the individual with even more choice. While the legal system, by definition, claims legitimacy for all its aspects, there is an ever-growing number of dissenting groups that claim legitimate 'civil disobedience' in the face of legal statutes and provide alternative legitimation for acts strongly disapproved of by the majority.

Another conflict between normative systems often arises when norms and values that an individual had internalized during childhood and adolescence clash with the expectations articulated by his or her respective present reference groups. Contrary to a widespread assumption, early-instilled inner controls can be rendered ineffective relatively easily through the respective individual's 'techniques of neutralization' (Skyes and Matza, 1957), whereas the importance of actual interactive social bonds and attachments to friends and companions are often underestimated in their capacity to steer an individual's actions. The more people are integrated in a social (group) relationship, the higher they tend to value it – and the more they are ready to do in order to maintain the love, esteem, respect or business contact that they are enjoying because of their belonging. The implicit or explicit threat of social exclusion and the loss of both material and immaterial resources actually constitutes quite a remarkable potential for control of any group over any individual. Anyone not wanting to be completely dominated by group norms is well advised to seek membership in many groups, and to move within and between a number of social circles. While this may balance some pressures, it also leads to new difficulties, since the individuals may very well face contradictory expectations that are hard to combine. This could force them to hide some of their behaviour from some of their friends, colleagues or other contacts. In the case that this information management fails, they may even be forced to reorganize the whole social network, to change friends or even move out of town – thus gaining a different kind of freedom, namely that which accompanies the role of the stranger (see Simmel, (1992) 1908: 509–12).

It is not without reason that most theories of crime and deviance nowadays do not part from any assumption about 'born criminals' or a specific 'criminal motivation' or the like, but from the much more trivial acknowledgement that social control is bound to work less than perfectly, that it is bound to have lacunae (see Box, 1981; Gottfredson and Hirschi, 1990; Hirschi, 1969; Sykes and Matza, 1957; Felson, 1994). Those 'deficiencies' of active or preventive social control allow the deviant motivation (which is, as Freud has convincingly demonstrated, common and well known to all of us) to develop into actual deviance which, thus, becomes an inescapable fact of life. While different social structures, educational systems and policy guidelines do have an influence on the number and ratio of murders, robberies, burglaries, etc., there is no social movement and no political system that could possibly eradicate crime and deviance and prevent such occurrences. The unavoidable lacunae of social control make deviance a normal feature of any social organization. This very simple fact – originally developed (albeit along a slightly different line of reasoning) by Emile Durkheim and often repeated since – engenders another one as its consequence, namely the simple fact that there will never be a society without the need to *react* to deviance.

*Reactions to deviance: informal, formal and sanction rules*
The imperfection of social control guarantees the perennial existence of deviance, thereby forcing every social organization not only to react to deviance on either an informal and/or a formal basis, but also to develop rules regarding the application of sanctions against infractors ('sanction norms' in the terminology of Heinrich Popitz, 1980: 86).

Informal social control is so much a part of everyday interactions that it is often hard to recognize. But every individual possesses a number of techniques to deal with other people's undesired behaviour. One may, consciously or unconsciously, either escalate verbal fights in order to clear the situation or begin to reduce or avoid contacts with the person(s) in question; one might complain to friends in the hope of finding support for one's own point of view or of excluding the annoying person(s) from one's circle of friends. If the annoying behaviour constitutes a serious offence, one might consider notifying the police in order to initiate some formal action. On a micro-level, informal controls that are much more subtle than this are being attempted innumerable times every day. For example, any slight modification of a married couple's everyday routine activities – like an unexpected kiss or lack of an anticipated one, an almost imperceptible avoidance of the other's look, a gift of flowers with no proper occasion – can either be meant as an (inclusive or exclusive) reaction to irritating spouse behaviour, and/or be seen as undesired and 'deviant' behaviour in itself, thereby occasioning demands for clarification ('what's the matter with you today, darling?') and/or reciprocal sanctions (from withdrawal from the common meal to have supper alone in front of an 'interesting' television programme that one 'cannot miss', all the way to withdrawal from the common bed). All in all, there is an enormously wide range of informal controls, ranging from joking, frowning, gossiping and scandalmongering over loss of honour and status, malediction and total exclusion from a group, through the firing of an employee and the boycotting of an undesired competitor, to all possible violent means, such as slapping a child or killing the seducer of one's wife, daughter or sister.

This should make it clear that the distinction between informal and formal controls is not identical with the distinction between 'soft' and 'severe' or 'inefficient' and 'efficient' means of control. While informal control is often rather light in the beginning, informal interventions also start at an earlier point in time, are more pervasive and usually have a greater impact on a person's self-concept, identity, career and life chances. Rather, the difference between informal and formal control lies in their organization. While you meet the authors of informal control in everyday life as mothers, teachers, peer groups, church pastors and the like, the authors of formal control are exercising a specific control job. That means, they work in institutions that were especially designed for the purpose of reacting to deviance – in the police force, the juvenile justice system, the courts or correctional institutions. They obey specific and mostly written formal rules ('sanction rules') that tell them how to proceed, how to punish and where to stop.

While the difference between informal and formal social control is in many respects essential, it should not be thought of as a clear-cut distinction. It is probably more correct to see formal and informal control as theoretically 'purified' ideal types (Max Weber) which, in reality, are often interwoven and hard to distinguish. There are, for instance, formal restrictions on informal control (penal procedures against parents who inflict brutal punishment on their children) as well as, on the other hand, informal codes of behaviour that influence the actions of policemen and other agents of formal social control. Terms like 'class justice', 'race justice' and others were all generated to describe or censure these clearly illegitimate, but existing interrelations.

Formal reactions to deviance usually achieve most of their effect by touching off informal reactions; what people often fear most is not the formal court sentence, but the loss of status and the restriction of life chances which usually come along with it. Therefore, the effect of formal sentences on the future behaviour of the delinquent can be extremely variable. A culprit who knows that none of his or her family and friends will let him or her down will bear a verdict much better (and will be affected by it to a far lesser degree) than one who, after an official verdict that labels him or her a criminal, may lose all social support.

There are other intriguing interrelations between formal and informal control. One example is the extensive use which formal control agents often make of the unparalleled quality of informal information systems (like the Paris police made use of the famous concierge system). The relation works vice versa when, for instance, criminal organizations try to control the illegal supply market (drugs, gambling, prostitution, weapons) by way of denouncing their competitors to the authorities. Another example is the possible substitution of formal by informal controls. Where agencies of formal control fail, other organizations may step in as their functional equivalents. In a little-known article, based on his own empirical research during a four-month visit to the United States in 1904, Max Weber described how religious sects managed to fulfil what normally would be considered state functions in frontier America (see Weber, 1978). Similarly, the Sicilian mafia stepped in as an institution of political control in the interest of the landowning classes when the Italian state apparatus was not able to protect them efficiently against rebellious peasants (see Hess, 1973).

The specific form that informal or formal social control may take depends to a large extent on the way a specific form of deviance is defined: in terms of 'crime' (= criminalization), of 'illness' (= medicalization) or as a 'minor incident' that does not threaten the validity of the normative order (= neutralization). Criminalized behaviour (in the widest sense) is regarded as intentional, and the actor is held responsible for it – and consequently eligible for punishment. To medicalize behaviour is to regard it as somehow pathological and to regard the actor as sick, that is, deviant but not of his or her own free will. Hence, the actor is eligible for certain types of help (treatment, therapy). Finally, social reaction can take the form of neutralization or insulation. In such cases, behaviour and actors are regarded as neither criminal nor sick, but silly. The behaviour may well be potentially disruptive and undoubtedly undesired, but it seems nevertheless best to let it run its course – to tolerate it as long as it stays within the limits of a specific context. Examples include subcultures like bohemianism, deviant institutions like prostitution, events like street carnivals or the (unfortunately also mostly passing) condition of being passionately in love. All these fields, times and situations are more or less insulated from 'normal standards' of behaviour and 'normal' social control, be it by avoidance, by informal contempt or by the assumption that people who engage in this kind of behaviour are 'a little bit out of their minds'. But in the very instance the behaviour in question exceeds the limits of toleration in terms of time or space or intensity, heavier forms of social control will set in. Which of these definitional strategies will be applied is not totally independent of the actors and their behaviour. More important, though, is the power of attribution, and the more powerful interactive partner or the more powerful group will define the situation and decide if and what kind of deviance there is and how it will be reacted to.

A significant element in this process is the attribution of responsibility. Once upon a time, in the era of animism, forces that we now regard as impersonal forces of nature were held responsible for the events they caused. When the Persian Emperor, Xerxes, could not cross a wild river with his army, he had his soldiers line up and whip the water. In the Middle Ages, dogs or pigs who had killed children were put on trial and actually hanged or decapitated (see Evans, 1987). Later, explanations of behaviour gradually shifted. Animals, but also the mentally ill and small children, were progressively seen as unable to bear criminal responsibility and unfit for criminal sanctions. A more acute awareness of the force of socio-economic conditions upon the actions of individuals (Marxism), as well as the discovery of the unconscious (Psychoanalysis), contributed to a further retreat of the notion of responsibility during the late nineteenth and early twentieth centuries. Therefore, while natural catastrophes were often regarded as crimes in past ages, it has become more and more common to interpret crimes as catastrophes – that is, situations in which the application of legal sanctions makes little or no sense at all.

Often one finds competing definitions of the same act: a conservative prosecutor may say 'crime', while a psychiatrist would point to an 'illness' and suggest the notion of an 'accident'. These and similar negotiations can be observed in all courts at all times, but also outside of the justice system on all levels of interaction. The actors themselves and their interactional partners may differ radically in their interpretations. While we are inclined to blame delinquency on deficient socialization, poverty and the like, and take responsibility away from the actors, we would probably be unhappily surprised if positive achievements like passing an exam or finishing a manuscript were not attributed to our own endeavours.

The differential attribution of responsibility has enormous consequences, not only for the forms of social control applied, but also for the behaviour of the actors themselves. Whoever is regarded as unable to steer his or her own actions (the 'sick junkie', for instance) is quite likely to acquire a kind of learned helplessness, and to regard his or her actions as determined by forces outside his or her own will and sphere of influence. Psychological research has shown that a radicalized idea of an external 'locus of control' can seriously impair a person's initiative and increase the seriousness of psychic problems – while also serving, at times, as a most welcome legitimation to continue destructive or self-destructive activities (see Peele, 1987).

*Ironies of social control*
Social control sometimes works as intended, but often enough it fails to work, producing surprising side-effects or even effects which run counter to its original intentions. Many times, it produces a mixture of desired, neutral and undesired effects. As David Matza (1969: 80) summed it up, 'the very effort to prevent, intervene, arrest, and "cure" persons of their alleged pathologies may, according to the neoChicagoan view, precipitate or seriously aggravate the tendency society wishes to guard against'. Ironically, too, the most focused and the most formal attempts at maintaining or regaining social order seem to be particularly likely to lead to undesired and even paradoxical consequences. Convincing demonstrations of this can be found at the juvenile courts, where interventions unwillingly, but systematically, seem to further exactly those criminal careers which they want to stop. Thus, they keep themselves busy with self-created 'secondary deviance', a phenomenon that occurs 'when the person begins to employ his deviant behavior or a role based on it as a means of defense, attack, or adjustment to the . . . problems created by the social reaction to it' (Lemert, 1948: 28).

This irony of formal control efforts was widely recognized in the 1960s. But from the 'diversion programmes' invented to avoid this paradoxical effect arose still another ironic result, which was to be discussed under the term of 'net-widening' – meaning the extension of social control to lesser forms of deviance, to the family and friends of the offender, and the intensification of control through psychological and therapeutic intervention that went much further than imprisonment. Formal social control spread out and moved from the institutions to the communities, until ever larger parts of the population were under some kind of surveillance. In a way, everybody became subject to some kind of control that used to be characteristic of institutions only, albeit maybe minimum security institutions. Hence the uncomfortable feeling of some critical criminologists that contemporary Western societies may be on the way to becoming 'minimum security societies' (see Blomberg, 1987).

While this criticism was to gain much and well-deserved momentum through the reception of Michel Foucault's works, it is certainly also not devoid of irony that the conservative defenders of the prison system could use many of Foucault's arguments, and those of the critics of diversion, to defend their anti-diversion position. Some reformers even accused a strange coalition of prison expansionists and radical criminologists of being responsible for the backlash which the prison reform and prison abolition movement suffered during the 1980s. While such an accusation may have exaggerated the importance of radical criminologists, it certainly would be an irony worth some consideration if their dystopian expectation of the total therapeutic or electronic state had somehow managed to contribute to a view of the prison as a symbol of the 'good old times' of a still limited and definable power of the state to punish.

But the irony does not stop here. Driving people into deviant roles and careers or producing stigmatized minority groups may in the end be very functional for social control purposes. Durkheim pointed out that the rituals of exposing crimes and punishing criminals help to clarify moral boundaries and integrate social groups. Freud described the criminal as a scapegoat of society. The id of all of us is a hell of deviant impulses which our Super-Ego holds in check by means of unpleasant guilt-feelings. We project our deviant impulses onto the criminals who dare enjoy the pleasure of acting them out and we thus satisfy our impulses symbolically. At the same time we revel in the punishment of criminals, because it satisfies our Super-Ego and makes us believe that we are superior to the criminal. The Danish scholar, Svend Ranulf, added an insightful sociological analysis to this explanation when he showed that:

> The disinterested tendency to inflict punishment is a distinctive characteristic of the lower middle class, that is, of a social class living under conditions which force its members to an extraordinarily high degree of self-restraint and subject them to much frustration of natural desires . . . the tendency in question tends to disappear in the middle class, as soon as it has acquired a certain standard of wealth and prestige. (1964: 198; 2)

Ranulf could indeed demonstrate that the tendency to inflict harsh punishment out of moral indignation did not exist in tribal societies or in aristocratic and upper class social strata. This explains the great attraction that crime and punishment have for readers of the tabloid press, as well as the soft abolitionist approach of bourgeois academics.

Pariah groups like Jews, criminals, witches, blacks, gypsies, drug addicts and others can play a functional role in stabilizing any given social order. The Jews, who ran the financial administration of many European princes in the seventeenth century, extracted money from the people to pass it on to their masters. Because of their pariah

condition, they were easy targets for hate and aggression, while divert-
ing the danger of popular revolts from the princes who probably
would have been the more 'correct' objects of popular resentment (see
Coser, 1974: 34–40). Similar processes can be observed today in the
ambivalent attitudes towards the leisure class of the super-rich as well
as towards drug addicts and other drop outs. While both the life-styles
of the people on these extremes of the social ladder and our attitudes
towards them have a number of common features (see Hofstätter,
1962; Matza and Sykes, 1961) – we admire them and look at their
happy-go-lucky approach to life with envy, but we also have aggressive
feelings towards them because of their 'undeserved' and often also
'immoral' lives at our expense – we normally show a split attitude
towards both groups. The admiration is directed towards the leisure
class, the aggression towards the pariah groups which, thus, help save
the leisure class from a lot of envious hate (see also Melossi, Chapter
3 in this volume, on social control through crime).

### Tendencies at the end of the millennium

On a grand scale, the history of social control reflects the power relations of each social formation. During the 'regulated anarchy' (Weber)
of pre-state egalitarian tribal societies, social control was characterized by retributive reciprocity and pacifying reintegration. In feudal
societies, and during the phases of early statehood, social control was
characterized by overt violence that was as vicious as it was selective.
The control apparatus was still rather weak and had to rely on selective brutal acts and their deterrent effect to try and keep the masses in
line. The capitalist mode of production overcame the need to rely on
overt force by the invention of paid labour and the simple act of with-
olding the surplus value while forcing the dispossessed working class
to continue offering their labour.

   Foucault in *Discipline and Punish* has worked out – in an ideal
type perspective – the different control styles of feudal and bourgeois societies, giving in the first chapter a detailed description of a
would-be regicide's painful public execution and later contrasting
this with the pervasive methods of discipline, panoptic surveillance
and institutional confinement. Evidently, all capitalist societies –
while having preserved assorted traces of the control forms of previous stages – rely on a combination of generalized social disciplinary
processes with a pervasive bureaucratic control. Present tendencies
are characterized by an increasingly technical element as part of a
general thrust towards ever more rationalization and commodification, but a more detailed view also reveals a number of contradictory
tendencies.

*Opiatization of control*

Both socialization and legitimation were far more successful in the earlier stages of human societies. In the times of small egalitarian societies, conformity was relatively easy to instil; and during the Middle Ages, the Catholic Church exercised a near-to-perfect ideological control over socialization and the legitimation of institutions. Since then, from the Reformation to the present time, the capacity of Western societies actively to produce conformity has been in decline. The emergence of a comparable apparatus of active social control has been prevented by the processes of secularization and rationalization, and the increasing social complexities of modern societies. Attempts to fill the gap on a grand scale by fundamentalist religious revivals as well as quasi-religious political ideologies (communism, fascism) have utterly failed, even if one must probably concede that the last word about the fate of fundamentalist alternatives to modern secularism has not yet been spoken.

At present, though, the main force in Western societies which seems able to instil conformity in people has nothing to do with church, religion or metaphysics, but rather with an intricate system involving the creation of material wants and what one may call 'the politics of desires'. This system is deeply rooted in both the capitalist production sphere as well as in a concomitant 'consumerist ethos' (Campbell, 1987) which is itself closely, albeit contradictorily, related to the unbroken tendency towards ever more rationalization, routinization and disenchantment of the world. As is well known, commodification requires the continual creation of new products and new markets, thus contributing to the desensitization of the individual and to the need for ever more stimulating experiences to produce excitement. And the more the capitalist system stresses cost-benefit rationality, purposive labour, etc., the stronger becomes the consumption ethic as its complementary component. Powerfully constructed and reinforced by the mass media and youth culture (advertising, popular music, etc.), it not only portrays and applauds a world of pleasure in commodities and commodified pleasures, but in effect also builds a surprisingly influential system of social control which we could refer to as a new 'opiatization' of society.

With all kinds of direct ideological control in decline, the creation of material wants and the striving for the satisfaction of these wants has thus become the pre-eminent agent of conformity. With most people having a stake in life – or at least a convincing illusion of it – few should want to risk that stake by committing undesired or even punishable acts. Put very simply: to attain self-realization and meaning in life, one must buy certain commodities that represent this meaning, for example security (life insurance, a home), experience of the inner self

(course in meditation, preferably in Tuscany), existential self-experi-
ence (free-climbing, bungee-jumping), complete relaxation (long and
expensive vacations in the sun), etc. To buy these symbolically-charged
commodities, one must conform to the work ethic. And the harder one
works, the more one needs to compensate everyday alienation in
leisure time. But with all leisure time compensations ever more linked
to commodified reifications, one must be ready to sell one's soul to the
only system that both creates, shapes and – at least partially or virtually – fulfills these wants, thus making capitalism something like a
latter-day catholic church.

Herbert Marcuse gives a profound analysis of this process in his
*One-Dimensional Man* (1964). His main thesis is that Western societies
are able to satisfy the basic needs and are at the same time solid enough
to tolerate quite a lot of variation in behaviour and even some deviance
– in sexual matters, for instance – thus producing a sense of freedom
which, in a deeper sense, actually results in a submission to ever
increasing processes of domination and manipulation. Postmodern
societies evidently make particularly considerable use of techniques
that are able to neutralize potential revolt through what he called
'repressive tolerance', that is, the harmless and sometimes only illu-
sionary satisfaction of real or artificially induced needs that pacifies the
working class and robs them of their revolutionary fervour.

Repressive tolerance works both ways, though. The endless creation of needs and material goals, and the accompanying ideology
that those goals should be attainable by everyone (see Merton, 1938),
creates at the same time an endless dissatisfaction – and, thus, the
motivation to do away with the restrictions or barriers on the roads to
achievement of the goals and to take illegitimate and illegal short
cuts. No wonder the opiatized consumer society is, paradoxically, also
a hotbed of unprecedented deviance, in which respect for the legal and
legitimate pathways to riches rapidly withers away when risks are perceived to be low. This applies as much to the juvenile shoplifter, who
does not yet have much to lose, as to corrupt officials, who feel protected by the consensual nature of their crimes and the resulting
difficulties of detection. Furthermore, even if the working classes are
and remain politically integrated, the system produces an ever larger
Lumpenproletariat of poor, permanently unemployed, homeless out-
casts whose stake in conformity is minimal (and on whom Marcuse, by
the way, rested much of his romantic hope for a social revolution).

*Socialization: birth of the 'dividual'?*
The 'romantic ethic and the spirit of consumerism' (Campbell, 1987)
are both an expression of and a guarantee for the further development
of a new type of socialization. It would be small wonder if this new

socialization that fits the 'mall' and the 'amusement park' life-styles ended up producing new types of personality. These new personality types would probably be different from those of the preceding phases in the process of civilization in that they would mark a turning point from an increase to a decrease of personal integration. While the medieval person, according to Norbert Elias, used to live with a low level of self-constraints and impulse controls, the fabrication of modern individuals – at least since the sixteenth century – was marked by a steady increase in internalization and psychic integration of those originally divergent personality components that Freud would later speak of as the *Es* (Id), *Ich* (Ego), and *Über-Ich* (Super-Ego).

A reverse tendency was discovered by research in socialization since the Second World War. The actions of the now emerging personality type seem to be much less geared to internalized norms and values and more to the demands of the respective situations, interaction partners and group commitments. Since people are apparently less steered by conscience and convictions than by situational expectations and role requirements, this new personality type has been characterized as a 'marketing character' (David Riesman), and others have brought up complementary evidence about the 'narcissistic' character of this personality (Christopher Lasch). This is a dramatic change that implies a whole array of highly ambivalent phenomena including, for example, the relation between adults and young persons. Whereas child rearing in the nineteenth century was structured often enough by command, repression and submission, giving rise to the authoritarian personality (Adorno et al., 1950), children today are much more respected and often treated on a close-to-equal basis. Children may take their meals with adults and speak at will (a phenomenon that would have defied imagination some generations ago). They may get into arguments with their parents without having to take account of spankings or other forms of retribution. Children have a say in family affairs such as holiday plans, schooling, and separation, divorce and remarriage of their parents. They dress like little adults, they watch much the same television programmes as their parents, and, finally, they owe much of their enhanced status to the fact that they are important consumers in terms of kids' wear, sweets, toys, cds, video games and cassettes, computer hard- and software, and the like.

Young people are being treated as equals in many ways, including some highly risky aspects linked with the commodification of sexual attractiveness (for example, young people's roles in television commercials, men's magazines and so on), but the positive and the negative potentials of this development are interwoven to such a degree that it is hard to predict which one will prevail. While narcissism is generally regarded as an undesirable trait, it is also true that the extreme relevance this new personality type attributes to self-realization and diversity also makes it comfortingly hard to imagine that this type of person could ever fall prey to authoritarian ideologies that altogether deny the individual's autonomy and right to be different. In terms of the production of conformity, the emerging type of socialization will, therefore, give rise to relatively independent, but inoffensive, unaggressive, and self-centred personalities who are difficult to homogenize in their behaviour by totalitarian ideologies or simplistic command structures, but who can easily be steered by (pleasurable) intervention in their motivation.

Given the increasingly external guidance of this personality type's actions, it is easy to imagine that there will be an increased tendency for individuals to show a substantial disintegration and fragmentation of their personality structure. The person's roles gain increased independence, and her or his ability to construct and maintain a coherent self is seriously impaired, which might transform the occidental 'individual' – in the long run at least – into what French philosopher Gilles Deleuze (1990) called the forthcoming 'dividual'.

*Techno-prevention and control by consensus*
The mechanism of these 'politics of wants' or 'politics of desires' works better in environments that are free of visible misery, antagonism and strife. In short, they work best in artificial environments that preventively allow access only to those who are materially and ideologically prepared to participate in the consensual pursuit of commodified pleasures. To prevent undesired things from happening by using landscape architecture and environmental design is clearly a more elegant way of exercising social control than having to arrest, prosecute and sentence people who only became offenders because of the lack of a more appropriate preventative design of the place. It is also an expression of a general move away from the reactive mode and towards a more proactive way of social control. To paraphrase Stanley Cohen, social control is shifting from its normal reactive style – only activated when rules are violated – towards a proactive mode: anticipating, predicting and calculating in advance. And since there is hardly anything that could fit this tendency better than the creation of artificial environments, many analysts have come to believe that one only has to turn one's attention to the malls, the amusement parks and the affluent suburbs of the metropolises to have a preview of things to come.

The huge, covered shopping areas just outside the metropolitan areas of North America and Europe look like laboratories for the construction of an artificially 'cleansed' society. In the midst of a snowy Canadian winter, you will find palm trees and waterfalls, flowers and exotic birds, and when the seasons change you will find respite in the cool spring-like mall when everybody else is sweating their souls out. The malls are little cities or mini-countries in their own right. They have border controls (private security have precise orders regarding who is and who is not to be granted entry) and internal policing (by private security firms), while the only real and ultimate sanction is expulsion from the artificial paradise. There are no beggars or loiterers, no (visibly) poor, nor will one find anyone who is not shopping (except, again, the omnipresent and helpful private security guard who makes a walk through the mall one of the safest experiences you can have).

The malls are a good laboratory for a new system of social control that works not by nineteenth-century command structures, but by unobtrusive politics of landscape (the malls are at a certain distance from the city, often with practically non-existent public transport connections, thereby preventing access of undesired people from the very start), defensible and sterile architecture with prefabricated pleasure stimuli (unobtrusive techno-prevention), and a consensual atmosphere that makes it the unavoidable duty of every visitor to obey cheerfully all the rules of the game.

The amusement parks are similar to malls, but they are even larger, making them more likely to represent a country or to simulate the world as it should be (Disney-Land, Disney-World). Amusement parks are geared not only towards the shopping adult, but to 'The Family', which is seen as a good-humoured, lovingly harmonious entity worth building a nation upon, and a worthy model for the structure of the global village (with the poor but happy countries in the role of the children). Everything must be safe, so everybody can have pleasure. Unlike the mall, the commodities that are for sale in the amusement parks are probably best described as highly standardized pleasurable experiences – and to the extent that pleasure is the ultimate end of most of our activities in life, what you buy in amusement parks is as close to a sense of life as one can get in a commodified universe. Safety control there is, to a large extent, unobtrusive. Things have been constructed extremely cleverly so as to allow as little deviance and accident as possible. Amusement park employees are gentle, often costumed and entertaining, and always lend a helping hand when anyone shows any sign of behaviour that is not perfectly in line with the expected routines. They act as unobtrusive engineers of consensus between the amusement park company, the parents, their children and the other visitors. There is no quarrel, no command, nor need to obey. Things work smoothly in what seems a universal consensus about the common goal of the community to have good, clean and safe fun.

There is an elective affinity between the very structures of the shopping mall and the amusement parks on the one hand and the ever-growing number of affluent suburbs that are beginning to cover the globe like a pattern of 'islands' or 'fortresses' of the very rich. Maybe it is here that the results of the social laboratories are finding their way into a 'real life' that, paradoxically enough, seems quite unable to shed the smell of the artificial in terms of social chemistry and social engineering, and is a sad simulation of what the ancient philosophers used to refer to as the 'good life'. The pattern of islands or fortresses is really a community of communities, unrelated geographically but structurally closer to each other than to their immediate environment where crimes of violence mingle with misery and desperation. On these paradise islands, there is no filth, no misery, no violence; the lawns are always well cut, the children happy and healthy, the people cheerful and positive in their thinking. Street crime is practically non-existent, and the dominant mode of social control is 'embedded, preventative, subtle, co-operative and apparently non-coercive and consensual' (Shearing and Stenning, 1987: 322) – that is, it is similar or identical to the type of social control that reigns in the amusement parks.

If the features of control that today shape the laboratories for future societies – the malls and amusement parks as well as the affluent suburban fortresses – were to be generalized in the next millennium, then things would have developed quite close to the sort of society described in Aldous Huxley's *Brave New World*.

> Within Huxley's imaginary world people are seduced into conformity by the pleasures offered by the drug 'soma' rather than coerced into compliance by threat of Big Brother, just as people are today seduced to conform by the pleasures of consuming the goods that corporate power has to offer. (Shearing and Stenning, 1987: 323)

The number of 'islands' or 'fortresses' structured along the lines described above is rapidly growing. This is for two reasons: one is the increasing wealth of those already at the top of the ladder since Reaganomics and Thatcherism turned the social welfare state's tide to a neo-liberal *enrichessez-vous*, the other is the exponential growth of the world's poor who are drawing suspicious attention from those inside the luxurious fortresses, like the nineteenth-century 'dangerous classes' once did in their respective societies. Those who can afford it flee into luxurious flats and homogeneous neighbourhoods which depend only to a very small extent upon state services, rather relying 'upon the voracious consumption of private security services' (Davis, 1990: 244). These services are innocuous for those who live there and fulfil more the function of a private army directed at the deterrence of, and if necessary armed defence against, invaders from the non-affluent and, therefore, 'foreign' environment – 'hence the thousands of lawns displaying the little 'armed response' warnings' (Davis, 1990: 244).

A comparable development on a larger scale is the attempt to fortify (by means of heavy border controls and restrictive immigration laws) a whole continent – 'Fortress Europe' – against the onslaught of waves of miserable Third-World asylum seekers.

For anyone familiar with European history, however, those phenomena are not as new as they might seem. Not only were towns, monasteries and even some village churches fortified against poor peasants, vagrants, bandits and other enemies of more civilized and more affluent inhabitants, but, inside the towns, the aristocrats or patricians used to live in buildings which turned strong and barren walls to the street and were easily defensible against the *popolo minuto* living around. Thus, the doorman-equipped buildings in Manhattan or the new downtown architecture of Los Angeles (as Mike Davis describes it in *City of Quartz*, 1990) will remind the reflective traveller of, for instance, the Renaissance towns of Tuscany or the Marais quarter in Paris. It is simply the typical situation that arises when the state is not yet (or not anymore) in a position to pacify the 'dangerous classes' of really down-trodden people, and the well-to-do have, therefore, to rely on their own private means.

*Privatization, commodification and expansion*
Privatization is one of the common denominators of today's laboratories for the future of social systems, and hence one of the traits most likely to continue to shape them. But privatization has many faces and means many things. While it is an attractive idea for all those who see the state as the source of all evil, it may also represent uncontrolled vigilantism and infringements of civil rights. More than anything else, it is likely to lead to an evermore unequal distribution of security, because privatization is also a very euphemistic term for what would be more correctly termed 'commodification' and 'commercialization' of security. Its growth corresponds to significant changes in property ownership. In North America, for instance, many public activities which used to take place in public community-owned spaces, now take place within huge privately owned facilities, which Shearing and Stenning call 'mass private property'. As examples, they cite the ever increasing number of 'shopping centers with hundreds of individual retail establishments, enormous residential estates with hundreds, if not thousands, of housing units, equally large office, recreational, industrial, and manufacturing complexes, and many university campuses' (Shearing and Stenning, 1983: 496). The considerable demand for both the services and goods of the security industry has already led to a reversal in the

ratio of public and private police personnel in the United States, with privates outnumbering the public service by almost three to one, and where four to one is a current forecast for the year 2000. In the USA, the private security industry's turnover was estimated at around US$50 bn in 1990 and in Germany estimates rose from less than DM11 bn in 1990 to more than DM14 bn in 1994 (see Nogala, 1995).

But demand alone is not the driving force of this market, as Nils Christie has recently demonstrated (Christie, 1993a). It is rather one of the markets that follow the rules of a supply-side economy (Galbraith, 1985). The more money and personnel are being invested in the detection of crime, the more this will reflect in rising crime rates, which in turn stimulate the demand for security goods and services as well as for prison capacity that is also increasingly being furnished by private corporations (which have even gone to the stockmarket and seem to promise a lucrative investment). According to Christie, for the security industry to prosper, there must be feelings of insecurity and these feelings must be focused on crime, even if they might in fact stem from shrinking job markets, rising prices for housing, the risks of modern technology or the deterioration of the environment. And with crime rates being one of the most convincing methods to focus these feelings on crime, crime rates are rather like a 'natural resource' for the crime control industry. The special feature of this resource is the fact that it is unlimited, since crime can always be created by simple legislative activity or multiplied by increased police budgets – or even only by initiating some more dark figure research. Its production depends on no more than investment in the combat of drug crimes, street crimes, hate crimes, environmental crimes and the like. As Christie said, the 'economic interests of the industry . . . will all the time be on the side of oversupply, both of police and of prison capacity', thereby establishing 'an extraordinarily strong force for expansion of the system' (Christie, 1993a: 110). If the trend towards commodification of security remains unbroken, the consequences could very well take the shape, as Christie puts it, of 'Gulags, Western style'.

*Limits to leisure and pleasure: of normalization and brutalization*

The gulag perspective presented by Christie implies a continued expansion of Western prison systems, operated by an ever-increasing 'Corrections-Commercial-Complex' (Lilly and Knepper, 1993: 164) which exerts a significant influence in sustaining so-called 'get-tough-on-crime politics'. Eventually this leads to the incarceration or internment in camps of substantial numbers of 'undesired', that is, marginalized and criminalized citizens (like inner-city young African-Americans in the USA).

Such a perspective is diametrically opposed by the perspective that has been developed by the philosophers Herbert Marcuse, Michel Foucault and, more recently, Gilles Deleuze. Their prediction does not imply the exponential growth of incarceration but, much to the contrary, suggests a withering away of all kinds of camps, prisons, factories, school buildings and other nineteenth-century means of spatial inclusion in large-scale buildings. In their analyses all kinds of institutionalization and incarceration have already become obsolete in view of the system's growing ability to manipulate motivations and monitor citizens' movements at all times and on all occasions. Their assumptions rest upon undeniable changes in the practice and potential of social control that indicate a shift away from the cruel punishments of the past to medicalization, to admonition instead of infliction of pain, to de-carceration and diversion instead of imprisonment, to normalization instead of exclusion, and to destructuring instead of centralization.

In this context the undeniable growth of the therapeutic realm,

and its invasion into areas previously dealt with through other forms of power/knowledge (the 'medicalization of deviance' thesis) are of major significance in the social control landscape. Even more important than therapeutic systems where coercion is involved (involuntary hospitalization, compulsory treatment of addicts, thought-control of political dissidents) is the construction of new therapeutic categories (diagnoses, syndromes, classifications) – in areas such as sexual deviance, family violence, hyperkinesis, learning disorders, eating disorders, etc. In advanced Western societies, this is perhaps the major site for emergence of new forms of deviance 'normalization' – and, hence, social control. (Cohen, S., 1994: 69)

But while many theorists seem to believe that these new techniques will soon push the outdated forms of social control such as total institutions, imprisonment, torture and the death penalty into well-deserved oblivion, there are at least two aspects that should dampen our hopes concerning any 'withering away' of the prisons. First, Horwitz (1990: 247) has stressed the fact that the therapeutic style of social control has 'only a narrow range of effectiveness. It can promote positive change when clients voluntarily cooperate and share common value systems with controllers. This is usually only the case when people share the educational, class, and cultural orientations of their therapists.' Second, one only has to take a look at the deepening trench between the world's affluent and afflicted parts, between the growing number of both the very rich and the very poor, to become aware of the possibility that the introduction of the new techniques of social control may find its limits right along the poverty line. While the new techniques will drive the old ones into oblivion at the top and maybe at the core of (post-) industrial societies, the old ones and even the very old ones will, more probably than not, be applied to those below and beyond the poverty line – that is, to the pauperized masses within and beyond the borders of the affluent world (see Sumner, Chapter 6 in this volume).

Those who live at the margins of society have little to expect from the gentle forms of medicalization, therapeutization, neutralization and normalization. There, beyond the enclaves of commodified happiness, the coming of age of young persons is not the continuous learning game with electronically geared reinforcements, but an often violent struggle in an environment that comes as close to the Hobbesian state of nature as any. And as far as the reactions to deviance are concerned, one will find all of them there – including the overt brutality of past stages of social formation that many theorists had long forgotten. Reactive social control still does rely on selective brutality that contains a peculiarly effective terrorizing element and which is regularly put into practice by powerful groups when they begin to define situations as critical for the survival of the(ir) system. On a grand historical scale, Mussolini, Hitler and Franco represent this method of controlling the working classes at a moment of dangerous social unrest. But one can also observe more restricted examples like the virtually unconditional crack-down on leftist terrorists in Germany during the 1970s, or the extreme persecution of drug traffickers in the United States and other countries. Seemingly outdated and premodern as it is, this control method – which includes coercion of masses in camps, long-term imprisonment, the death sentence, extra-legal killings by death squads and/or corrupt police, etc. – will become ever-more important, being linked to the extent that structural unemployment, international mass migration, youth violence and a restless lumpenproletariat will continue to grow, while social consensus continues to decline.

## Conclusion

As far as the public perception of the status quo is concerned, an apparently discrepant discourse points to the dangers of an all-too-mighty state that reduces its citizens to mere objects of control on the one hand (leading to what one could call 'the transparent-citizen-panic') and to the risk of a complete breakdown of order on the other hand (which leads to 'the breakdown-of-social-control-panic'). The first panic is being fuelled by the analyses of Herbert Marcuse and Michel Foucault. It capitalizes on therapeutic control and computerized surveillance, and gives rise to the fear of an increasingly wider and deeper-reaching net of social control, depriving individuals of their liberty by subtle but all-the-more effective means, and turning them into transparent pieces of glass under the gaze of the powerful. The second perspective contradicts this and points to the fact that the individual has never been as transparent as in early tribal societies or medieval villages. It was in those comparatively small human groups, when everybody knew and was able to supervise everybody else in a closed kinship-regulated system, that peer control reached its unparalleled peak. Top-down control also was certainly more powerful in medieval times and had another climax in the totalitarian states of the twentieth century (which not by chance gave rise to Orwell's dystopia). Since then the efficiency of control has actually declined.

Of course, computer surveillance, data matching, profiling and the like are very impressive new means of control. 'Visions of the central all-knowing computer and Kafkaesque nightmares lurk on the horizon' (Marx and Reichman, 1987: 202) and there is no doubt about the repressive potential of such technology. But, on closer scrutiny, the accuracy and efficiency of this technology seem severely limited due to shortcomings in data-gathering and errors in data-processing which, for an all-too-human bureaucracy, become ever-more difficult to control the more information there is. In addition, the technology's vulnerability to manipulation and even complete neutralization by knowledgeable violators who deliberately produce false data and manage to obscure detection of the correct ones (Marx and Reichman, 1987) should not be underestimated. Moreover – and this point is often neglected – those extraordinary control methods have only become necessary because the state's grip on its subjects has loosened, and those subjects have become extraordinarily difficult to control due to their great number, diversification, mobility, anonymity, in addition to the enormous differentiation of societies into subsystems and subcultures. Relatively speaking, the new control methods might be and probably are less effective than the old ones, in view of their respective control problems. Today's news from the front of the police's 'thin blue line' can easily give the impression that we are headed for a complete breakdown of social control, at least in the no-go areas of the inner cities, where poverty, homelessness, joblessness and lawlessness, drugs and violence, vandalism, truancy and teenage parenthood seem to reign supreme. Furthermore, heterogeneous phenomena such as international mass migrations, the apparently independent behaviour of multinational corporations, the drug and arms trade, the peddling of uranium, international terrorism and the handling of poison gas by doomsday sects or, for that matter, pilfering at the workplace and tax evasion – which all appear to be out of control of any national or international legitimate political authority – certainly nourish the same impression. These seemingly contradictory fears of a coming totalization of social control on the one hand, and a complete breakdown of social order on the other, may, nevertheless, become compatible when we see them as a reflection of different risks associated with different areas of the social system.

Internal polarizations of societies and the creation of an ever-deepening gap between the fortresses of the affluent and the migrating miserable masses are developments that are resulting in a marked bifurcation of control styles. The prospects are normalization and de-institutionalization for the 'in-groups', and an increasing brutalization at the margins for the 'out-groups'. Each control style, in turn, generates its own dangers and panic-discourses. The amusement park scenario entails the risk of a totalized benevolent submergence of the individual in an ocean of techno-prevention and manipulated consensus, while the scenario at the margins justifies the vision of a complete breakdown of social order and entails the danger of brutal top-down control measures.

*Sebastian Scheerer is Professor of Criminology at the University of Hamburg. Henner Hess is a professor in the Faculty of Education at the University of Frankfurt.*

# 6

# The Decline of Social Control and the Rise of Vocabularies of Struggle

## Colin Sumner

I want to engage in a little polemic. In a recent essay, Massimo Pavarini claimed that criminology is 'now facing a crisis of identity so profound that we may have serious doubts about its capacity for survival as presently constituted' (Pavarini, 1994a: 43). On the contrary, I would say, it is not so much a crisis as a normal and permanent condition for a modernist science. There are many reasons for this. One of the most important is that criminology is, among other things, part of the social control movement initiated by Ross and Park, and that project is now in tatters. Although severe, the crisis of identity in criminology is less profound and consequential than the demise of the vision and reality of social control. Besides, criminology will survive – because it has a strong and well-defended nest inside another, more legalistic, vision: that of penal repression and crime prevention. But, if we are concerned with sociology and some notion of socialism, we must be concerned more broadly with the character and implications of the demise of the political project of social control in North America and Northern Europe, its originating centres. This is not just a Northern, metropolitan concern, as we have indicated throughout this volume, it is a concern which cuts to the very heart of sociology and social democracy, because the concept of social control, in its heyday, lay at the centre of both those enterprises.

Implicit in these opening remarks is the contention that, contrary to Dario Melossi (see Chapter 3 in this volume), the concept of social control became inextricably linked in the first quarter of the twentieth century with the *political* project of American social democracy. Writers like Mead and Park were also active reformers, and Roosevelt's New Deal bore all the hallmarks of the subsumption of penal law within the general framework of social policy (for more on all of this, see Sumner, 1994: Chapter 3). Social control, it is my contention, is not just an academic concept which evolved out of the bright minds of social scientists but is most fully understood as an idea which was part and parcel of the social-democratic political movement in the USA. It is a piece of knowledge interconnected with a particular condensation of power, to use Foucault's language. To use Marx's terms, it is a scientific concept which could only have been thought under certain historical conditions and which hitherto has borne the ideological and cultural marks of its moment of formation. I shall argue, contrary to Scheerer and Hess (Chapter 5 in this volume), that it is not an innocent general concept but an historically loaded artefact of modern culture and that it requires considerable reworking before it can rise above its times.

The vision of the new social-democratic society which social control contained is now very difficult to imagine, so often, since the 1960s, has that whole vision been deconstructed, denounced, resisted and de-mystified by both Left and Right, or just rendered plain inoperable by major social-structural changes. The concept of social control itself is a fractured shadow of its former glory, now a tired and disintegrated collection of soundbites disconnected from its earlier periods of vitality. It deserves an old folks' home, but the state will not foot the bill. When the cost-benefit analysis rules, old social-democratic concepts are left to die alone in the hypothetical and hypothermic community, ironic victims of the epoch of the fiscally driven market-state obsessively deconstructing all social welfare provision and unintentionally reconstructing the social conditions which gave rise to the concept of social control in the first place. However, there will be no rejuvenation of the concept as a force for social democracy, in my view; the policy of 'let them rot', on a global scale, means that any future the concept has will be as a concomitant of militaristic self-defence by autonomous communities attempting to weather the icy blasts of state neglect and isolation/exclusion.

The official story in the tabloids is that social control was weakened by the poor care given by single-parent families and then so violently mugged by black, inner-city youth and other disorderly elements from 'yob culture' that it never recovered. It has been replaced by more prisons, high-tech private security operations and reduced welfare benefits, alongside a commitment to winning the next election. Its ideological driving forces, the ideologies of social democracy and liberal sociology, are much weakened. The word 'social' is reserved for parties of the alcoholic rather than the political kind and even ultra-right-wing ideologues only dream of getting 'control' of the situation.

The very words 'social control' have lost their meaning and their postmodern critics observe, with their usual literary acuity, that there has been a slippage in the signifiers. What this loss actually mediates or reflects is not so much a literary lapse as a series of major economic and political transformations. The fantasy of 'control' of social affairs has been replaced by the more modest, and much more desperate, dystopia of the 'management' of 'trouble-spots'. Social control is constantly subverted by the subcontracting-out of vital policing and servicing functions by the fire-brigade-state's hit-squads of trained accountants, merchant bankers and experienced line-managers – that is, when the state officials are forced to abandon their daily denial that there is actually any trouble at all. Normally, the accountants and the public relations teams brush away the reality of 'social problems' (another old concept dying a death by accountancy), thereby enabling the fire-brigade state to be cost-effective in the extreme – it only comes out to 'deliver' its goods when the city is burning or the baby dying, when the massacre is half-over, and when the media payoff is maximized.

I exaggerate a little perhaps, but in the hyperrealism of rule by accountancy the vision of social control is clearly replaced by the spreadsheet of managerialism. Slowly but surely, in Britain, following North America, we see the old-style, local-level and 'hands-on' management by the professionals (doctors, teachers, senior police officers, etc.) replaced with management by people with MBAs, budget-management 'skills', and invaluable prior experience managing factories and sports centres, selling used cars or reading the news. Intra-community, intra-institutional regulation – so central to the old social control project – is sacrificed to the quickly learned universalism of a servile management science, notably the ability to 'cut' according to long-discredited market-economy principles so revered by the shrunken society of the accountancy-state. Not entirely accidentally, of course, the political power of what was 'the new petty bourgeoisie', an often critical and radical class fraction whose members frequently leaned towards social democracy or socialism, has been severed at source.

Not only is social control disappearing in the face of the market and the new marketeers, but the very constitution of society itself is being restructured: infrastructure is replacing or dominating superstructure at all points. Culture, as the accumulated wisdoms of a people, is prefixed by enterprise. Social control has not only been intellectually abandoned to its fate on the mean streets of the enterprise culture, it is being politically divested of its class roots. The political power of its driving force, the liberal petty bourgeoisie, has been 'cut-back' at source and their political parties are in decline or, at least, struggling to maintain their integrity in an age of survivalism.

Social control terminally declined as a concept in the late 1970s at the same time as social democracy and consensus politics. For some sociologists, it was substituted by Left Realist criminology (see Pavarini, Chapter 4 in this volume). A more realistic answer from the Left, in my view, would have been a 'new idealism' which would have countered the criticisms of social democracy, socialism and social control with a new vision of social regulation at the end of the century. That may yet emerge, although few such visions could be optimistic. In any case, the irony is that the 'new realism' was an anachronistic idealism. The Left Realist renewal of the old vision of social control and of social-democratic socialism – in the face of some terrible internal weaknesses within the Left, and some harsh political and financial realities – was, in effect, to postpone an opportunity to redefine the political agenda of the socialist and social-democratic movements.

In summary, as we enter the mid-1990s, we are faced with an end of century which threatens to leave us back in the nineteenth century, with its free trade, gun boats, repression and political disintegration – yet we persist in making the prospect more frightening still by facing the wrong way and not looking at the future head on. What is needed is a vision of social counter-organization which can fire a new mode of counter-cultural co-operation. The connections between visions of social transformation and theories of social regulation need to be renewed. Abandoning such connections to a micro-pragmatism which restricts itself to the parameters of parochialism and the politics of immediate 'relevance' is to give up on the social itself.

## Back to the roots

In his *American Journal of Sociology* article of 1921, Park raised the question which so troubled Durkheim: 'How does a mere collection of individuals succeed in acting in a corporate and consistent way?' (Park, 1921: 5). This he explicitly defined to be the problem of social control. The Durkheimian drive to cultivate social regulation in a morally deregulated society was thus reproduced in Park's thought. What mattered to Park was that, following Durkheim's view of modernity, the touchstone of a society over a collection of individuals was 'corporate action' (Park, 1921: 19), not likemindedness. Social unity in modernity could not be based on imitation or 'herd consciousness' but had to be rooted in the unified and unifying practices of different individuals from a plurality of cultures: the classical problematic of twentieth-century liberal pluralism, with all its merits and deficiencies. It is this problematic that logically and politically generated the modern(ist) concept and problem of social control. Social control, in this Chicagoan sense, involved the participation of informed and diverse publics in the construction of associations that are meaningful to those publics and which function to regulate the terrible consequences of unregulated capitalism. Its watchwords were communication, voluntarism, persuasion, diversity, culture, participation and self-regulation.

The concept of social control arose more out of the turbulent melting pot of cities like Chicago than the abstractions of Harvard students of social administration: its conversion into a metaphor for the enforcement of conformity in the 1950s was merely an imposed conservative mangerialism. Social control was always a grounded, praxis-linked conception. In essence, it was a practical plan for authentic public involvement in the creation of communities out of chaos. It emerged triumphant with the rise of the New Dealers of the 1930s and was a genuine attempt to rescue capitalism from its intrinsically destructive and divisive contradictions, so evident in the USA by 1932. The alternatives asserted elsewhere were National Socialism and Stalinism. From the beginning, as Melossi (1990) rightly points out, social control was an alternative to rule by decree and was to be centred around self-control. Effective social regulation had to be meaningful for, and chosen by, the individual in conscious relation to his or her immediate community.

Social control, in this sense, had to take multicultural divisions, poverty and class polarity as its starting point – as the difficult raw material out of which some coherence had to be worked. As such, it could be claimed with some force, as Melossi implicitly does (ibid.), that it was a concept ahead of its time in some ways and whose time may well yet not be done. I am not so confident. Certainly, it was never an unrealistic concept and should never have been parodied as blind to deep social divisions, as it was much later. Indeed, it could be added that it grew up explicitly aware of the constant slippage of signifiers in a mass-mediated society containing many languages and little in the way of a shared universe of discourse (see Wirth, 1936, discussed in Sumner, 1994: 89–100). The political problematic of the twentieth century, for the autonomous capitalist societies of the North, especially of the 'New World', has revolved precisely around how to integrate pluralistic societies. Social control, and inevitably part of criminology, have been fundamental, both intellectually and politically, to this strategy. As Park himself concluded, social control is the central problem of society. No more, nor less.

Equally, however, we must note, social control is not a concept which is likely to emerge as a powerful force in the societies of the periphery (see Bergalli, Chapter 2 in this volume) except in so far as they have put social democracy on the political agenda. It is still not a concept with much analytic weight in the Fourth World of the super-poor or within the metropolitan ghettoes of permanent unemployment. It is a concept for societies that believe they can integrate their diverse populations into a functioning totality. For that reason, we may conjecture, it may not be an attractive concept in Bosnia – but it might never again have any purchase in Britain either. Some old societies may well have past the point where the social control project is operable. Concepts are historical creatures: they rarely apply well in all times and places and some applications simply fail. The idea of general labour, as Marx observed, may not have been thinkable in ancient Greece, with its sharp hierarchies, and, I would add in retrospect, it is not an idea that can be applied well to those times.

Park had defined sociology itself as merely a 'method for investigating the processes by which individuals are inducted into and induced to co-operate in some sort of corporate existence which we call society' (1921: 19). That is the exact significance of the whole field of the sociology of deviance and social control. It has been logically and politically at the heart of the philosophy of liberal pluralism, the project of corporatism, the science of sociology, and the theory of social democracy for the whole of the twentieth century. Seen from the standpoint of the 'roaring twenties' in Chicago, it is obvious why. Social control seemed, and was, so important. Without some degree of self-regulation rooted in some genuine collective unity, its inhabitants were faced with an unlimited civil war. Moreover, at the international level in the 1930s, without co-operation and regulation a further world conflagration was predicted to arise – and it duly did. Social control has, not surprisingly, therefore, been part of the central conceptual matrix of American sociology throughout the twentieth century (see Chunn and Gavigan, 1988) and has had an enormous influence on world sociology as a result.

Mead, the social-psychological inspiration of the Chicago school, drew very similar conclusions about law and social control to those of Durkheim (Mead, 1918). He observed that the strength of the law lay in our respect for its symbolic values, not in its deterrent value. Punishment, he flatly declared, 'preserves a criminal class' (1918: 583). Law, however, did unite a population around some common ideals and interests, even though punitiveness itself did nothing towards rehabilitating the offender or eradicating crime. 'Seemingly, without the criminal the cohesiveness of society would disappear and the universal goods of the community would crumble into mutually repellent individual particles (ibid.: 591). But, unlike later writers such as Tannenbaum (1938), Mead could not see how crime control by law could be combined with crime regulation through 'comprehension of social and psychological conditions' (1918: 592). The two approaches seemed to him to be totally contradictory. In the end, Mead felt that the more mature approach was the latter, a 'social control' guided by the positive objectives of social reconstruction, the nurturance of a healthy self within the offender, and a move beyond war (both civil and international). His philosophy was clear: only when we can regulate our societies without attempting to annihilate offending individuals will we know that we have conquered the roots of our civil and existential insecurity.

Social control was from the beginning a project that entailed reflexivity, communication, democratic discourse, meaningful associations and participation. It was also always a project which assumed the perpetuation of capitalism, the power of the state and the ubiquity of cultural heterogeneity. It never assumed harmony, consensus, understanding and freedom from want; it dreamed of them. It had a political project built into its very centre. Now, on the basis of these few outlines of the historicity of the concept, let us proceed further.

**The radical critique of the concept of social control**

Looking back, we can easily see that the late 1960s' critique of the concept of social control was slightly unfair. A few words of admonition are not out of order.

That critique supposed its target to be an eternally conservative perspective that was blind to the ills of capitalism and which asserted a non-existent cultural and moral consensus. Indeed, the structural-functionalist theory of social control in the 1950s, which was its target, did display those characteristics, but that functionalist perspective was not the only theory of social control and it did depart significantly from the historic centre of the social control project which I take to be best expressed by Park. In thus reducing social control to one of its variants, the radical critique – with its constant reference to persistent class divisions – glossed over the attempt of the social control project to deal with multiculturalism and somewhat missed the point that American sociology of the late 1930s did address class directly in its analysis of blocked opportunities and structurally induced anomie. The critique thereby avoided addressing the awkward subject of the dangers of over-inflated ideologies of upward mobility and universal acquisition – dangers not unknown to subsequent socialist ideology and practice, especially in the Third World. The critique thus also leapt to a solution within some kind of Marxist, or at least anti-élitist, exposé of established powers, as if Marxism had ever offered any detailed analysis or solution of multiculturalism and as if the old class structures of Europe were never going to be transformed by capitalist development towards something resembling the complex political and cultural configurations of North America.

The radical critique was, thus, a little disingenuous. The cruder versions supposed a workers' revolution which had long been off any realistic agenda and showed even less signs of being revivable in post-Treaty of Rome Europe. Moreover, the products of such revolutions were coming apart at the seams in an Eastern Europe long criticized by its people, and by Western European neo-Marxism, for its oppressive conditions. Even the libertarian Marxism of the late 1960s and early 1970s had little to offer to those who demanded democratization and equal rights. The 'taking rights, democracy, welfare, women, and crime seriously' movement which developed in the late 1970s was too little, too late. Socialists rarely offered serious alternatives to the concept of social control until the 1980s and, when they did, they needed recourse to political ideas from the 1930s (see, for example, Hirst, 1986).

In addition, this radical criticism of the concept of social control did not really come to terms with the fact that social control was always understood by Park and his kind to be an alternative to state decree. In many senses, social control was to subsume state prohibition; or, alternatively, the state was to become sufficiently sociologically aware to recognize the limits of legal repression – and so much early sociology of law emerges from within this problematic. In either case, state power was to be regulated and guided by the power of associations with roots in the community. This was the hallmark of the continuity with Durkheim which the social control movement undoubtedly sustained. By dismissing all aspects of state-sanctioned social control as the ideological expressions of the class state, Althusser's work being the extreme case, the baby was thrown out with the bathwater. The point missed was that social control was very much a critique of the old, corrupt, patriarchal form of state and a celebration of popular democratic, multicultural forces. No one who has studied the history of the USA from 1918 to 1939 could mistake that fact (again Melossi's book of 1990 is very welcome in this respect; see also Sumner, 1994: Chapters 2–3). To reject the social control project was not just to reject a critique of law, statism and authoritarianism, it was to reject a liberal critique of the patriarchal and very undemocratic form of the capitalist state. Indeed, it was a rejection which gave a very broad meaning to the slur 'liberal'. That becomes very clear when we listen to Václav Havel talking of 'the aims of life', in contrast to what he calls the 'post-totalitarian' systems of Eastern Europe: 'Life, in its essence, moves towards plurality, diversity, independent self-constitution and self-organization, in short, towards the fulfilment of its own freedom' (Havel, 1985: 29). Park and Mead would have wholeheartedly approved.

Now we are well into the brutally selfish times of the 1990s, the emphasis of the social control project upon community development, voluntary associations, citizen participation, open information and local welfare groups does not seem as merely liberal as it did in the 1960s. We are reminded that capitalism seems to go in cycles and that what looks tame in one period can look radical in another.

*A revised critique of social control theory*
None of the above 'critiques of the critique' amount to a papering over the weaknesses in the liberal-pluralist conception of social control. The critiques of the last 20 years did make several telling points and these will be restated and creatively developed in the following subsections.

*Lack of historical specificity*  The social control project does not distinguish between types of social formation or forms of state within capitalist societies. It is a universal panacea. The social control recipe, therefore, could have less than liberal implications in some societal or epochal contexts. For example, forming neighbourhood watch committees to engage in or assist in the policing of crime does not, in the 1980s, amount to an extension of participatory democracy but more of an extension of state policing under a 'law-and-order' government. General concepts are undoubtedly necessary for social science (see Scheerer and Hess, Chapter 5 in this volume), but this particular one, social control, is loaded with evaluative, utopian content – for example, concerning the character of human interaction, the possibility of local power and the supremacy of reason over passion – and is not separable from its generative political project without a great deal of analytic and political work. Concepts may rarely be able to evacuate such evaluative content, but in this case the weighting is substantial and the concept looks difficult to apply in pre- or postmodern settings. Only if we reduced the concept to a very bare minimum would it survive this criticism and, even then, I cannot see how the concept would survive the argument that one group's social control system is another group's mindless violence.

Bearing in mind Marx's discussion of general concepts in the *Grundrisse* (1973), it is difficult to see the concept of social control as being of the same order as the concept of production. It seems more akin to the less simple, less concrete notion of population and is, therefore, always in need of breaking down into its constituent parts. Social control is a synthetic general concept and is, therefore, all-too-capable of a multiplicity of radically different historical meanings. It is precisely this capacity which gives it a weighty historicity: it is always loaded with conjunctural, political meanings and is, therefore, not conducive to use as a transhistorical concept.

*Informalism, local control and the central state*  The emphasis on local and informal controls within the community completely glossed over the possibility that these might be hi-jacked, manipulated or even attacked by the institutions of the central state. The government is assumed to be in favour of local and informal social control, an assumption that bore no relation to reality in, for example, Thatcher's Britain. Thatcherism was a political project which was determined to smash the power of certain kinds of local and informal social regulatory systems, for example, socialistic local government. Central government can be remarkably selective about which kind of social control it will support or tolerate. That selectivity is usually political in type.

What this points up is the fact that the Parkian project assumes that central and local government are not themselves at war, and are usually working together for the good of the whole. This assumption is mistaken in the long run, given that the general tendencies of capital accumulation must sustain the existence of a relative surplus population (Marx's category), both within Western cities and on a global scale, and that the central state will only tolerate the political activities of the local level in so far as they do not seriously threaten to change the continued marginalization and social exclusion of this surplus population. Moreover, if it is also true that the capitalist state has a long-run tendency to enable its officials to accumulate private capital in one way or another from the benefit of their offices, we would expect a long-term inclination towards the marginalization and political exclusion of local authorities.

Overall, there are reasons to believe that informal or community-level social control will be constantly subjected to central-state interference and regulation, and that such local social control as relates to the permanently marginalized and excluded sections of the working class, the politically most pivotal form of informal social control, will follow a long-run tendency towards constant absorption into, or domination by, the imperatives of the central state.

*Autonomism, underclasses and independence struggles*    If the above is correct, then it will also follow that the classes and class fractions, ethnic groups, nations and other groups which would, in principle, benefit the most from the Parkian project of social control will, actually, be those who are least likely to benefit from it. Indeed, arguably, the best they could hope for is the development of an internal social control system which sustained their autonomy, cultural integrity, political institutions and military forces (see Bergalli, Chapter 2 in this volume, on the Autonomies of contemporary Spain). Such a conception is well beyond the scope of Park's ideas. Unfortunately, this is one of the most important potential developments in the theory of social control in the 1990s.

Communities, regions, nations or peoples that have been dominated, assaulted, punished, marginalized or excluded are not showing a massive inclination to being incorporated into larger corporate hegemonies. Whether it is in South Africa, Latvia, Bosnia, Britain, Germany or Canada, aboriginals or long-settled groups with distinct linguistic, cultural and political identities are neither content to accept immigrant or second-class citizen status, nor the punitive forms of social control so often developed to deal with immigrants. Consequently, one of the most striking forms of social control of the Parkian type in the 1990s, if such a thing can be said to exist at all, is that developed as self-protection against the interference or assaults of the hegemonic state and as a weapon for self-advancement in the political assault on that state. Now, this phenomenon has important ramifications for the concept of social control and its associated theorizing: first, it directly challenges the criminologists' statist acceptance of the definition of many of these counter-hegemonic forms of action as crimes – criminology must now really decide whose side it is on because it cannot be on both sides; second, one sociologist's social control is now another's serious crime, and vice versa – social control must now be uncoupled from its traditional association with the state; and, third, at long last, theorists of social control must face up to the question as to which exact values they think social control is to promote or be guided by (for example, the right to self-determination or the need for the unity of the nation-state).

My own, somewhat pessimistic, view is that, just as we have begun to understand that we must uncouple the social control movement and the concept of social control from its historical linkage with the central state, the state in many countries is deciding to uncouple, or at least reorganize the political status of, those recalcitrant regions of autonomy with the effect of permanently disenfranchising them. Whether this takes the friendly form of subordinate integration or the less friendly forms of disintegrative abandonment, expulsion, military conquest or ethnic cleansing, such uncouplings amount to state withdrawal from the idea of positive assimilation or multicultural integration, and thus from the spirit of the social control project. In such a scenario, which is certainly contemporary, the question is not so much how we social scientists should reformulate the conception of social control as to what exactly will replace, in harsh political reality, a social control movement in decline. In my view, what we are faced with from the year 2000 is a two-tier system: social control in all its full Parkian glory for the rich, high-tech and included (in the private citadels of the wealthy North), and the full panoply of repression, abandonment, distanced interference and 'Bantustanization' for the excluded remainder. Reintegrative shaming, (see Braithwaite, 1989), for the rich; famine, repression and alienation for the poor.

*Lack of intrinsic meaning* As Chunn and Gavigan (1988) also observe, the concept of social control is a very undifferentiated one. Any association or action, according to post-1945 usage, can be seen as an agency of social control, whatever its form, content, purpose, practice or place within the social system. This feature gives it a certain monumental vagueness as a concept and enables it to be used as a catch-all with little intrinsic or denotative political or ideological meaning – and a lot of latent connotation. It could thus refer to either a liberal welfare-state interventionism in the hands of social democratic sociology or, in the hands of radical sociology, a totalizing, almost totalitarian form of state repressiveness permeating all nooks and crannies of society. Too few observers have made the simple point that the key questions about any alleged instance of social control are: (a) what is social about it? (b) whom does it control? and (c) for what purpose? The constituent elements of social control are always in need of specification in each and every instance; it is not a concept that speaks for itself with much volume or clarity. What is necessary if we want to continue using the category, it seems to me, is a relational analysis of the forces that are clashing, an account of the circumstances and conditions which colour and prejudice that clash, and a theory of the ideological and cultural mediation of those forces and circumstances through the categories of social censure (see Sumner, 1990, on the concept of social censure). Only with such a form of analysis could one begin to escape the problems around the definition of what is social control and what is censured as violence. As Garland found in *Punishment and Modern Society* (1990: 191–209), a conception of social censure is necessary to move from an analysis of punishment as an institution to an account of punishment as a cultural form (see Sumner, 1996, on the sociological relation between censure and punishment). Such a sociology does not bracket off the evaluative overlay within ruling philosophies of social control but consciously builds it into the explanation of the exact character of the social censure. It is precisely those evaluations, in all their cultural, ideological and historical specificity, which give shape and targets to the punishment.

It might be as useful, however, to consider social control from the standpoint of what it is not: its Other or exterior. For the last 40 years, the Other of social control has, generically, been social deviance. All too often, social control is simply defined as the normative dimension of social life which defines and censures deviance. Now, given that the concept of deviance is a deeply problematic one, for many reasons, and can be seen to have lost its historic meaning and function (Sumner, 1994), the concept of social control has lost its theoretical partner – its exterior – and thus much of its sense or definition. For example, social deviance is now widely accepted to have little fixed behavioural reference – what is censured varies enormously with time, place, person, context and culture – and, thus, is really only defined as that which is censured or socially controlled. If we now accept that social control has, at a minimum, lost its Other or, more persuasively, has been disentangled from social deviance, then we too could begin to move with the times and uncouple social control from social deviance theoretically. Simple effects would follow, such as the abandonment of assumptions like (a) social control is triggered off by deviance, (b) deviance is followed by social control, and (c) social control and deviance define each other. Such a move delivers ideas such as the autonomy and arbitrariness of social control (there is smoke without fire, because this is not a natural relation), the non-deviance of censured actions (it is not necessarily cool to break social rules but sometimes downright traditional and conformist), and the definition of deviance according to independent, autonomous, cultural codes rather than social convention. And so on. From this standpoint, we could begin to analyse the respective cultures which clash and the social relations which precipitate the collision, without slipping into statism or romanticism. Simply by making these key analytic uncouplings, we would also automatically make some progress in the general deconstruction of our ideas of the Generalized Other (the degenerate, the inadequate, the incontinent, the mad, the bad and the sad, etc.) through rendering the obviousness of those categories as insults or censures within a socially structured relational collision.

## Official social control and disciplined resistance

The criticisms above indicate that the whole social control project, as it was originally conceived in liberal American sociology, was an important corrective to patriarchal, repressive, corrupt state forms but nevertheless a very limited creature of its time. It was still locked into a conception of the value of the centralized state form of governance, a notion of society as state-centred. It certainly had no idea that the 1980s would see the emergence of right-wing governments which would, paradoxically, denounce statism in their rhetoric and in their practice increase the power of the central government over local authorities. Nor did it anticipate the current inclination of statist governments to privatize every conceivable industry or service and thus retain effective control, via the logic of the market, over the direction and *motif* of all such privatized sectors. Both these instances illustrate the fact that central government has many ways of controlling the details and organization of social practice, but, more importantly, that governance need not depend upon the state-centredness of society.

It has become more important than ever to acknowledge the role the so-called voluntary sector can play in organizing welfare relief, charitable projects, cultural associations, political institutions, media of communications and military forces. The power of people to organize their own institutions, autonomously from – and even in direct opposition to – the central state, is the other side of the dialectic of social control. This power is, to the social controllers, the deviant side of politics, often carrying, in their eyes, the barest of legitimacy and often being brutally criminalized or annihilated. Acknowledgement of the resistant forms of power or 'alternative' forms of social control is, paradoxically, to emphasize that the current trend, partly stemming from Foucault's work, to stress the ubiquity and fragmentation of power and therefore everyone's relative autonomy, only succeeds at the expense of so much forgetting. It forgets the monumental social power which is accumulated in the hands of central government and private capital, and the monumental effort and courage it takes to survive and self-protect through building alternative, oppositional forms of power. Power may be ubiquitous, but it is more ubiquitous for some than for others. For those for whom it is somewhat less than ubiquitous, it has to be fought for – over long periods of time and often in conditions of great hardship.

This means that we ought to begin to understand a different meaning of social control, namely that of the collective discipline required for resistance and self-protection. In this register, surveillance, discipline, self-examination, self-care, self-protection, community defence and even military (or militaristic) tactics are not system impositions tending us towards conformity but chosen strategies for survival, despite or against the system. Foucauldianism, on the question of power, can be an irritating illustration of the middle-class intellectual game of making distinctions and playing with words without any grounded or realistic sense of their implications: it may now be time to recover a meaning of social control for the excluded Other (the working class, women, minority ethnics, subordinate or peripheral nations, and the colonized) which would stress the positivity of disciplined resistance and self-protective withdrawal into supportive community.

Official social control has been invalidated intellectually by critical sociology, and rendered increasingly ineffective by the activities of the fiscal state. If there was anything that was truly social about the class-ridden, male-dominated, white-ruled practices of official social control, then it is now being sold off – along with so much else – to private capital. Official social control is being privatized; and it will probably remain just as class-ridden, male-dominated and white as it always was. In societies where alienation, in both its objective and subjective senses, is ubiquitous, the state rules and individuals struggle to retain any sense of control over their lives, their definition of their selves, and their language. Vocabularies of motive were for Mills, ultimately, expressions of socially legitimate accounts for individual actions – or alienated disguises for the truth in a world where propaganda ruled. Vocabularies of struggle are perhaps the only ones where an authentic degree of social control is exercised. The ultimate political truth about social control – a highly political concept – is that it was, and remains, a Utopia for the disenfranchised, a myth of repossession, and an antidote to alienation. It may be that now is the time to begin reconstructing our vocabularies of struggle as part of the restoration of that Utopia, and again social control might stand for our attempts to preserve the power of autonomous communities. This time, however, it would not be to insert those communities into a representative democracy that is doomed to inequity from the start but rather to withdraw and protect them from any further destruction by the decentralized state and its hired hands.

In this way, contrary to Dario Melossi (1990), the state is no longer the state of social control, nor is the concept of state an ideological one in comparison with a concept of social control which non-ideologically reflects the multiplicity of viewpoints. Rather, since 1945 the state has hi-jacked most of the developed forms of social control and is now insouciantly selling many of them off to private bidders. Official social control was, thus, a political project within liberal ideology that was taken over, rendered powerless, abolished or sold by the free-marketeer statism of the 1980s' new conservative ideologues. The claim that we had entered the 'end of ideology' epoch (Bell, 1960) is now revealed to have been as temporary as we always imagined. The 'new' dominant ideology is that of the power of the free market to solve all problems. Social control is thus no more free of ideological construction than it ever was. Indeed, more than ever, it is clear that there is an 'official' social control which belongs to the state, in one way or another, and another social control which is distinctly 'unofficial' and stands autonomously from the state in protection of its own. The dialectic that really matters now is not between social control and the state but between the different, and opposed, forms and forces of social control: between central and local government, between efficiency and democracy, and between the tiny minority in control of social and economic power and the large majority of officially and financially powerless. Each local sector or unit must fight its own corner in the fearsome swirl of an inhuman free market. The weak are losing regularly and, ironically, the social seeds for a new 'social control' project are being sown daily, one which may not be mass-integrative so much as group-protective.

## Recovering the power of self-regulation

In the current period, the mistake would be to look backwards, either to a myth of American democracy or to a myth of social-democratic labourism. Time moves on. As I have indicated, the existing concept of social control has lost its ideological drive. The assimilationist objectives of the 1920s, the social-system Utopia of the 1950s, and the egalitarian-progressive karma of the labelling perspective in the 1960s have all exhausted their limited possibilities. Faith in such visions has withered in the face of the stridency and power of the new conservative right and of the relentless self-examinations of the disintegrated, nihilistic left. The future, as always, lies in the politics and political forms of the unincorporated, disadvantaged, 'deviant' sections of society and their struggle with the international economic order and its corresponding state forms: they have chosen new routes, ones which emphasize the right to be different and the right to self-determination. Social control is not especially a part of their Utopias, although self-regulation certainly is. The social for them is part of their oppression and, therefore, their task, in so far as it constitutes a generalizable unity, is either to recover the social and to reconstruct it in the process, or, more pessimistically, to distance themselves from the social and construct their own alternative bonding system. It is that future we must face head-on in the twenty-first century.

Essentially, the abandonment of any desire for a substantial hegemony by the new Right has made debates about assimilation, systemic-ness and equity redundant or at least marginal. With the tactics of ruthless selfishness and victory at all costs uppermost, the politics of the free market have liberated the Left from the need for any commitment to forge an impossible total consensus. Conversations with the fiscal élite are now of marginal interest and relevance. Capitalist instrumentalism is now so divorced from any moral base or any political ambiguity that the task for communities or groups in struggle must be to renew a general moral vision and connect it to a viable political strategy for survival and independence.

Any such renewal of the progressive moral vision must contain a substitute programme for social control. However hopeless it seems to propound ideas of social co-operation in this age of rampant individualism, the task is necessary because social progress is dependent upon it. Without social co-operation and self-regulation, individualism can only deliver its undoubted fruits to the privileged few – as the 'roaring twenties' and the selfish eighties demonstrated. Crime does indeed become a problem for all in deregulated capitalism. The 'new realists' in criminology were right to say we must take it seriously, along with the problem of order. Hyper-individualism must lead to an increasing disregard for any rules of civilized conduct and to explosions of frustration, anger and violence within the ranks of the dispossessed, disenfranchised, disillusioned and distressed.

But this is not a time for Utopias. Our task at present is to construct a coherent defence of a positive kind, one that thereby has an outgoing programme based on moral and political principles which may sustain electoral victory but more importantly found a worthwhile form of life beyond that. Not an easy task. In the first instance, it seems clear that in an age of amoralism the first objective must be to reconstruct our moral vision. The final collapse of Stalinism has only vindicated our persistent critique of its roots in orthodox Communist political dogma. That dogma relegated morality, rights and equity to the paradise waiting to be produced by scientific socialism. It mistakenly thought that they were extrinsic to the production of a decent life, a luxury to come after the revolution rather an intrinsic component of any real revolutionary process. As we have been saying for decades now, there is no real revolution without a revolution in consciousness. Undemocratic rule is the same whatever it chooses to call itself, whether that be the new conservatism, communism, social democracy or feminism. So too is unethical rule, whatever its practical guise. Recent calls for a new ethics are on the right track – our task is to give these calls a more focused direction in relation to the concept of social control.

If concepts of social control have always had their roots firmly within the political imperatives of their day, then ours should be, and will be, no different. Our political imperative, and it is urgent, is to reforge and reformulate the connections that have been shattered by the recent waves of neo-conservatism. New alliances and organizations of democratic forces need to be constructed, not just to limit state power or to gain electoral victory but, crucially, to answer to urgent popular needs and to articulate the moral-ethical critique inherent in the subjective feeling of those needs. This is something that social-democratic parties, and some of the new progressive groups, have singularly failed to do. Some of these have statist social control programmes, belonging to a bygone time, that simply fail to reflect the popular and angry moral critique of the new conservatism and the hard fact of enormous structural disintegration. Others are only concerned with advancing their own rights, powers and benefits – in the name of the abstract worker, woman, minority ethnic or native – and thus frequently reproduce forms of political process more familiar to the Hitler–Stalin period.

The new vision of social control, the substitute programme, must be an expression of the popular moral critique of *laissez-faire* politics. It must capture the essential *cri de coeur* that we hear daily. This vision, therefore, cannot be a reflection of the 'folk mores' of W.G. Sumner or the household values of Roscoe Pound, of the societal need for assimilation demanded by Park or of the systems-needs described by Parsons, or of the demands of equity articulated by liberal sociology – not even of the radical call for the overhaul of capitalism or patriarchy. It must return the search for co-operation and justice to the actual needs of recalcitrantly independent publics, however diverse and uncomfortable those needs are to progressives. Any new social control movement must, quite simply, be an expression of the views and will of the majority whose needs are currently not being met. In this sense, it will probably be best described as the popular regulation of power – through the expression of popular censure of its current mode of exercise. This mode of social control may be understood as the recovery of a popular common sense that has been swamped by the dogmas of parties, the blinkers of the accountants, and the judgement of the experts. It is a social control that amounts to a recovery of democracy.

Such a social control has as its first axiom not the word assimilation, nor integration, nor limitation, nor revolution, but the word recovery. Its goal is the reconstruction of a social world which once again holds out the potential of becoming a truly global one. This goal is also its method. Process is more important than product. The 'social' needs to be recovered from the predators, opportunists, bullies, dictators and parasites; they have hi-jacked it. At the moment, it is lost and, therefore, all talk of 'new social control' must be put in inverted commas. It is in formation. The social control we are currently talking about, that we now need so badly, is not yet a full social entity. It exists in spirit, at least, because of centuries of subordination, and in some places takes the concrete forms of autonomous power or self-empowerment, but its forms are only partially constructed. Its full recovery as a social entity is, therefore, best described as popular recovery or pre-social reconstruction: essentially, the recovery of social process.

Elsewhere I have argued that the recovery of social process demands a new concept of moral health to replace the concepts of crime and deviance (Sumner, 1990). Crime, as a category, was always limited by the tendency of crime control to amount to a protection of the state and private property, a tendency which inevitably constricted its emancipatory value for the mass of the people. Deviance was always limited by its roots in psychiatric notions of abnormality and in political beliefs of the possibility of moral consensus. Neither any longer helps us to define what is wrong with our world. Crimes of the state and the powerful are as important as those of the powerless, and what is criminal excludes much that is socially unhealthy, harmful or wrong. Current normality is criminal and thus crime stands compromised as a meaningful category. What is defined as deviant by the authorities is often popular, and the crimes and ways of the powerful are often popularly defined as deviant. Psychiatry has little to do with it when power rules over the definitions of popular morality. Current normality is deviant and thus deviance has lost its intelligibility as a descriptor of a type of behaviour. What we need now is a new category to provide the yardstick by which we reconstruct our moral tables as to what is right and wrong, acceptable and unacceptable, appropriate and inappropriate. It seems to me that, for all the difficulties, this category must be a new notion of moral health.

Such a category of moral health must be recaptured from the transcendental debates of the privileged and the mysterious expertise of the doctors. It needs to emerge from the common-sense and moral-political instincts of the disenfranchised publics. We do not need more blueprints from intellectuals – New Age or Stone Age – as to what health is. What we do need is free debate about the many dimensions of moral and social health. This is not a demand for alternative health education, but a call for a new public debate as to exactly what is unhealthy about the many matters which have or have not been defined as criminal and deviant. In the confusion caused by the cynicism, hypocrisy and double-standards of the 1980s, many no longer have any sense of certainty as to what is bad or unhealthy, or in what context. No social world can healthily exist for long in such a nihilistic vacuum.

As all proponents of some form of social control have argued, there has to be some moral binding between the individual and the social, some ties which validate and inspire participation, or else commitment to the social aspect of life must decline. That is what is happening now – there is a clear decline in the social control (as self-regulation) which arises voluntarily when individuals feel bound to social order, institution or process. The destruction or absence of a truly social process leads to a decline in social control. It is a self-fulfilling prophecy. The new conservatives cannot complain of the rise in crime when they have done so much to destroy the social bonding which disinclined people to commit it. They are the ones who are ultimately responsible for the decline of social control and it is our task, ironically, to begin the search for the new forms of communal and political bonding which might begin to stem the tide of disaffiliation from any social involvement. Such a new form of social control must renew voluntary social binding alongside the facilitation of popular critique; its concomitant sociology, therefore, must understand the moral and political critique involved in popular common sense.

Maybe it is time to constitute a new equivalent to Parkian social control which retains its original Rossian sense as a limitation on arbitrary power and the irrationality of the purely economic. This would not be so much a class-based, welfare movement as a broad-based overhaul of establishment values (or valuelessness); not a 'social' as opposed to a 'natural' control and not a 'control' as opposed to a spontaneous unification, but rather a concept more appropriate to our hyper-individualistic, socially conscious age of anti-imperialism; a concept of the need for mutual self-empowerment in conditions of peace, emotional interconnection and economy ruled by friendship; a world where censure was a last resort and only destruction, violence and unwanted domination would be censured. Only under such conditions could we constitute ourselves socially as amiable, reflexive, intelligent, creatures devoted to the common good – as truly social beings.

# 7

# Unsolved Mysteries and Unforeseen Futures of Social Control

*Roberto Bergalli*

Broaching the subject of social control at the end of the millennium is by no means an easy task. And this task becomes even more complex if one tries to approach it from a multidisciplinary angle, which, given the innumerable contributions that have been made this century, is the most comprehensive way of dealing with it. However, I believe that my modest contribution could limit itself to those aspects which allow one to prolong a discussion about the way the concept of social control is used, at the same time trying to apply some of the analyses made both previously and here by the rest of the contributors to this volume.

Bearing in mind the ideological origins of this concept (see Bergalli, 1980, 1989) and the instrumental uses which have been made of it (Bergalli, 1993), and which I have taken the liberty of pointing out, I am going to leave out all matters referring to its application in specific disciplinary fields. Nevertheless, I should make it clear that in spite of the effort involved in designating it a critical and emancipating potential, which would completely counteract the conservative political undertone which the concept has hanging over it (see Malinowsky and Münch, 1975: 2), it is not possible to ignore its intrinsically ideological nature.

The detailed analysis which Melossi (1990) made suffices to make the disciplinary transition undergone by the concept of social control quite clear although, as Hess did (1983b), it is still worth pointing out its deep anthropological roots. Initially used within the framework of general sociology, it later played an important role in the emerging social psychology of the Chicago School. Immediately afterwards it was included within the systemic Parsonian vision, from where it was established as a central but vague category in any subsequent functionalist analysis. However, it was Melossi himself who recovered it for political and legal philosophy, trying to connect it to those levels of analysis which allow the lack of ingenuity of the concept to be understood when examined in the light of specific projects of political domination.

Seen from this ample and cross-disciplinary perspective, social control undoubtedly becomes a vital element of political debate and, as a result, I believe that it is in this field – the political field – where proposals for the future, together with the possibilities of making semantic use of the concept, should be made. This does not only not exclude but even *obliges* us to reinterpret the term scientifically, which is in fact the moving force behind this book.

## A global perspective

There is something which I am sure everyone agrees upon when the discussion on social control enters into a political key, and that something is the lack of ingenuity in the way the concept is used as a tool to maintain a specific social order.

It may well be true that when Ross used the concept for the first time in his attempt to explain social organization he was not thinking within an explicitly defined model of society. Nevertheless, another early exponent of the concept, as again observed by Melossi (1990: 114), developed the idea of how to build democratic society upon free communication and the recognition of the diversity of the individuals and groups which comprise it (Cooley, 1983: 154, quoted by Melossi, 1990). The social model became evident when the first Chicagoans began to talk about social control; their first searches to find contact points between an individual and his or her surroundings underlined the need to harmonize these two spheres which, up until that time, had not received adequate attention. Along these lines, the work carried out by Mead (especially 1925) was obviously precursory, and the later symbolic interactionism built a way of thinking that was capable of penetrating the network of relationships between individuals and society, which are vital when outlining a model of the latter. The tensions and conflicts revealed during the period of so-called 'social disorganization' had to be analysed first and controlled afterwards, without reducing or restricting the democratic spirit which was behind industrial society in a period of uncontrollable growth. However, at the same time it was also vital to maintain and extol the individualism which the fabric of society was supported by – more so if this individualism contained a strong sense of valorization of a new subjectivity, researched in depth by the first social psychologists and criminal sociologists. And yet it limited the resurgence of true historical subjects which were going to be the main players of the period dawning upon North American society. Against this backdrop of sociological knowledge development, social control acted as a clearly limiting element to the efforts of ethnic and social integration of the many waves of immigration.

However much this model of democratic but individualistic society had a firm footing in the United States, it was not until later that it received its consolidation and expansion through the systemic vision of Talcott Parsons (1951). The Parsonian social system was founded upon a basic, but very strong idea of social control, combining psycho-sociological demands of a Freudian nature with political and legal characteristics.

*The contribution which the legal and normative world has made to social control*
The political and legal characteristics which Parsons (1962) gave to the concept of social control provided the necessary impulse for the world of legal culture to accept it. So, even though Durkheim had not been indifferent to the idea of the law as the main tool of social organization, it was only with the complete entrance of functionalist sociology into the legal universe that law became systematically regarded as a vital part of social control (see Luhmann, 1972: II).

Afterwards, this idea was extended to other legal fields and hence in criminal law, for example, it is quite normal to find in Europe the idea that punitive intervention satisfies an important function of social control that is vital for organizing democratic society. This has become evident both in legal theory (for example, Jakobs, 1991), and in the fields of politics and criminal justice studies which are a lot more sensitive to contact with sociological knowledge (see, for example, Hassemer, 1973, in Germany or Muñoz Conde, 1985, in Spain). At the present time, when dealing with any functionalist approach, it seems impossible to advance any hypothesis about using the penal system without taking into account its supposed ability to solve conflicts, which means that it can be identified as a mechanism of social control.

But this ability is completely false, as has been shown by research within what has been called 'critical' criminology. Some tendencies of critical criminology, especially the Scandinavian and Dutch abolitionist movements, foster the idea of substituting the penal system, together with the punitive ideology which supports it, because they claim that this system not only expropriates the ability which the perpetrators themselves have of solving the conflicts, but also worsens the repercussions. Other currents of thought, without moving away from criminal law although recovering its ability to guarantee the fundamental rights of those people affected by punitive intervention, try to re-channel punitive intervention within the limits of a state with a rule of law. But even in this case, as I said previously, the idea of social control as being something essential to criminal law disappears, or at least moves down to a lower plane.

Why has the tradition of understanding criminal law as a mechanism of social control been so abruptly interrupted? Some reasons can be found. I am going to refer to two here, two which Pavarini (Chapter 4 in this volume) mentions: the first relates to social control as a sociological question; and the second to social control as a political question.

## Social control as a sociological question: deviant behaviour

I completely agree with Pavarini in the sense that if we consider social control as a sociological category then it should be interpreted from paradigms or viewpoints such as: the motivation behind the action, social integration and socialization. All these points of view can be recognized in a consensual type of society and, as a result, a person who does not subject him or herself to social order receives the label 'deviant'. And so deviation is seen as something negative.

This consideration reflects the great functionalist tradition, in the heart of which the sociology of deviation was elaborated. The theory of deviant behaviour which is rooted in the vision which Durkheim had of the social order (which is based on normative consensus and the social division of labour) represented the triumph of a dominant culture because it had within its grasp the power to impose values and norms. A culture which, thanks to the Allied victory in the Second World War, expanded from the United States to Europe and then, in virtue of the hegemony established in different world markets, on to other continents.

According to Pavarini, the negative meaning which was given to the word deviation meant a denial of 'alterity' and, with this denial, a return to the consideration that someone who shows this sort of behaviour is in some way suffering from pathology.

This vision of what is deviant remained intact for several decades and was the axis of much social, psychiatric and medical treatment carried out to help those 'deviants' who had least or who were suffering. Basically it was what legitimized the welfare state to use all of its interventionist techniques in favour of the needy and the suffering.

But criminal behaviour was also considered as deviant behaviour, and the normative value of this assimilation was perhaps what legitimized, to a great extent, both the origin and strength of sociological criminology. Even when Durkheim removed this category of 'pathology' from sociological vocabulary, it still remained firmly rooted within the treatment of criminal behaviour, especially in institutional circles. So, with the sociology of deviant behaviour, all the 'ghosts' of criminological positivism were reborn with renewed strength.

However, this is not all. Sumner (1990 and 1994) gave a very complete description of the implications involved in the sociology of deviance. He maintained that any form of labelling as deviant is really just a modern type of censure, a form of moral and political judgement; that is, that the recognition of a discipline's ability to transfer its knowledge content from the supposed scientific objectivity with which it is studied to the field of moral evaluation converts this discipline into an ideology. And this is in fact what both criminology and the sociology of deviance have done. If we consider the possibility of building a sociology of social censure, that is, an analysis which regards crime and social deviation as mere extensions or reflections of the systematic, intellectualized or false conscience of group interests, then it will also be possible to remove the deviant labels from the far-reaching fields of knowledge, power and meaning which criminology and the sociology of deviance were useful for.

If we accept this radical way in which Sumner questions the sociology of deviant behaviour, then all the theories which recent authors have put forward about the study of social control are debatable; especially those which use the paradigm of the reaction to deviation (such as Clark and Gibbs, 1965), although there are also some who attempted a redefinition even within the same paradigm (such as Black, 1984, or Horwitz, 1990). With regard to these latter authors, it is precisely Scheerer and Hess, Chapter 5 in this volume, who attempt to underline the inefficiency of continuing to analyse social control by basing oneself exclusively on its reactive qualities.

## Social control as a political question: the role of deviation

Pavarini (1993) still says that the consideration of social control as a political question supposes the imposition, transformation or conservation of a specific social order. In order to understand the concept of social control in this way, it is necessary to bear in mind some of the categories of political or legal science such as: power, control, state, law, repression, authority. And this has to be so, because the substratum upon which one attempts to build social order takes for granted that there exists a network of conflict within which each group or class is struggling to protect its own interests.

Within this framework, deviant behaviour has to be understood in a positive light. The recognition of its alterity confers upon the person with deviant behaviour an ability which he or she was previously unknown to have, since, once the potential of this behaviour is admitted, one accepts at the same time the idea that, in reality, the reiteration of this behaviour is not so much a challenge to social values, but rather proof that these values are no longer truly values. In this case, the deviant person is someone who brings innovations and who can become an agent of transformation – that is, he or she becomes a political actor, and may even be revolutionary.

So, as has been argued earlier, the role which deviant behaviour plays in the perspective of observing social control in a political manner is of extreme importance. This is because not only does the concept of social control have its apparent neutrality removed, but also, in certain social contexts, it can play a mobilizing or even destabilizing role.

It is clear that however acceptable the suggestive reflections of Pavarini may be, it will be difficult, the way things are today, for them to receive full recognition. At the end of the 1960s, this interpretation of deviant behaviour was the standard bearer of the critical criminology movement emerging at that time, and during the 1970s its founders raised it as a flag of the vindications which they sought.

I am sure all of you have in mind the first meetings of the National Deviancy Conference composed of radical British sociologists, and the repercussions which these meetings had upon the community of all the criminologists who had a share in their original proposals; these repercussions were felt across Europe and coincided with those that were coming from California. A similar situation arose with the European Group for the Study of Deviance and Social Control, which still meets but which is convinced now that the semantic message of the concepts of deviant behaviour and social control have another content. The translations of works by these British sociologists became guidebooks in countries in Latin America where even now the belief exists that critical criminology is still that which was proposed in the 1970s; there is little difference with what is happening in Spain, although there the reasons why this situation persists are slightly different. In this matter, it is true that many Europeans are responsible for not having explained in good time how great a transformation European criminological thought was undergoing, especially in the UK.

As a result, these are some of the difficulties which I believe the reflections of Pavarini, which I mentioned earlier, present. But I will discuss them in more detail later on. First, I should like to say that Sumner would not accept these reflections either, since, as has already been seen, he completely rejected any use of the sociological category of deviant behaviour because of all the ideology which it had hanging over it. In fact, he has recently described it as:

> One thing that has not lost its roots. It is a censure of unintegrated or unintegrable social fragments that are perceived as a threat to the unity (or desired unity) of the social whole – a censure precipitated and recurrently activated by cultural conflicts following major labour migrations in societies aspiring to social democracy. (Sumner, 1994: 34)

So he also rejects the idea because of its bias against social heterogeneity and, as a result, for its political leaning towards traditionalism. Here I should like to point out the way in which Sumner and Melossi's analyses coincide on the role played by the sociology of deviance during, the American social-democratic period. The somewhat clinical tone which the concept of social deviation obtained in North American society (see Sumner, 1994: 135), replacing the remains of a theory of degeneration, inspired the combination of a fear of what is different (and of crime) with the appreciation of cultural conflict in a multicultural society. Obviously the catalytic role in the social conscience played by the category of deviation meant at the same time a task of homogenization around the values and norms which organized the welfare state and also the legitimization of state intervention both in social and in other fields.

The building of a strong state based upon the idea of social-democracy allowed the expansion of an internal consensus which, together with the leadership position which the United States had reached after the Second World War at an international level, gave the state a capacity of control which until then had been completely unheard of in the modern age.

But the international economic order which was established and which was based upon this position of leadership did not just bring to Europe the fashions, customs and values which had been built up during an era of full employment and growing consumption, it also brought with it a set of theories and models of social research. The Marshall Plan helped to rebuild the productive capacity of many European countries, but at the same time the financial resources necessary to get academic activity and scientific research going were supplied to universities by large American foundations. This enabled direct flow and continual contact between American and European scholars. It seemed natural, therefore, that structural-functionalism, as a way of considering society, should immediately be adopted by renewed European social science; it was just as logical that the construction of democratic welfare states should be carried out from a social-democratic perspective which, based upon important agreements (between trade unions, businessmen and politicians) also needed a concentrated effort at consensus. This was how, in a very similar way to what happened in the United States, the category of deviation not only enabled Europe to rethink criminology but also enabled other social sciences, which until that moment had been very distant, to begin a process of coming together. Pitch (1975) gave a very precise explanation of this process and of the expansion of the idea of deviant behaviour in a piece of work that became a classic, not only in Italy but also in the Spanish-speaking world.

So the welfare culture grew considerably in Europe after 1950. First with the experience of the Scandinavian countries but later with what became known as social constitutionalism – which was developed by the Constitutions of the Repubblica Italiana (1948) and the Bundesrepublik Deutschland (1949), and then much later by the Constitution of the Reino de España (1978). This enabled the widening of the social-democratic regime. In this way, social policies became a constant worry for European governments and the temptation to achieve a more equal society consolidated this regime even more (see Ashford, 1979).

The results of all this process on the strategies of social control were obviously 'anti-institutionalizing'. A 'soft' approach was used when dealing with deviant behaviour and especially with crime. The phenomenon of de-institutionalization and territorialization of control, even penal control, was moved to all those fields where deviation had been 'trapped'. It was undoubtedly Foucault who best foresaw this cycle and in three of his most important works, *Madness and Civilization, The Birth of the Clinic* and *Discipline and Punish*, it is possible to see the guiding line which was to unleash this process.

But what this 'freedom' of control did was transfer to 'free' society a mythology. The recognition of deviation and crime as normal phenomena did not come about through approval. It was more the mass media, thanks to amazing technological progress, which substituted for traditional agencies of social control, creating an expansive and broad society. It was through the mass media that the social construction of problems became notably accelerated. Deviant behaviour and crime acquired the status of 'daily myths', upon which everything bad in post-industrial society was loaded. As a result, control over specific groups of individuals created a new social divide and it was against this backdrop, and as a result of the trauma which the first oil crisis of 1973 caused to the capitalist system, that the fall of the welfare state began.

### Now that the welfare culture has disappeared, what is social control and how is it to be carried out?

The second half of the 1970s and the whole of the 1980s witnessed a pulverization of social policies. The empire of 'market forces' made unsustainable progress through the emergence of Reaganomics and the 'exemplary' hardness of Thatcherism. The results of the combination of these two essential dimensions of neo-liberalism can be seen clearly, and little need be added about the deliberate abandoning of all social policies in favour of financial-monetarist policies. The establishment of a dual society, with a great polarization of wealth and an extreme dissemination of misery, is no longer just something which exists in Third World countries; it exists in those same societies which are at the centre of capitalism, starting with the United States.

So the important attempt which social-democracy had made during the 40 vigorous years after the Second World War, to try and balance the 'natural' imbalances of capitalism, has been brought to nothing. And together with this, the end of the Cold War and the fall of the Berlin Wall, which also meant the downfall of the Soviet-Stalinist empire, has given strength to the idea of creating a single world market. In this situation, the globalization of the economy as an attempt at rebuilding capitalism is something which is ideal for the strongest centres of the system, particularly Europe and the United States, to control. 'Realism', as palpable evidence of the new situation, has begun to dominate ideologies and the announced 'end of history' – which some people hurriedly proclaimed – is going to be the last and short-lived moment of true world hegemony.

What this brief period of neo-liberal euphoria was truly like can now be seen. Rather than an exhaustion of ideas, what we really saw during this period was the exaltation of one single ideology. The obvious structural weakness of those countries who freed themselves from the Stalinist yoke has left impoverished masses of population clinging to ancient nationalisms which have produced a tidal wave of irrationality and violence. Historical ethnic intolerance is changing the map of Europe both in the Balkans and the Urals, and is even being felt quite severely in Western Europe. On the other hand, the so-called German reunification (which perhaps would be better called *Anschluss* or reconnection) has meant that the 'engine' of Europe has slowed down the process of European unification and has generated a series of negative repercussions in the rest of Germany's European 'partners'.

The Presidential change in the United States, on the other hand, is having to deal with the legacy of the conflicts which the military-industrial complex had encouraged in different parts of the world. The strategic transformation which became clear with the Gulf War underlined how the force of weapons and the will to intervene can produce a boomerang effect on the capacity of authority and control. But not only this, when facing the failure of military efficiency, we have reached the limit of the manipulative strength of international bodies (UN, NATO) – something which is having serious repercussions on the very theory or principle of international law. These are basically the principles of what has come to be known as an 'international community', based upon the respect for state sovereignty and the fundamental rights of citizens, which is precisely what is being questioned right now.

The situation which I have just described has given final judgement on the end of the Welfare Age. Especially in the United States at the moment, there is a great deal of tension between those forces which want to carry on privileging the use of the financial markets and others which have comprehended the need to strengthen social policies once again. Evidence of this tension can be seen in the way President Clinton is attempting to introduce a new Public Health Law which would oblige the Federal government to assume the protection of public health. Undoubtedly the struggle to get Congress to accept NAFTA is another illustration of how in US domestic policy, the interests of those people who want to open up the labour market and those who are still hanging on to the profits of financial enterprise are firmly opposed.

### Is the sociology of social control still valid? Unsolved mysteries?

The conditions of helplessness which millions of people, even in Europe and the United States, are living in and the situation of violence, death and environmental aggression which affects almost all the inhabitants of the Third World make it impossible for sociologists and criminologists to carry on using the categories of social control and deviant behaviour which were used to elaborate a sociology of social control during the years of social-democratic exaltation. Given the situation at the moment, it stands to reason that studies on social control are not going to undergo the 'real explosion' of vitality which occurred in the 1930s (Melossi, 1990: 138, n. 1).

If it is true that during this period, United States policy found the intellectual tool in the concept of social control to achieve social cohesion (see Melossi, ibid.: 116), then it would be worth asking ourselves now about the validity of a sociology which researches into the efficiency of control mechanisms to regulate the actual situation of atomization and fragmentation which contemporary society is going through at the moment.

What Lyotard (1984) said about the 'great narrations' being characteristic of postmodern society seems true. And it seems that the 'great narration' of social control, which was the central axis of functionalist and interactionist sociology, no longer possesses the ability to explain those processes which are needed to maintain the cohesion and social solidarity that was reached during their reign. It would seem, therefore, that sociology is going to have to be orientated towards searching for other ways of avoiding chaos and disintegration.

As Sumner (1994) showed, the sociology of deviance emerged in the twentieth century as a liberal version of criminology and as part of a sociology of social control. During the 1929–30 crisis, the social phenomena of unemployment, mental disturbance and crime could be dealt with by social administration, that is, those interventions of social policy which characterized social democracy. The wide consensus which allowed a New Deal to be established, and its positive results, meant that through this policy a social differentiation could be carried out. Therefore, the concept of deviant behaviour was absolutely functional to the political organization of society and, for that reason, it became a partner par excellence of social control.

Nowadays, however, when it seems to be more and more difficult to obtain consensus and when social conflict is becoming more and more acute, the forms of exercising social control are becoming less efficient and more merciless. The term 'deviation' is no longer a useful partner, since as unemployment grows, with mental disturbance and crime, to almost exasperating limits, it would hardly seem reasonable to carry on calling deviant a type of behaviour which is becoming more and more generalized. Apart from the uselessness of the concept, it is also well worth bearing in mind the severe criticism which Sumner (1990) makes of it when he points out its profound ideological content.

## The unforeseen future

To be quite honest, there is no clear path to follow in order to obtain a recomposition of the actual incapacity of sociology and criminology. I find it unacceptable to carry on thinking about reactive means of control since if, as Hess (1986) maintained, both the formal and the informal reactions are going to carry on down the expansive, technocratic and violent path which he indicates for them, then very little can be expected from a social control which is based upon these traditional forms. Similarly, it is enough simply to look at the 'industry of crime control' to understand the worrying development of the criminal justice system in the United States (see Christie, 1993a), and for there to be a profound rejection of any use of reactive social control as a general panacea.

However, there does remain the possibility of carrying on talking about the active forms of social control. Here, undoubtedly, the debate has to be situated within the widest possible framework of discussion of the democratic forms of social life. If mass mediation and the forms of political representation are putting in evidence the most abject corruption, then perhaps the time has come to rethink democracy, and to do this we have in our hands the new expressions of a political subjectivity which was unheard of 50 years ago. The feminist movement, the recognition of minorities and, in general, all those social movements which have unsatisfied demands, possess an initiative which can regenerate the basis of democracy.

The different crises which contemporary society has gone through – crises of rationality, legitimation and motivation (see Habermas, 1979) – have left the social world without any impulses or motivations upon which to base the individual–society link. The phenomena of fractured community and exacerbated individualism which are the basis of current social behaviour incline people to retract any personal effort towards adaptation to situations of economic need.

With this very pessimistic outlook towards the future, it is vital to encourage a new sociological imagination which would allow us to substitute the sociology of social control with a sociology of social justice and democracy.

# References

Adorno, T.W., Frenkel-Brunswick, E., Levinson, D.J. and Sanford, R.J. (1950). *The Authoritarian Personality*. London: Norton.

Ahire, P.T. (1991). *Imperial Policing: The Emergence and Role of the Police in Colonial Nigeria 1860–1960*. Milton Keynes: Open University Press.

Ajmone, T. (1992). 'Un'osservatorio sulla sicurezza a Modena', *Sicurezza e Territorio*, 2: 29–32.

Ajmone, T. and Pavarini, M. (1992). 'Azioni di prevenzione nel quartiere Reno', *Sicurezza e Territorio*, 4: 7–10.

Alvazzi de Frate, A., Zvekic, U. and Van Dijk, J.J.M. (1993). *Understanding Crime: Experiences of Crime and Crime Control*. Rome: UNICRI.

Arroyo Zapatero, L. (1981). 'La reforma de los delitos de rebelión y de terrorismo por la LO 2/1981, de 4 de mayo', *Cuadernos de Política Criminal*, 15: 379–404.

Ashford, D.E. (1979). *The Emergence of the Welfare State*. Oxford: Basil Blackwell.

Austin, J.L. (1955). *How to Do Things with Words*. Cambridge, MA: Harvard University Press.

Balkin, S. (1979). 'Victimisation rates, safety and fear of crime', *Social Problems*, 26 (3): 343–7.

Baratta, A. (1984). 'La teoria della prevenzione-integrazione: Una "nuova" fondazione della pena all'interno della teoria sistemica', *Dei Delitti e Delle Pene*, 1: 5–30.

Baratta, A. (1985a). 'Vecchie e nuove strategie nella legittimazione del diritto penale', *Dei Delitti e Delle Pene*, 2: 247–68.

Baratta, A. (1985b). 'Principi di diritto penale minimo: Per una teoria dei diritti umani come oggetti e limiti della legge penale', *Dei Delitti e Delle Pene*, 3: 443–73.

Baratta, A. (1993). 'I nuovi orizzonti della prevenzione', *Sicurezza e Territorio*, 2: 9–14.

Basaglia, F. and Basaglia-Ongaro, F. (1974). *La maggioranza deviante: l'ideologia del controllo sociale*. Milan: Einaudi.

Baudrillard, J. (1991). *La Guerre du Golfe n'a pas eu Lieu*. Paris: Editions Galiée.

Beaumont, G. and Tocqueville, A. (1833). *On the Penitentiary System of the United States and its Application in France*. Philadelphia: Carey, Lea and Blanchard.

Beck, U. (1994). 'The debate on the "Individualization Theory" in today's sociology in Germany', *Soziologie*, 3: 191–200.

Bell, D. (1960). *The End of Ideology*. New York: Free Press.

Bell, D. (1973). *The Coming of Post-Industrial Society*. New York: Basic Books.

Bentley, A.F. (1908). *The Process of Government*. Cambridge, MA: Harvard University Press.

Bergalli, R. (1980). 'La ideología del control social tradicional', *Doctrina Penal*, 3: 805–18. Also 'L'ideologia del controllo sociale tradizionale', *Sociologia del Diritto*, VII-3, 57–69.

Bergalli, R. (1982). 'Hacia una criminología de la liberación para América Latina', in *Crítica a la Criminología*. Bogotá: Temis, 173–92.

Bergalli, R. (1983). 'América Latina: nuevos caminos críticos', in R. Bergalli, J. Bustos Ramírez and T. Miralles (eds), *El pensamiento criminológico: un análisis crítico*. Barcelona: Peninsula, Bogotá: Temis.

Bergalli, R. (1984). 'Sentido y contenido de una sociología del control penal para América Latina', in *Criminología Crítica I. Seminario*. Medellín, Colombia: Universidad de Medellín.

Bergalli, R. (1989). 'Introducción' (España), in R. Bergalli and E.E. Mari (eds), *Historia Ideológica del Control Social ( España Argentina, Siglos XIX–XX)*. Barcelona: Colec.

Bergalli, R. (1991). 'El sistema penal español como el ámbito menos conocido del control social', *Doctrina Penal*, 55–6: 403–20.

Bergalli, R. (1993). 'Orígines conceptuales y usos instrumentales del concepto de control social', *Revista de Derecho Penal y Criminología*, 2: 173–84.

Bergalli, R. and Mari, E.E. (eds) (1989). *Historia ideológica del control social*. Barcelona: PPU.

Bianchi, J. (1996). 'Pitfalls and strategies of abolition', in H. Bianchi and R. van Swaaningen (eds), *Abolition: Towards a Non-Repressive Approach to Crime*. Amsterdam: Free University Press.

Birkbeck, C. and Martínez Rincones, F. (1992). *La criminología en América Latina: balance y perspectivas*. Mérida, Venezuela: Universidad de Los Andes.

Black, D. (1976). *The Behavior of Law*. New York: Academic Press.

Black, D. (ed.) (1984). *Toward a General Theory of Social Control*. 2 vols. New York: Academic.

Blomberg, T.G. (1987). 'Criminal justice reform and social control: Are we becoming a minimum security society?', in J. Lowman, R.J. Menzies and T.S. Palys (eds), *Transcarceration: Essays in the Sociology of Social Control*. Aldershot: Gower.

Bone, S. (1989). *Safety and security in housing design: A guide for action*. London: Royal Institute of British Architects.

Box, S. (1981 (1971)). *Deviance, Reality and Society*. London: Holt, Rinehart and Winston. (2 edns).

Braithwaite, J. (1989). *Crime, Shame and Reintegration*. Cambridge: Cambridge University Press.

Bricola, F. (1973). 'La teoria generale del reato', *Muovissimo Digesto Italiano*, XIX: 47–137.

Brodeur, J.-P. (1993). 'La pensée postmoderne e la criminologie', *La Criminologie*, XXVI: 73–121.

Broom, L. and Selznick, P. (1955). *Sociology*. New York: Harper and Row.

Brown, J. (1990). *Insecure Societies*. London: Macmillan.

Bueno Arús, F. (1986). 'Principios generales de la legislación antiterrorista', *Revista de la Facultad de Derecho de las Universidad Complutense*, 11: 135–66.

Bustos Ramírez, J. (1987). 'Criminología crítica y derecho penal', in J. Bustos (ed.), *Control social y sistema penal*. Barcelona: PPU.

Cain, M. (1989). *Growing Up Good: Policing the Behaviour of Girls in Europe*. London: Sage.

Campbell, C. (1987). *The Romantic Ethic and the Spirit of Modern Consumerism*. Oxford: Basil Blackwell.

Cappetti, C. (1993). *Writing Chicago: Modernism, Ethnography, and the Novel*. New York: Columbia University Press.

Cardoso, F.H. (1976). *Ideologías de la burguesia industrial en sociedades dependientes*

*(Argentina y Brasil)*. Mexico: Siglo Veintiuno. (5th edn).

CEPAL-ONU (1994). *Informe anual: balance preliminar de la economía de América Latina y el Caribe*. Quoted in *El Pais*, 23 December 1994.

Christie, N. (1981). *Limits to Pain*. Oslo: Universtetsforlaget.

Christie, N. (1993a). *Crime Control as Industry: Towards GULAGS, Western Style?* Oslo: Universitetsforlaget.

Christie, N. (1993b). *La industria del control del delito: La nueva forma del Holocausto?* Buenos Aires: Editores del Puerto.

Chunn, D.E. and Gavigan, S.A.M. (1988). 'Social control: analytic tool or analytic quagmire?' *Contemporary Crises*, 12: 107–24.

Clark, A. and Gibbs, J. (1965). 'Social control: a reformulation', *Social Problems*, 12: 398–415.

Clark, R.P. (1990), *Negotiating with ETA: Obstacles to Peace in the Basque Country, 1975–88*. Reno, NV: University of Nevada Press.

Cohen, S. (1973). *Folk Devils and Moral Panics*. St. Albans: Paladin.

Cohen, S. (1985). *Visions of Social Control*. Cambridge: Polity Press.

Cohen, S. (1990). *Intellectual Scepticism and Political Commitment: The Case of Radical Criminology*. Amsterdam: Stichting W.A. Bonger Lezingen.

Cohen, S. (1994). 'Soziale Kontrolle und die Politik der Rekonstruktion', in D. Frehsee, G. Löschper and K.F. Schumann (eds), *Srafecht, soziale Kontrolle, soziale Disziplinerierung*. Opladen: Westdeutscher Verlag.

Cohen, S. and Scull, A. (eds) (1983). *Social Control and the State*. Oxford: Martin Robertson.

Cohn-Bendit, D. and Schmid, T. (1994 (1992, *Heimat Babylon*)). *Patria Babilonia: la sfida della democrazia multiculturale*. Rome: Theoria.

Conklin, J.E. (1975). *The Impact of Crime*. New York: Macmillan.

Cooley, C.H. (1983 (1909)). *Social Organization: A Study of the Larger Mind*. New Brunswick, NJ: Transaction Books.

Cooper, B. (1989). *The Management and Prevention of Juvenile Crime Problems*. London: Home Office, Crime Prevention Unit.

Coser, L.A. (1974). *Greedy Institutions*. New York: Free Press.

Coser, L.A. (1982). 'The notion of control in sociological theory', in J.P. Gibbs (ed.), *Social Control: Views from the Social Sciences*. Beverly Hills, CA: Sage.

Council of Europe (1987). *Urban Violence and Insecurity: The Role of Local Politics*. Strasbourg: Council of Europe, Standing Conference of Local and Regional Authorities of Europe.

Council of Europe (1989). *Local Strategies for the Reduction of Urban Insecurity in Europe: Proceedings of the International Conference at Barcelona, 17–20 November 1987*. Strasbourg: Council of Europe, Standing Conference of Local and Regional Authorities of Europe.

Council of Europe (1990). *Bulletin d'information pénitentiaire*. Strasbourg: Council of Europe.

Cox, A. (1986). 'First Amendment', *Society*, 24 (1): 8-15.

Creazzo, G. (1994). '"Nouva prevenzione": vivere una citta sicura', *Sicurezza e Territorio*, 13: 27–30.

Croce, B. (1956 (1925)). *Etica e politica*. Bari: Laterza.

Cuber, J.F. (1940). 'Some aspects of institutional disorganization', *American Sociological Review*, 5: 483–8.

Davis, M. (1990). *City of Quartz: Excavating the Future in Los Angeles*. London: Verso Books.

Davis, M. (1993). *La Città di Quarzo: indagine sul futuro a Los Angeles.* Rome: Manifestolibri.

de Benoist, A. (1993–4 (1991)). 'The Idea of Empire', *Telos*, 98–9: 81–98.

de Castro, L.A. (1981). *Conocimiento y orden social: criminología como legitimación y criminología de la liberación.* Maracaibo, Venezuela: Instituto de Criminología, Universidad del Zulia.

de Castro, L.A. (ed.) (1990). *Criminología en América Latina.* Rome: UNICRI.

de Leo, G. (1986). 'Il crimine come problema e la sua spiegazione: nuovo realismo e doltre', *Dei Delitti e Delle Pene*, 3: 453–68.

de Otto, I. (1987). *Derecho constitucional: sistema de fuentes.* Barcelona: Ariel.

Deegan, M.J. (1988). *Jane Addams and the Men of the Chicago School, 1892–1918.* New Brunswick, NJ: Transaction Books.

del Olmo, R. (1987). 'Criminología y derecho penal: aspectos gnoseológicos de una relación necesaria en la América Latina actual', *Doctrina Penal*, 10: 23–43.

Deleuze, G. (1990). 'Das elektronische Halsband: Innenansicht der kontrollen Gesellschaft', *Neue Rundschau*, 4: 5–10.

Della Porta, D. (1992). *Lo scambio occulto: casi di corruzione politica in Italia.* Bologna: Il Mulino.

Delmas-Marty, M. (1985). 'L'enjeu d'un code penal, reflexions à propos de l'inflation de lois penales in France', *Melanges Legros*, 165–84.

Dershowitz, A. (1976). *Fair and Certain Punishment.* New York: McGraw-Hill.

Downes, D. (1988). *Contrast in Tolerance: PostWar Penal Policy in Netherlands and England and Wales.* Oxford: Clarendon Press.

DOXA (1992). 'La percezione della delinquenza', *Bollettino Della Doxa*, 19–20: 216–47.

Dumm, T. (1987). *Democracy and Punishment: Disciplinary Origins of the United States.* Madison, WI: University of Wisconsin Press.

Duprez, D. (1991). 'De l'anomie de la gestion social aux représentations de l'insécurité', *Deviance et Société*, 15 (3): 275–92.

Durkheim, E. (1964 (1893)). *The Division of Labour in Society.* New York: Free Press.

Durkheim, E. (1938 (1895)). *The Rules of Sociological Method.* New York: Free Press.

Elias, N. (1987). 'The retreat of sociologists into the present', *Theory, Culture and Society*, 4 (2/3): 223–48.

Erikson, K.T. (1966). *Wayward Puritans.* New York: John Wiley and Sons.

Espinosa, E.L. d. (1980). 'Social and legal order in sociological functionalism', *Contemporary Crises*, 4: 43–76.

Espinosa, E.L. d. (1989). *Delitos sin víctimas: orden social y ambivalencia moral.* Madrid: Alianza Universidad.

Etzioni, A. (1992). 'Communitarian solutions – what communitarians think', *Journal of State Government*, 65 (1): 9–11.

Eurisko (1993). *Ciò che fa più paura agli Italiani, Indagine condotto per conto dell' osservatorio permanente sulla comunicazione.* Rome: Ministero dell'Interno.

Evans, E.P. (1987). *The Criminal Prosecution and Capital Punishment of Animals.* London: Faber and Faber.

Ewen, S. (1976). *Captains of Consciousness: Advertising and the Social Roots of the Consumer Culture.* New York: McGraw-Hill.

Fanon, F. (1967). *The Wretched of the Earth.* Harmondsworth: Penguin.

Farrington, D.P. (1989). *Implications of Criminal Career Research for the Prevention of Offending.* Cambridge: Institute of Criminology, University of Cambridge.

Feeley, M. and Simon, J. (1992). 'The New Penology: Notes on the emerging strategy of corrections and its applications', *Criminology,* 4: 449–74.

Felson, M. (1994). *Crime and Everyday Life.* Thousand Oaks, CA: Pine Forge Press.

Fernández Calvet, J. (1986). *Terra Lliure 1979–85.* Barcelona: El Llamp.

Ferrajoli, L. (1985). 'Il diritto penale minimo', *Dei Delitti e Delle Pene,* 3: 493–524.

Ferrajoli, L. (1989). *Diritto e ragione: teoria del garantismo penale.* Naples: Laterza.

Ferrajoli, L. (1994). 'Il diritto penale minimo: Un programma', *Il Manifesto,* 20 February.

Findlay, J., Bright, J. and Kevin, G. (1990). *Youth Crime Prevention: A Handbook of Good Practice.* Swindon: Crime Concern.

Fish, S. (1994). *'There's No Such Thing as Free Speech . . . and It's a Good Thing Too.* New York: Oxford University Press..

Foucault, M. (1978 (1976)). *The History of Sexuality, Vol. 1.* New York: Random House.

Foucault, M. (1977 (1975)). *Discipline and Punish: The Birth of the Prison.* Trans. A. Sheridan. London/New York: Allen Lane/Pantheon.

Freud, S. (1955 (1921)). *Group Psychology and the Analysis of the Ego.* In *The Standard Edition,* vol. 18. London: Hogarth.

Fries, S.D. (1973). 'Staatstheorie and the New American Science of Politics', *Journal of the History of Ideas,* 34: 391–404.

Fuller, R.C. (1942). 'Morals and the criminal law', *Journal of Criminal Law and Criminology,* 32: 624–30.

Fuller, R.C. and Myers, R.R. (1942). 'Some aspects of a theory of social problems', *American Sociological Review,* 6: 24–32.

Galbraith, J.K. (1985). *The New Industrial State.* 4th edn. New York: Houghton Mifflin.

Gambetta, D. (1992). *La Mafia Siciliana: un'industria della protezione privata.* Turin: Einaudi.

García, San Pedro, J. (1993). *Terrorismo: Aspectos criminológicos y legales.* Madrid: Centro de Estudios Judiciales, Ministerio de Justicia.

García Valdés, C. (1991). 'La represión de la delincuencia terrorista en el ordenamiento jurídico vigente y en el Anteproyecto de Código Penal de 1992,' unpublished paper, *El IV Seminario Duque de Ahumada,* Aranjuez-Madrid.

Garland, D. (1990). *Punishment and Modern Society.* Oxford: Clarendon Press.

Gatti, U., Fossa, G., Marugo, M.I. and Materazzi, V. (1991). 'Le inchieste di vittimizzazione: problemi metodologici e primi risultati di uno studio-pilota condotto nella città di Genova', *Rassegna Italiana di Criminologia,* 2 (4): 363–85.

Geertz, C. (1973). *The Interpretation of Cultures.* New York: Basic Books.

Gehlen, A. (1974 (1940)). *Der Mensch: seine Natur und seine Stellung in der Welt.* 10th edn. Frankfurt: Athenaion.

Gibbs, A.P. (1989). *Control: Sociology's Central Notion.* Urbana, IL: University of Illinois Press.

Gibbs, J.P. (1981). *Norms, Deviance and Social Control.* New York: Elsevier.

Gibbs, J.P. (ed.) (1982). *Social Control: Views from the Social Sciences.* Beverly Hills, CA: Sage.

Giddens, A. (1984). *The Constitution of Society: Outline of the Theory of Structuration.* Berkeley, CA: University of California Press.

Gitlin, T. (1991). 'Confrontation in the Gulf: The peace movement, the war movement, the media and democracy', Lecture, 13 February, Institute of International Studies, University of California, Berkeley, CA.

Gottfredson, M. and Hirschi, T. (1990). *A General Theory of Crime.* Stanford, CA: Stanford University Press.

Gouldner, A.W. (1975). *For Sociology.* Harmondsworth: Pelican.

Graham, J. (1990). *Crime Prevention Strategies in Europe and North America.* Helsinki: Helsinki Institute for Crime Prevention and Control.

Gramsci, A. (1975 (1929–1935)). *Quaderni del carcere.* 4 Vols. Turin: Einaudi.

Grandi, R., Pavarini, M. and Simondi, M. (eds) (1985). *I segni di Caino: l'imagine della devianza nelle comunicazioni di massa.* Naples: ESI.

Greenberg, S.F. (1985). *Informal Citizen Action at a Neighborhood Level.* Washington, DC: US Government Printing Office.

Gusfield, J.R. (1957). 'Moral passage: the symbolic process in public designations of deviance', *Social Problems*, 15 (2): 175–88.

Gusfield, J.R. (1963). *Symbolic Crusade: Status Politics and the American Temperance Movement.* Urbana, IL: University of Illinois Press.

Habermas, J. (1979). *Legitimationsprobleme im Spätkapitalismus.* Frankfurt: Suhrkamp Verlag.

Habermas, J. (1994 (1992)). 'Citizenship and national identity,' in B. van Steenbergen (ed.), *The Condition of Citizenship.* London: Sage.

Hall, S., Critcher, C., Jefferson, T., Clarke, J. and Roberts, B. (1978). *Policing the Crisis: Mugging, the State, and Law and Order.* London: Macmillan.

Hassemer, W. (1973). *Theorie und Soziologie des Verbrechens: Ansätz zur einer praxisorientierten Rechtsgutlehre.* Frankfurt: Europäische Verlagsanstalt.

Hassemer, W. (1986). *Sozialwissenschaften im Strafrecht.* Darmstadt: Neuwied.

Havel, V. (1985). *Living in Truth.* London: Faber and Faber.

Hess, H. (1973 (1970)). *Mafia and Mafiosi: The Structure of Power.* Westmead/Lexington: Saxon House. (2 edns).

Hess, H. (1983a). 'Probleme der sozialen Kontrolle', in H-J. Kerner, H. Goeppinger and F. Streng (eds), *Festschrift für Heinz Leferenz.* Heidelberg: C.F. Müller.

Hess, H. (1983b). 'Il controllo sociale: società e potere'. *Dei Delitti e Delle Pene*, IV–2, 187–213.

Hess, H. (1986). 'Criminalitá come mito quotidiano: una difesa della criminologia come critica dell'ideologia', *Dei Delitti e Delle Pene*, IV–2: 187–213.

Hirschi, T. (1969). *Causes of Delinquency.* Berkeley, CA.: University of California Press.

Hirst, P.Q. (1986). *Law, Socialism and Democracy.* London: Allen and Unwin.

Hobbes, T. (1962 (1909) (1651)). *Leviathan.* New York/Oxford: Collier Books/Oxford University Press.

Hofstätter, P. (1962). 'Eliten und Minoritäten', *Kölner Zeitschrift für Soziologie und Sozialpsychologie,* 14: 59–86.

Hollingshead, A.B. (1941). 'The concept of social control', *American Sociological Review*, 6: 218–24.

Hope, T. and Shaw, M. (ed.) (1988). *Communities and Crime Reduction.* London: HMSO.

Horwitz, A.V. (1990). *The Logic of Social Control.* New York and London: Plenum.

Hulsman, L. and Bernat de Celis, J. (1982). *Peines perdues: le systéme pénal en question.* Paris: Le Centurion.

Hunt, A. (1991). 'Postmodernism and critical criminology', in B.D. MacLean and D. Milanovic (eds), *New Directions in Critical Criminology.* Vancouver: Collective Press.

Imbeni, R. (1994). *La Cittadinanza Europea.* Bologna: Gruppo del Partito del Socialismo Europeo.

Jakobs, G. (1991 (1983)). *Strafrecht. Allgemeiner Teil. Die Grundlagen und die Zurechnungslehre.* Berlin/New York: W. de Gruyter.

Janowitz, M. (1975). 'Sociological theory and social control', *American Journal of Sociology,* 81 (1): 82–108.

Jáuregui Bereciartu, G. (1994 (1986)). *Decline of the Nation-State.* Reno, NV: University of Nevada Press. (2 edns).

Jellinek, G. (1901 (1895)). *The Declaration of the Rights of Men and Citizens.* New York: Holt.

Joas, H. (1985 (1980)). *G.H. Mead: A contemporary Re-examination of His Thought.* Cambridge Polity. (2 edns).

Johnson, E.H. (ed.) (1987). *Handbook on Crime and Delinquency Prevention.* New York: Greenwood Press.

Kairys, D. (1982). 'Freedom of Speech', in D. Kairys (ed.), *The Politics of Law: A Progressive Critique.* New York: Pantheon.

Kaiser, G., Kury, H. and Albrecht, H.J. (eds) (1991). *Victims and Criminal Justice.* Freiburg: Max Planck Institute.

Kelsen, H. (1924 (1922)). 'The conception of the state and social psychology', *International Journal of Psychoanalysis,* 5: 1–38.

King, M. (1988). *How to Make Social Crime Prevention Work.* London: HMSO.

Lab, S.P. (1988). *Crime Prevention.* Cincinnati, OH: Anderson.

Lagrange, H. (1992). 'Appréhension et préoccupation sécuritaire', *Deviance et Société,* 16 (1): 1–29.

Lagrange, H. and Zauberman, R. (1991). 'Introduction: du débat sur le crime et l'insécurité aux politiques locales', *Deviance et Société,* 15 (3), 233–55.

Lakoff, G. (1991). 'Metaphor and war: The metaphor system used to justify war in the Gulf', *Postmodern Culture.* Available from the PMC Talk file-list as LAKOFF ESSAY.

Lamarca Pérez. C. (1985). *Tratamiento jurídico-penal del terrorismo.* Madrid: Centro de Publicaciones, Ministerio de Justicia.

LaPiere, R.T. (1954). *A Theory of Social Control.* New York: McGraw-Hill.

Le Bon, G. (1960 (1892)). *The Crowd.* New York: Viking Press.

Lefton, M., Skipper, J.K., Jr. and McCaghy, C.H. (eds) (1968). *Approaches to Deviance.* New York: Appleton-Century-Crofts.

Lemert, E.M. (1942). 'The folkways and social control', *American Sociological Review,* 7: 394–9.

Lemert, E.M. (1948). 'Some aspects of a general theory of sociopathic behaviour', *Research Studies, State College of Washington,* XVI 1: 23–9.

Lemert, E.M. (1951). *Social Pathology.* New York: McGraw-Hill.

Lemert, E.M. (1967 (1972)). *Human Deviance, Social Problems, and Social Control.* Englewood Cliffs, NJ: Prentice-Hall.

Lewis, J., Jhally, S. and Morgan, M. (1991). *The Gulf War: A Study of the Media, Public Opinion and Public Knowledge* (Doc. No. P-8). Amherst, USA: Center for the Study of Communication, Department of Communication, University of Massachusetts.

Lilly, J.R. and Knepper, P. (1993). 'The Corrections-commercial complex', *Crime and Delinquency,* 39 (2): 150–66.

Luhmann, N. (1972, 1983, 1987). *Rechtssoziologie.* Opladen, Westdeutscher Verlag. (1st, 2nd, 3rd edns).

Lyotard, J.-F. (1984). *The Postmodern Condition: A Report on Knowledge.* Manchester: University of Manchester Press.

McChesney, R.W. (1993). *Telecommunications, Mass-Media, and Democracy: The Battle for the Control of U.S. Broadcasting, 1928–1935.* New York: Oxford UP.

Machiavelli, N. (1977 (1513)). *The Prince.* New York: W.W. Norton.

MacKinnon, C. (1993). *Only Words.* Cambridge, MA: Harvard UP.

Malinowsky, P. and Münch, U. (1975). *Soziale Kontrolle ( Soziologische Theoriebildung un ihr Bezug zur Praxis der sozialen Arbeit)*. Neuwied und Darmstadt: Kritische Texte-Luchterhand Verlag.

Marcuse, H. (1964). *One-Dimensional Man*. London/Boston: Routledge and Kegan Paul/Beacon.

Marx, G.T. and Reichman, N. (1987). 'Routinizing the discovery of secrets: Computers as informants', in J. Lowman, R. Menzies and T.S. Palys (eds), *Transcarceration: Essays in the Sociology of Social Control*. Aldershot: Gower.

Marx, K. (1964 (1844)). 'Contribution to the critique of Hegel's *Philosophy of Right: Introduction*', in T.B. Bottomore (ed.), *K. Marx, Early Writings*. New York: McGraw-Hill.

Marx, K. (1973). *Grundrisse*. Harmondsworth: Penguin.

Marx, K. (1977 (1867)). *Capital. Volume 1*. New York: International Publishers.

Mathiesen, T. (1984). *The Politics of Abolition*. Oslo: Universitetsforlaget.

Matza, D. (1969). *Becoming Deviant*. Englewood Cliffs, NJ: Prentice-Hall.

Matza, D. and Sykes, G.M. (1961). 'Juvenile delinquency and subterranean values', *American Sociological Review*, 26 (5): 712–19.

Mayer, J.A. (1983). 'Notes towards a working definition of social control in historical analysis', in S. Cohen and A. Scull (eds), *Social Control and the State*. Oxford: Martin Robertson.

Mead, G.H. (1964 (1918)). 'The psychology of punitive justice', *American Journal of Sociology*, 23 (5): 577–602. Reprinted in A.J. Reck (ed.), *G.H. Mead: Selected Writings*. Indianapolis, IN: Bobbs-Merrill.

Mead, G.H. (1934). *Mind, Self, and Society*. Chicago, IL: University of Chicago Press.

Mead, G.H. (1964 (1925)). 'The genesis of the self and social control', in A.J. Reck (ed.), *G.H. Mead, Selected Writings*. Indianapolis, IN: Bobbs-Merrill.

Melossi, D. (1988). 'Incarcerazione, vocabolarili punitivi e ciclo politico-economico in Italia (1896–1965): rapporto su di una ricerca in corso', *Inchiesta*, 79–80: 13–18.

Melossi, D. (1990). *The State of Social Control: A Sociological Study of Concepts of State and Social Control in the Making of Democracy*. Cambridge: Polity. (1992), *El Estado del Control Social*, Siglo XXI, México D.F.

Melossi, D. (1993). 'Gazette of morality and social whip: Punishment hegemony and the case of the USA, 1970–92', *Social and Legal Studies*, 2: 259–79.

Melossi, D. (1994a). 'State, identity, and social control: The current case of Europe', paper presented at 13th World Conference of Sociology. Bielefeld. 18-23 July.

Melossi, D. (1994b). 'The "economy" of illegalities: Normal crimes, elites and social control in comparative analysis', in D. Nelken (ed.), *The Futures of Criminology*. London: Sage.

Melossi, D. and Pavarini, M. (1981 (1977)). *The Prison and the Factory*. London: Macmillan. (2 edns).

Memmi, A. (1965). *The Colonizer and the Colonized*. Boston, MA: Beacon Press.

Merrin, W. (1994). 'Uncritical criticism? Norris, Baudrillard and the Gulf War', *Economy and Society*, 23: 433–58.

Merton, R.K. (1938). 'Social structure and anomie', *American Sociological Review*, 3: 672–82.

Mills, C.W. (1956). *The Power Elite*. New York: Oxford University Press.

Mills, C.W. (1963a (1939)). 'Language, logic and culture', in I.L. Horowitz (ed.), *Power, Politics and People*. New York: Oxford UP.

Mills, C.W. (1963b (1940)). 'Situated actions and vocabularies of motive', in I.L. Horowitz (ed.), *Power, Politics and People*. New York: Oxford UP.

Mills, C.W. (1967). *Power, Politics and People*. (ed. by I.L. Horowitz) London: Oxford

University Press.

Ministry of Justice (1990). *La prigione in Italia: storia, evoluzione e prospettive*. Rome: Poligrafici dello Stato.

Mir Puig, S. (1982). 'Sobre la posibilidad y límites de una cienca social del derecho penal', in S. Mir Puig (ed.), *Derecho penal y ciencias sociales*. Barcelona: Universidad Autónoma de Barcelona.

Muñagorri Lagúia, I. (1985). 'Algunas notas sobre el proceso penal como momento de criminalización y de control social, con comentarios a la reciente normativa española', in R. Bergalli (ed.), *El poder penal del estado*. Buenos Aires: Depalma.

Muñoz Conde, F. (1985). *Derecho penal y control social*. Jerez, Spain: Fundación Universitaria.

Nelken, D. (1985). 'Community Involvement in Crime Control', *Current Legal Problems*, 38: 39–67.

Nelken, D. (ed.) (1994). *The Futures of Criminology*. London: Sage.

Neppi Modona, G. and Violante, L. (1978). *Poteri dello stato e sistema penale*. Turin: Tirrenia Stampatori.

Newman, O. (1972). *Defensible Space*. New York: Macmillan.

Nogala, D. (1995). 'Was ist eigentlich so "privat" an der "Privatisierung sozialer Kontrolle"? Anmerkungen zu Erscheinungen, Indikatoren und Politökonomie der zivilen Sicherheitsindustrie', in F. Sack and M. Voss (eds), *Privatisierung: Rückzug oder Stärkung staatlicher Sozialkontrolle?* Opladen: Westdeutscher Verlag.

Norris, C. (1992). *Uncritical Theory*. London: Lawrence and Wishart.

Oestreich, G. (1969). 'Strukturprobleme des europäischen Absolutismus', in G. Oestrich (ed.), *Geist und Gestalt des frühmodernen Staates. Ausgewählte Aufsätze*. Berlin: Duncker and Humblot

Oreja Aguirre, M. (ed.) (1994). *La Constitucion Europea*. Madrid: Actas.

Osborn, S. and Bright, J. (1989). *Crime Prevention and Community Safety: A practical Guide for Local Authorities*. London: Safe Neighbourhoods Unit.

Palidda, S. (1993). *Sapere di polizia e sicurezza a livello locale*. Florence: Istituto Universitario Europeo.

Park, R.E. (1921). 'Sociology and the social sciences: The social organism and the collective mind', *American Journal of Sociology*, 27 (1): 1–21.

Park, R.E. (1950). *Race and Culture*. Glencoe, IL: The Free Press.

Park, R.E. (1972 (1904)). *The Crowd and the Public*. Chicago, IL: University of Chicago Press. (2 edns).

Park, R.E. and Burgess, E.W. (1969 (1921)). *Introduction to the Science of Sociology*. Chicago, IL: University of Chicago Press.

Park, R.E., Burgess, E.W. and McKenzie, R.D. (1967). *The City*. Chicago, IL: University of Chicago Press.

Parsons, T. (1937). *The Structure of Social Action*. New York: McGraw-Hill. (2nd edn).

Parsons, T. (1951). *The Social System*. New York/London: Free Press/Routledge and Kegan Paul.

Parsons, T. (1962). 'The law and social control', in W.M. Evan (ed.), *Law and Sociology*. New York: Free Press.

Passerin d'Entréves, A. (1967). *The Notion of the State*. Oxford: Clarendon Press.

Pastore, M. (1993). 'Frontiere, conflitti, identitá: a proposito di libera circolazione e nuove forme di controllo sociale in Europa', *Dei Delitti e Delle Pene*, 3 (3): 19–37.

Pateman, C. (1988). *The Sexual Contract*. Cambridge: Polity Press.

Pavarini, M. (1985). 'Il sistema di diritto penale tra abolizionismo e riduzionismo', *Dei*

# 172    Social control and political order

*Delitti e Delle Pene* 3: 325–53.

Pavarini, M. (1992a). 'Strategie discplinari e culture dei servizi', in L. Pepa (ed.), *La nostra bastiglia: la sfida della formazione tra repressione e presa in carico della devianza.* Torino: Gruppo Abele.

Pavarini, M. (1992b). 'Vivere una città sicura', *Sicurezza e Territorio,* 1: 11–14.

Pavarini, M. (1993). 'Perché correre il rischio della prevenzione', *Sicurezza e Territorio,* 2: 27–30.

Pavarini, M. (1994a). 'Is criminology worth saving?', in D. Nelken (ed.), *The Futures of Criminology.* London: Sage.

Pavarini, M. (1994b). *I nuovi confini della penalitá: introduzione alla sociologica della pena.* Bologna: Edizioni Martina.

Pavarini, M. (1994c). 'The New Penology and politics in crisis: The Italian case', *British Journal of Criminology,* 34: 49–61.

Paz, O. (1990 (1979)). 'Mexico and the United States', in O. Paz, *The Labyrinth of Solitude.* London: Penguin Books.

Peele, S. (1987). 'A moral vision of addiction: How people's values determine whether they become and remain addicts', *Journal of Drug Issues,* Spring: 187–215.

Pepa, L. (1992). *La nostra bastiglia: la sfida della formazione tra repressione e presa in carico della devianza.* Turin: Gruppo Abele.

Pepa, L. (1994). 'Una esperienza di "nuova prevenzione" in un quartiere di Bologna', *Sicurezza e Territorio,* 13: 31–4.

Pfohl, S. (1985). *Images of Deviance and Social Control.* New York: McGraw-Hill.

Pitch, T. (1980 (1975)). *La teoria de la desviación social.* Mexico: Editorial Nueva Imagen. (2 edns).

Pitch, T. (1986). 'Viaggio intorno alla criminologia: discutendo con i realisti', *Dei Delitti e Delle Pene,* 3: 469–89.

Pitch, T. (1989). *Responsabilità limitate: attori, conflitti e giustizia penale.* Milan: Feltrinelli.

Pitch, T. (1994). 'Sentirsi sicure, sentirsi sicuri', *Sicurezza e Territorio,* 13: 23–6.

Popitz, H. (1980). *Die normative Konstruktion von Gesellschaft.* Tübingen: Mohr.

Pound, R. (1930). *Criminal Justice in America.* New York: Henry Holt.

Pound, R. (1942). *Social Control through Law.* New Haven: Yale University Press.

Poyner, B. (1983). *Design against Crime: Beyond Defensible Space.* London: Butterworths.

Ranulf, S. (1964 (1938)). *Moral Indignation and Middle Class Psychology. A Sociological Study.* New York: Schocken Books.

Ricolfi, L. (1994). 'Elezioni e mass media: quanti voti ha spostato la tv', *Il Mulino,* 43: 1031–46.

Ritzer, G. (1993). *The McDonaldization of Society.* Newbury Park, CA: Pine Forge.

Robert, P. (1990). 'L'insécurité: représentations collectives et question pénale', *L'Annee Socioloiques,* 40: 313–30.

Ross, E.A. (1969 (1901)). *Social Control: A Survey of the Foundations of Order.* Cleveland, OH and London/Boston, MA: The Press of Case Western Reserve University/Bacon.

Rothman, D. (1983). 'Social control: The uses and abuses of the concept in the history of incarceration', in S. Cohen and A. Scull (eds), *Social Control and the State.* Oxford: Martin Robertson.

Sack, F. (1993). 'Strafrechtliche Kontrolle und Sozialdisziplinierung', in D. Frehsee, G. Löschper and K.F. Schumann (eds), *Srafecht, soziale Kontrolle, soziale Disziplinierung.* Opladen: Westdeutscher Verlag.

Sapelli, G. (1994). *Cleptocrazia: il 'meccanismo unico' della corrupzione tra economia e politica*. Milan: Feltrinelli.

Savelsberg, J.J. (1987). 'The making of criminal law norms in welfare states', *Law and Society Review,* 21 (4): 529–41.

Schaefner, G.F. (1991). 'International choices: The rise and fall of subsidiarity', *Futures,* 23 (7): 681–94.

Scheerer, S. (1983). 'L'abolizionisme della criminologia contemporanea', *Dei Delitte e Delle Pene,* 1 (3): 525–41.

Schlesinger, P. (1992). 'A question of identity', *New European,* 5 (1): 10–14.

Schmitt, C. (1921). *Die Diktatur.* Liepzig: Duncker and Humblot.

Scholte, E.M. (1989). *Social Control Theory, Educational Intervention and the Prevention of Delinquency in Netherlands.* Leiden: University of Leiden, Psychology Department.

Serrano-Piedecasas, J.R. (1988). *Emergencia y crisis del estado social: análisis de la excepcionalidad penal y motivos de su perpetuación.* Barcelona: PPU.

Sewell, W.H. (1992). 'A theory of structure: Duality, agency, and transformation', *American Journal of Sociology,* 98 (1): 1–29.

Sgubbi, F. (1990). *Il reato come rischio sociale: ricerche sulle scelte di allocazione dell' illegalitá penale.* Bologna: Il Mulino.

Shalin, D.N. (1988). 'G.H. Mead, socialism, and the Progressive agenda', *American Journal of Sociology,* 93: 913–51.

Shearing, C.D. and Stenning, P.C. (1983). 'Private security: Implications for social control', *Social Problems,* 30 (5): 493–506.

Shearing, C.D. and Stenning, P.C. (1987). 'Say "Cheese!": The Disney order that is not so Mickey Mouse', in C.D. Shearing and P.C. Stenning (eds), *Private Policing.* Newbury Park, CA: Sage.

Sighele, S. (1985 (1891)). *La folla delinquente.* Venice: Marsilio.

Simmel, G. (1992 (1908)). *Soziologie – Untersuchungen über die Formen der Vergesellschaftung.* Frankfurt: Suhrkamp.

Simon, H.A. (1991). *Models for My Life.* New York: Basic Books.

Skinner, Q. (1978). *The Foundations of Modern Political Thought.* 2 vols. Cambridge: Cambridge UP.

Skogan, W.G. (1990). *Disorder and Decline: Crime and the Spiral Decay in American Neighbourhoods.* New York: Free Press.

Smart, C. (1990). 'Feminist approaches to criminology or postmodern woman meets atavistic man', in L. Gelsthorpe and A. Morris (eds), *Feminist Perspectives in Criminology.* Buckingham: Open University Press.

Smart, C. and Smart, B. (eds) (1978). *Women, Sexuality and Social Control.* London: Routledge.

Smauss (1980). 'Vuoto teorico e servilismo politico nelle ricerche KOL', *La Questione Criminale,* 2–3: 363–400.

Smith, D. (1988). *The Chicago School: A Liberal Critique of Capitalism.* Basingstoke: Macmillan.

Smith, D.E. (1976). 'The ideological practice of sociology', *Catalyst,* 8: 39–54.

Spigel, L. (1992). *Make Room for TV.* Chicago, IL: University of Chicago Press.

Spinelli, A. and Rossi, E. (1991 (1941)). 'Manifesto di Ventotene', in A. Spinelli (ed.), *Il Manifesto di Ventotene.* Bologna: Il Mulino.

Stedman Jones, G. (1983). 'Class expression versus social control? A critique of recent trends in the social history of "leisure"', in S. Cohen and A. Scull (eds), *Social Control and the State.* Oxford: Martin Robertson.

Steinert, H. (1995). 'Soziale Ausschließung – das richtige Thema zur richtigen Zeit',

*Kriminologisches Journal*, 27: 82–8.

Sumner, C.S. (ed.) (1982). *Crime, Justice and Underdevelopment*. London: Heinemann.

Sumner, C.S. (ed.) (1990). *Censure, Politics and Criminal Justice*. Milton Keynes: Open University Press.

Sumner, C.S. (1994). *The Sociology of Deviance: An Obituary*. Buckingham: Open University Press.

Sumner, C.S. (1996). 'Censure, culture and punishment', *Dei Delitti e Delle Pene*, 3: 127–36.

Sykes, G. and Matza, D. (1957). 'Techniques of neutralization: A theory of delinquency,' *American Sociological Review*, 22: 664–73.

Tannenbaum, F. (1938). *Crime and the Community*. New York: Columbia University Press.

Ter Wal, J. (1991). 'Il linguaggio del pregiudizio etnico', *Politica e Economia*, 4: 33–48.

Terradillos Basoco, J. (1988). *Terrorismo y Derecho*. Madrid: Tecnos.

Thomas, C.Y. (1984). *The Rise of the Authoritarian State in Peripheral Societies*. New York: Monthly Review Press.

Thomas, W.I. and Znaniecki, F. (1958 (1918–1920)). *The Polish Peasant in Europe and America*. Chicago, IL: University of Chicago Press.

Tinland, F. (1985). 'Hobbes, Spinoza, Rousseau et la formation de l'idée de démocratie comme mesure de la légitimité du pouvoir politique', *Revue Philosophique*, 2: 195–222.

Tocqueville, A. de. (1961 (1835 and 1840)). *Democracy in America*. 2 vols. New York: Schocken.

Trentin, S. (1945). *Stato, nazione, federalismo*. Milan: La Fiaccola.

Trenz, H.-J. and Zaitch, D. (1995). 'Terrorismo y control social: estrategias, funciones y conflicto simbólico', in D. Melossi (ed.), *Social Control, Political Power and the Penal Question: For a Sociology of Criminal Law and Punishment*. Oñati: Oñati Proceedings, IISL.

Turner, R.H. (ed.). (1967). *Robert E. Park: On Social Control and Collective Behaviour*. Chicago, IL: University of Chicago Press.

Uría, A. (1983). *Miserables y locos: medicina mental y orden social el la España del Siglo XIX*. Barcelona: Tusquets.

Van Dijk, J.J.M. and De Waard, J. (1991). 'A two-dimensional typology of crime prevention projects, with a bibliography', *Criminal Justice Abstracts*, 23 (3): 483–503.

Van Dijk, J.J.M. and Mayhew, P. (1993). 'Criminal victimisation in the industrial world: key findings of the 1989 and 1992 international crime surveys', in A. Alvazzi de Frate, U. Zvekic and J.J.M. Van Dijk (eds), *Understanding Crime. Experiences of Crime and Crime Control*. Rome: UNICRI.

Van Dijk, J.J.M., Matthew, P. and Killias, M. (1990). *Experiences of Crime Across the World*. Kluwer: Deventer.

Van Dijk, T.A. (1993). *Elite Discourse and Racism*. London: Sage.

Van Krieken, R. (1991). 'The poverty of social control: Explaining power in the historical sociology of the welfare state', *The Sociological Review*, 1: 1–25.

Vidmar, K.H. (1994). *Living in Difference: The 1950s Television and Representation of History*. Unpublished paper. Department of Sociology, University of California at Davis, CA.

Vincent, G. (1896). 'The province of sociology', *American Journal of Sociology*, 1 (4): 473–91.

Waever, O., Buzan, B., Kelstrup, M. and Lemaitre, P. (1993). *Identity, Migration and the New Security Agenda in Europe*. London: Pinter.

Watts, A. (1992). *The Wisdom of Insecurity*. London: Rider.

Weber, M. (1958 (1904–5)). *The Protestant Ethic and Spirit of Capitalism*. New York: Scribner's.

Weber, M. (1978 (1920)). 'Die protestischen Sekten und der Geist des Kapitalismus', in M. Weber, *Gesammelte Aufsätze zur Religionssoziologie*, Tubingen: Mohr.

Weinberg, J., Hinkle, G.J. and Hinkle, R.C. (1969). 'Introduction', in E.A. Ross, *Social Control: A Survey of the Foundations of Order*. Cleveland, OH and London/Boston, MA: The Press of Case Western Reserve University/Bacon.

Wirth, L. (1936). 'Preface', in K. Mannheim, *Ideology and Utopia*. New York: Harcourt Brace.

Wirth, L. (1940). 'Ideological aspects of social disorganization', *American Sociological Review*, 5: 472–82.

Wrong, D. (1961). 'The oversocialized conception of man', *American Sociological Review*, 26: 184–93.

Young, J. (1989). *Criminology: A Realistic Critique*. London: Sage.

Young, J. and Matthews, R. (eds) (1992a). *Rethinking Criminology: The Realist Debate*. London: Sage.

Young, J. and Matthews, R. (eds) (1992b). *Issues in Realist Criminology*. London: Sage.

# Index